Cut from the Same Cloth?

ESSAYS BY

Negla Abdalla
Zahra Adams
Fatima Ahdash
Sabeena Akhtar
Mariam Ansar
Shaista Aziz
Suma Din
Khadijah Elshayyal
Ruqaiya Haris
Fatha Hassan
Raisa Hassan
Sumaya Kassim
Rumana Lasker Dawood
Suhaiymah Manzoor-Khan
Asha Mohamed
Sofia Rehman
Yvonne Ridley
Aisha Rimi
Khadijah Rotimi
Sophie Williams
Hodan Yusuf

Cut from the Same Cloth?

MUSLIM WOMEN ON LIFE IN BRITAIN

Edited by
Sabeena Akhtar

unbound

This edition first published in 2021

Unbound
Level 1, Devonshire House,
One Mayfair Place, London w1j 8aj

www.unbound.com

Text design by Ellipsis, Glasgow

A CIP record for this book is available from the British Library

ISBN 978-1-78352-945-2 (hbk limited edition)
ISBN 978-1-78352-944-5 (trade pbk)
ISBN 978-1-78352-943-8 (ebook)

Printed and bound by Clays Ltd, Elcograf S.p.A

3 5 7 9 10 8 6 4 2

With special thanks to the patrons of this book

Jannatul Shammi
Tilted Axis Press

CONTENTS

INTRODUCTION

Let me begin as Muslims often do: with thanks. Thanks to Allah, the most merciful, most high, without whom we would be nothing.

Thanks to Unbound for providing us with the space to share our words, and to you, the reader, for your ongoing support. Thanks to my Muslim sisters, in all our struggles, joy and configurations – this book is for you.

When Unbound invited me to work on an anthology by visibly Muslim women, I jumped at the chance. Like so many Muslim women I had sat on the sidelines time and time again, growing frustrated with negative portrayals and tired stereotypes. While 'Muslimness' is, of course, not limited to a piece of cloth, so often we as hijab-wearing women find ourselves judged by our visibility without being afforded ownership of the narrative that surrounds it. I sometimes think of the hijab as a mirror. What is projected onto it is often a reflection of a person's own character, politics and baggage, it is seldom about the woman underneath. Even in the midst of the global pandemic, we find that (unrelated) images of women in hijabs have become weaponised, accompanying many of the negative COVID-19 news stories in order to further malign communities that are already disproportionately suffering at its hands.

The effect of wide-scale securitisation, hostility and surveillance of the Muslim community has also increasingly manifested itself in the palpable othering of hijab-wearing women, who are perceived as the visual representatives of Islam. What we are reduced to are the passive enablers of 'violent' Muslim men or the radical Other, and, in the case of Shamima Begum, both. She is presented in her black khimar devoid of context, stripped of citizenship, due legal process and even humanity. She has not *been* radicalised, she *is* radical. Her predisposition to violence is read as innate. Yet, despite all of this co-opting and projecting onto the hijab, as visibly Muslim women we are rarely afforded an opportunity to discuss our experiences on our own terms and, crucially, through the prism of our spirituality. In books and in the media we are spoken on behalf of, often, by men, non-hijab wearing women and non-Muslims. Too often we are seen to exist only in statistics, while others gain a platform off the back of the hostilities we face. Yet it can sometimes feel as if we are inundated with endless op-eds, 'behind the veils' and thinkpieces about hijab and Muslim women. I invite readers to ask why this is, what the purpose behind the pieces is, what their appeal is and, most importantly, who are they written for? As my dear friend and contributor Sumaya Kassim pointed out in an update for this project, 'often, it feels like Muslim women are only valuable when they're selling something, or when they're oppressed/ silenced. As silent, invisible beings, Muslim women serve specific political purposes: we make mainstream feminists feel good about being liberated, we make secular liberals feel progressive, we provide anti-Islamic media outlets and YouTubers with plenty of revenue, and an excellent excuse for the government to commit all manner of crimes in the name of saving us'. But what of our own stories, religiosity, hopes and creativity? I wanted to create a space for visibly Muslim women to speak freely about their lives and interests without being reduced to passive inhabitants in them, and not because we have something to prove or disprove, but simply *because*. Perhaps naively, I did not anticipate how political a collection of personal essays written by visibly Muslim women would be.

The path to publication of this anthology has not always been easy. Along the way we have been told by some claiming to be feminists that as women who are visibly Muslim or have had the experience of being visibly Muslim, we are oppressed and should hence be no-platformed. They would rather shut down the voices of some women than engage with that which contradicts their own preconceived colonial values. Such is the twisted logic of some corners of liberalist thought. We've been accused of being everything from the ominous 'traditionalists with agendas' to 'rabid feminists', social-justice warriors and, more recently, critical race theorists (apparently a slur) simply because we wanted to write a book. As many random strangers have hypothesised about what lies within these pages, perhaps we should begin with what this is not. It is not a polemic on the hijab and why we wear it, or a litmus test of our relatability to the white gaze. It is not a group of hijab-wearing women looking down on the women who don't wear it. It's a hijab, not a halo. Our experiences do not negate or take precedence over any other.

There will be no grand 'unveilings', and we will not be making or breaking any stereotypes today; nor will there be any justification or condemnation of our various religious standpoints. This book is not a pulpit or minbar, it is not data for analysis, it is not an opportunity for voyeurism and it is certainly not a government-funded initiative. It is but a small snapshot of the many and varied lives, concerns and issues important to women across race and class who have simply had the shared experience of being visibly Muslim in Britain today. Though we cover a broad range of topics, many of the pieces deal with how we, at the various intersections of our identities as Muslim women and girls, are perceived and taught to perceive ourselves, and how we can recognise and resist the distorted lens through which we are regarded. Asha examines how the education system embeds racial hierarchy at a young age, while Negla reflects on how we internalise inferiority and the impact that has on Black Muslim women in particular. Hodan expands on how Black Muslimahs are often unsafe both outside and within the Muslim community, and Sumaya, Rumana, Ruqaiya, Khadijah R. and Raisa discuss how stereo-types, social media, beauty standards, ableism and racial perceptions taint the relationships we have with ourselves and our creative output. Mariam, Aisha, Suma, Khadijah E. and Fatha explore our relationships with physical spaces, place, motherhood, COVID-19 and men. Fatima laments the treatment of Arab Muslims in the human-rights sector, and Yvonne, Sophie and I discuss the political and mental impact of hypervisibility and invisibility, the starkest example of which can be seen through Zahra and Shaista's piece on Grenfell. Suhaiymah reaches the conclusion that the questions put to us as Muslim women are themselves an exertion of power that control the narrative, irrespective of the answer, while Sofia engages scholarship and the Qur'an as praxis for understanding what she calls the 'triple consciousness' of being Muslim, British and woman.

While we differ in our understanding and approaches to the many perceptions of Muslim women, all of us in the various stages of our journeys find solace and liberation in the submission to Allah. As a writer I have experienced first-hand the appetite for stories by Muslim women that fit a reductive blueprint, ironically often centring Muslim men and our reactions to their perceived oppressions, or measuring our worth or relatability through capitalism or secularism – preferably devoid of any spirituality, despite this being a religious identity. Diversity among Muslim women is often presented as falling within the binary of extremist versus culturally Muslim. I wanted to scratch beneath the headline-grabbing dichotomies and hear from women like me, who are often overlooked or tokenised in our own stories by audiences that prefer women who are more relatable to Western hegemonies, who are able to dismiss or fulfil stereotypes about who it is thought we are: oppressed or radical, passive or pint-drinking, religious or 'liberated', boring or skateboarding.

I simply wanted a space to discuss our unique experiences without expediency or agenda.

I wanted to capture the true, warts-and-all nature of the British Muslim community that I know and love. The one that includes Muslims of all races, that captures our different age and class experiences as well as the differing experiences of disabled and non-disabled Muslimahs. I wanted to include women who have never before been published, who may speak English as a second language, and to place as much value in the words and experiences of mothers and working-class Muslimahs as we do in those of academics and scholars. To capture our joy, humour and the comfort of spirituality, in addition to interrogating our shortcomings, such as anti-Black racism, misogyny and the very specific issues we face from within and outside our communities.

A recent House of Commons report commissioned by the Chair of the Women and Equalities Select Committee, Maria Miller MP, found that Muslim women who wear hijabs are routinely discriminated against. 'The evidence was very strong that ... it was seen as acceptable to discriminate against Muslim women and that [people] almost didn't see it as discrimination', she wrote.

And while we didn't need an MP to tell us what we already knew, so it goes.

Muslim women, particularly visibly Muslim women, are harangued at work, at home and in politics. So when this unique opportunity arose, I grabbed it, and gave only one pre-requisite to my sisters and co-authors – *write what you want*. There were no buzzwords, titles or topics to cover; we just wanted to provide Muslim creatives with a space to write the things they most wanted to share. The task was harder for some of us than we initially envisaged: Muslim women writers are so used to being commissioned into caricatures of ourselves that many of us struggled with the creative freedom. We persevered to create something truly affecting and meaningful.

What follows are the honest and heartfelt words of a group of brilliant women. Some are angry and painful, others are reflective and funny. Each is personal, sincere and invites you, the reader, Muslim or not, to interrogate your own perceptions and biases.

Sabeena Akhtar
Spring 2021

I AM NOT AN ANSWER,
I AM THE QUESTION

Suhaiymah Manzoor-Khan

O you who believe! Stand out firmly for justice, as witnesses to Allah, even as against yourselves, or your parents, or your kin, and whether it be against rich or poor.

Surah An-Nisa, Qur'an, 4:135

Living as we did – on the edge – we developed a particular way of seeing reality . . . a mode of seeing unknown to most of our oppressors, that sustained us, aided us in our struggle.

bell hooks, *From Margin to Center*

The year I started university, I turned nineteen before term even began. There is a photograph of me from that day, blissfully unaware of the precipice of change on which I stand. Back then, even though it is not so long ago, I was assured about the simplicity of what I believed in: equality, fairness and the readjustment of the world so everybody had more of the same. The idea was simple and based in my experience. My grandparents were immigrants, my parents grew up through the 'Paki-bashing' years and I went to the local (Leeds) state school, where I watched as poorer and more vulnerable class-mates were constantly put in isolation and eventually excluded. I wanted equality. Gender, racial, sexual and class equality. That was the deal of the day. I was easily and happily a feminist in that sense. If boys could stay out late, I wanted the same. If men were paid more than women in the same jobs, I wanted the same. I ardently believed there should be more Black, brown, female, disabled and queer MPs. As I look into my nineteen-year-old eyes I see how straightforward it would have been.

However, a month before my nineteenth birthday I was accepted by Cambridge University to study history. As a grandchild of immigrants and a state-school kid, that seemed like reaching the height of 'equality'. I was shoving a foot onto a rung of the ladder that we weren't meant to be on – ostensibly getting 'the same' as the most privileged. But my time at Cambridge proved my definition of equality wrong. Merely doing what powerful people do isn't equivalent to holding or redistributing power or accessing resources. Moreover, I began to question whether I wanted power or resources on the basis that powerful people had those things. Did I really want 'the same as' people whose social and economic capital, and value as humans, came from the historic subjugation and contemporary exclusion of others deemed less valuable?

My easy relationship with feminism was sent into disarray at Cambridge too. I didn't straightforwardly share experiences with the majority of women there just because we were women. The majority were white, meaning society saw them differently to me, rewarded them better and blessed them with a humanity it didn't see fit to grant me. I realised that power imbalances existed not merely between men and women, but within those very categories and around their boundaries too. Other women were able to weaponise racist tropes and sexist Islamophobic stereotypes to exclude and silence me. I suddenly found myself overlooked in feminist spaces, as if my colour or hijab compromised my value as a woman worth fighting for – exposing the unspoken identity of who was assumed central in all 'feminist' conversations. Studying history, I began to recognise the unspoken identity of the subject assumed central in all my modules too. He was not only someone who occupied historical worlds different from those of my ancestors, but whose history was actively or complicitly involved in the colonial oppression of theirs. Even in the most mundane interactions at Cambridge, racist assumptions about my intelligence, civility and ability seeped through. Such experiences pushed me to reconsider my desire for, and definition of, 'equality'.

If I wasn't equal to other women, how could I be equal to men? If our histories weren't told equally, and our subjectivities weren't given equal validity, and if all men weren't equal, then which men and what type of subject did I want equality with? To be a man of equivalent race, religion and positionality as my woman-self would barely see me enter a world of equality! I was joined in my questions by other women of colour at Cambridge who introduced me to rich histories of writing by Black feminists and anti-colonialists.[*] I learned how feminism was used historically by hypocrites like Lord Cromer and Winston Churchill, who passionately opposed women's rights and suffrage in Britain, but justified colonial occupation and the decimation of foreign economies by professing a concern for foreign women who needed 'saving' from the misogyny of 'uncivilised' men. This trope was reproduced throughout the twentieth century to justify conquests like the invasion of Afghanistan in 2001 as a feminist intervention, rather than viewing it as a destruction of women's worlds, security and autonomy. This trope of 'saving' Muslim women hounded me in many feminist circles I engaged with, in which my opinions and priorities were of secondary relevance to assumptions about me.

Motivated by these injustices, I organised on campus through my various positions on the Women's Campaign, as college BME Students' Officer, Access Officer and Islamic Society Activism Officer. I facilitated workshops and talks about intersectional feminism, cultural appropriation and micro-aggressions, gender and Islam, and initiated the 'Faith & Feminism' campaign, critiquing secular feminist narratives. By the time I graduated, however, I realised that even this sort

---

[*] See, ed. Younge, Odelia, *A Fly Girl's Guide to University: Being a woman of colour at Cambridge and other institutions of power and elitism* (Verve Poetry Press, 2019)

of 'intersectional feminist' lens had its limits. Some of the conversations I witnessed became overly preoccupied with individual 'identities' to the detriment of focusing on the structures and conditions which produced them through oppression. This sometimes disintegrated the collective nature of our original intentions – especially as neoliberalism more widely was catching up with and co-opting the language of intersectionality. The resulting ambiguity in direction meant that, unfortunately, feminist rhetoric in some circles became increasingly complicit in the failure to hold anything or anyone accountable for oppression. At the same time, in society more widely, accountability for gendered and sexual oppression was increasingly and singularly burdened onto Muslim men/men of colour. Persecution of such men through state surveillance, detention and extrajudicial punishment was therefore increasingly justified through a feminist lens (think 'grooming gangs' rhetoric). This hurt me. It meant that even working towards gender and racial equality in more nuanced ways could be co-opted. The survivors and victims of sexual violence always got erased in the fray.

Therefore, the battle that became more meaningful to me at that stage was one for *liberation*. Upon reflection I could see now how my desire for 'equality' had failed to comprehensively interrogate oppressive structures. For example, wanting more MPs of 'diverse backgrounds' was based on an assumption that representation in Parliament was good in and of itself – not questioning the role and authority of Parliament in upholding violence through austerity, necropolitical distribution of resources, racist policing and imperial domination. Further, if modern nation-states were born from the colonial capitalist system working always to exclude and dehumanise 'outsiders', would the presence of 'more diverse people' in nation-state governance automatically undo patriarchy and racism? I had been too long a student at Cambridge not to know that the answer to such a question was a categorical no.

My existing as a woman of colour at Cambridge had not dismantled the elitism and norms of colonial white supremacy that suffused the institution both materially and ideologically. Moreover, graduating from Cambridge would not keep me safe from racialised misogyny or the unavoidability of being surveilled and criminalised by the state for being Muslim. While the social capital I gained (in conjunction with the Yorkshire accent I lost, RIP) at Cambridge perhaps equipped me with an advantage over students who wanted to become corporate lawyers or MPs (neither things that I ever had an interest in becoming), it could do nothing to counteract the fact that between 2013 and 2016, while I was studying, being Muslim in Britain had become an unambiguous security issue. Specifically, counterterrorism's racist logics had fully seeped into the bedrock of society by 2015, when Prevent legislation was made a statutory duty upon all public-sector employees to 'prevent people being drawn into terrorism' by looking out for (incredibly vague) 'signs of radicalisation'. (This has been discredited by hundreds of academics who show that such 'signs' merely criminalise identity and ideas by pathologising violence as inherent to certain 'identities' or 'ideologies' based on pseudoscientific research which does nothing to interrogate the contexts that cause violence.) My existence was therefore suspect, my body hyper-visible, my behaviour regulated and my freedom to criticise curtailed. Doing 'the same as powerful people' had not liberated me.

My shift away from a politics aimed at 'equality' was informed not only by these disillusionments, but also by the debates around 'decolonising' that abounded in my final year at Cambridge. In light of the Rhodes Must Fall movement and 'Why Is My Curriculum White?', I was involved in discussions about what it could mean to decolonise an institution like Cambridge – one of the world's foremost training grounds for elites who historically and contemporarily commit imperialist violence and racist atrocities; and which had endowments and wealth that could be directly and indirectly linked to colonial looting and the transatlantic slave trade. The idea of decolonising seemed to strike at the heart of what liberation might look like beyond achieving 'equality' in contexts that were fundamentally unjust. It was a project to historicise how the world had come to be as it was, and unlearn the reasons *why* certain things/ideas/people and not others were deemed successful, valuable or intellectual, as well as to restore or repair the material consequences and inequities caused and justified by these ideas. I found myself confronting my own assumptions and questioning how my education had limited my thinking.

Did it matter that my history degree had taught me practically nothing about the world beyond Europe? Did it matter that it had taught me about Europe devoid of its reliance on the world beyond? Did it matter that modules on world history were taught from the coloniser's point of view?

This line of questioning took me on to a scholarship for Postcolonial Studies at London's School of Oriental and African Studies (SOAS) the week after my twenty-second birthday. At this stage my feminist politics had mutated, so that I disagreed with most who declared themselves feminist due to the way they were still able to oppress and exclude women who were racialised, Muslim, migrant, detained, disabled, refugee, queer, trans or living on colonised or formerly colonised land. In fact, I increasingly distanced myself from labelling my politics in general. Instead, due to my recent self-reflection, I found myself engaging more deeply with the place of my submission to Allah in my politics. For a long time it felt as if Islam was an isolated element of my life, secluded to five-times-daily worship and private principles and prayers. However, since the British context had made 'Muslim' my most apparent identity by my early twenties, I, too, began to pay it more heed in all elements of my life. In fact, as an independent study during my Cambridge degree I'd looked at the dialogues between Islam and socialism in the postcolonial Arab world, immersing myself in writings by the likes of Hassan al-Banna, Sayyid Qutb and Ali Shariati. This opened the door to my engagement with a tradition of understanding the Qur'an and hadith as a framework for social justice, and it also made me aware for the first time about the norms of secularity that I had unthinkingly internalised (e.g. the notion of private/public split of self; or my notion of my 'religion' and 'politics' as separate entities).

Secularism was inherently entangled with the making of the modern colonial world and yet it was the one bastion of coloniality that had managed to evade my previous attempts at denaturalising the world I lived in – I would also argue it is the one bastion of coloniality that most people engaged in 'decolonising' work in the UK and Europe fail to interrogate, undermining the wider project. In my re-engagement with Islam as an adult I therefore found a rigorous guide and template for fighting structural and historic injustice from its root, rather than simply seeking equal access to power in oppressive systems. Musa (AS) had asked Pharaoh not for more representation of Israelites in his tyrannical regime but for Pharaoh to submit to the authority of Allah and, in so doing, relinquish his stranglehold on the marginalised. Islam made liberation of the most comprehensive and holistic kind I had considered not only viable, but mandatory.

At the same time, during the course of my master's degree, the most stimulating ideas I studied were in a Queer theory module. Here I encountered a crucial tool for attempting to 'unlearn': questioning. Questioning my every assumption and unpicking easy sentences to see the layers they were made up of. Queer theorists talked about 'queering' not only in relation to identity, but as an ideological method of disrupting norms and destabilising power dynamics through exposing them (by asking about them) and non-compliance. This felt like the most 'decolonial' approach to knowledge I had engaged with so far, and during this time I began to see the radical 'queer-ness' – as a rupture of norms – that was Islam itself. Prioritis-ing and adhering to Islamic principles was a truly disruptive, non-compliant act in the modern/colonial/secular world. There is nothing quite so unpalatable to knowledge norms and academic institutions as prioritising knowledge that stems from the Word of Allah. For me, at that time, the radical potential of Islam lay in the fact that submission to Allah disrupted the hierarchy of power and norms of respectability/secularism and truth/'objectivity' that we are taught to assume are 'the way things have always been' throughout the educa-tion system. By disrupting I found myself in a more exciting space, one from which I could ask where such norms come from, why they masqueraded as 'objective' and 'universal', and who benefited from them. Submission solely to Allah subse-quently entailed the freedom to ask questions about the power, authority and value of everything else. No human, institution or set of norms – no matter how old – had an innate right to stand above questioning.

I cannot express how this revelation and embracing this liberating epistemology of taking knowledge of Allah as my only premise revolutionised my politics. In attempting to *be* Muslim as a praxis beyond an identity, I realised that most feminist and anti-racist politics I had engaged with up until that point were shallowly asking the wrong questions. Most of the questions being asked were not *my* questions at all. So much of my educational and consciousness-raising work had been the work of answering questions posed by others (whether asked aloud or not). For example, much of my work was haunted by questions such as, '*Are* you oppressed by Islam?', '*Do* Muslim women really have autonomy?' and '*Are* Muslims anything but "backwards" and subhuman?' All, in a way, the same question: the demand to justify my existence. Writer and professor Toni Morrison alluded to this in her recognition that the function of racism is distraction, and that 'there will always be one more thing.'

What I realised through attempting to take only Allah as my premise and thus unlearn, destabilise and question the norms around me, was that to be truly free my existence had to stop being solely an answer to other people's questions. I had to try to exist in Allah's gaze alone, not in the perpetual space of trying to appease a man-made gaze. That meant that instead of being a continuous set of answers, my existence could be a question. Subsequently, rather than prioritising achieving 'equality' in an unjust system, or explaining how oppression works (which I do still commit to though, because it is a form of redistributing knowledge/blessings and tools of understanding reality outside of the lens of Power), I decided that the work that would truly be *for my liberation* would be a politics of questioning things for the sake of Allah.

What do I mean by a politics of questioning for the sake of Allah? I mean committing myself to stop being an answer to other people's questions and gazes in order to exist fully and intentionally for Allah. Even in writing this essay there is the underlying pressure to use the word count to answer an ever-present question like 'Why do you really wear a hijab?' But by committing to not being an answer to other people's questions I commit to allow myself to exist as more than merely Other – as more than just in relation to white supremacy, Islamophobia, patriarchy, secular modernity and colonialism. It is a commitment to liberation in the sense of submission only to Allah. This commitment is, I believe, true to my nineteen-year-old self. A commitment that would enable her to want more than merely what the people who benefit from her oppression have, and do more than merely answer, prove or disprove questions. Instead, that commitment would enable her to *ask* questions, knowing nothing is beyond questioning, and be a constant question herself.

Breaking stereotypes is the most obvious form of being an answer to other people's questions that exists for Muslim women. It does nothing for us but waste our time. Stereotypes do not exist to be broken, they exist to break us. Therefore, I am no longer placing value on disproving other people's assumptions. This refusal is a form of non-compliance in a world that says Muslim women's humanity and worth are conditional upon proving it. In not complying with that world, we can become questions to it instead. *Why* is our humanity conditional? Why is the onus on us to prove it?

A politics of questioning *is*, to me, inherently Islamic. Was questioning norms not the very thing Allah's Prophets did? Ibrahim (AS) questioned the legitimacy of his father's gods, Musa (AS) questioned the basis of Pharaoh's authority, Isa (AS) questioned the norms of his society, and Muhammad (SAW) questioned a tradition of idolatry and culture of greed and competition. Nothing but Allah is worthy of worship (la ilaha illallah), and yet most of everything else violently asserts itself as godlike in its right to be, to control, to judge, to exclude and to harm. A politics of questioning is a refusal to apologise for that certainty of submission, or to justify it and distance myself from my Otherness, and unpalatability – to not explain it or disprove it – but to exist so fully in it, submitting to Allah, that I am a constant question to the world itself.

I am talking about not attempting to be respectable to get a look in on being 'human', but through existing as dehumanised, being the very question asking why humanity is not, in fact, universal. I am talking about not trying to meet impossible conditions such as 'assimilate/integrate to deserve fair treatment', but instead, through existing, being the very question that asks why assimilation/integration is called for if it can never be truly accepted from those of us excluded in the first place. I am talking about recalibrating our goals so that our ideas of liberation are not merely attempts to reproduce power relations based in the violent histories we see around us – to not simply want a seat at the table with oppressors, but to ask how the table was made at all. I am talking about liberation in the sense of being able to look at the world and ourselves through our own eyes, and to trust them – even though doing so will make us 'crazy'. In fact, a politics of questioning will have the whole world telling us we're mentally unstable at worst and liars with victim-complexes at best. This is the punitive response to our refusal to answer and the threat of our questioning which exposes the historicity and construct of the contexts we live in. People will patronise, ridicule, demand answers and coerce us into definitions, but by refusing to answer and by persisting in asking there is a type of liberation that can be reached beyond what I have known before. An Islamic praxis of questioning is the only thing that has provided me with a tool to disrupt oppression itself like this. It is to be free before asking permission.

Existing as a Muslim woman is itself a question to the world. It is a question about essential categories, Otherness, our relationship to colonial-rendered nation-state identities and their necessity, as well as our relationship to Allah. The position of Muslim women is one which exposes how state violence invokes both race and gender and how feminist politics mobilise 'religion' to condone state violence and racialised notions of humanity. I am not saying that being a Muslim woman makes one inherently revolutionary; in fact, radical politics are disincentivised for Muslim women due to our precarious position threatened by racism, Islamophobia and misogyny. However, I am saying that Muslim women exist in a margin where we are oppressed in the most intimate ways by the state and carceral capitalism infringing on our families, bodies, right to raise children, etc., and that such experience gives us a particular way of seeing reality which is potentially radical. Our power lies in whether we allow ourselves to look with our own eyes and not deny the forms of tyranny and violence that we find. Our marginal and multiply oppressed position gives us – to use cultural theorist bell hooks' analogy about African-American women in the 1980s –

> a special vantage point ... to criticize the dominant racist, classist, sexist hegemony as well as to envision and create a counter-hegemony ... the margin is more than a site of deprivation ... It offers to one the possibility of a radical perspective from which to see and create, to imagine alternatives, new worlds.
>
> – *From Margin to Center*, p.15

I hope not to appropriate hooks' point but would like to take it in a new direction. Is not the margin the site of Islam? Prophets were social, political and/or ideological pariahs (or became so due to receiving revelation). Their marginality, resulting from their submission to Allah, was (with Allah's plan and permission) what made it *possible* for them to revolutionise their societies in the ways they did. Muslim women today occupy one of the most monstered sites of marginality

23

that exists in Britain/Europe/'the West'. The statistics are widely available and speak for themselves, but the embodied pain and psychological trauma speak even louder. For us, then, to use our marginality as a way to question the world around us, we stand the best chance of proposing alternatives – and, as ever, ones that benefit *everyone*, regardless of how maligned we are by them. The struggles of trans women, sex workers and other monstered and non-conforming people to survive, have access to safety, freedom from harm and be granted humanity have often benefited *all* criminalised people and bodies made suspect by the state – making them safer and less liable to unjustified harm as well as connecting the violence of e.g. the border, capitalism and misogyny (Mac and Smith, 2018) – and the struggle of Muslim women will do the same while also harbouring the potential of meta-physical revolution of our relationships to ourselves which undergird our world. Alternative futures are not possible if we remain merely answers, we have to be God-conscious questions, refusing to submit to any other power, and thus exposing every other power that asserts its inevitability.

As I finish writing this essay, it is September again, I have just turned twenty-four. I do not know a lot and I hope I don't sound so arrogant as to seem like I think I do. I am confident I will look back on this essay soon and cringe, but such is the nature of believing – we must have the vulnerability and humility to be sincere but also learn more and do better when we know better. But I do know some things *right now*. I know that the decision to see with my own eyes and to stop answering people's questions about my existence has been one of the most liberating decisions I have ever made. I also know that submitting only to Allah is the liberation before the liberation. I know that a lot of people will reject me for that, and that many feel strange about my commitment to Allah – but I also know that this stems from the fact that I am refusing to answer the unspoken question of explaining myself. And I know that that infuriates.

To be a question rather than an answer is to be a provocation and rupture in the story the world tells about itself. It is to expose the master's tools, which is surely a step towards no longer using them. It is to be the threat of dismantlement. To be a question, rather than an answer – a tick in the box, a book on a reading list, a representative, quota, debate or accompanying photograph – is to be truly unacceptable. And being unacceptable *is* the start of liberation because it is a question about who decides what is acceptable in the first place. The power of unpalatability and of embracing our monstrosity is surely the way of the Prophets. They named and exposed the oppressive structures of their times. They disrupted norms, refused to explain their right to exist, and did not seek conditional acceptance because they were committed singularly to obeying the authority of Allah. They simply called, through their existence, for us to pursue another world, a world that collectively bent in that humble submission. They saw the illusion of this life that declared itself the only reality. And so, in the spirit of trying to follow their examples, trying to submit to Allah, and trying to be fair to others – as my nineteen-year-old eyes still plead in that photo – I declare that I am not an answer, and refuse to give you one.

I am not a feminist, socialist, radical or Islamist. I am not an essay to show your friend 'what Muslims think about X'. I am not a punchline or an 'eye-opening response'. I am not a poet, performer, writer, commentator or activist. I am not an example. I am not a subject of your research. I am merely a question. That is the closest thing to freedom I have found: to not sate the appetite of the voyeur I was told to spend my life answering to. I do not apologise that such existence is unacceptable, I ask you *why* it is. Why is being a Muslim woman who sees the world through her own eyes and refuses to prove, disprove or explain it so uncomfortable? Why is finishing reading this essay so dissatisfying?

Abu Huraira reported: 'The Messenger of Allah, peace and blessings be upon him, said, "Islam began as a something strange and it will return to being strange, so blessed are the strangers."'

(Sahih Muslim 145)

HIDDEN

Asha Mohamed

If an African makes a contribution to the world but a European is not there to record said contribution, did it actually occur?

How exhausting and demoralising it is to have whiteness be the lens through which we look at everything. There is a poster in the London Underground for a visit to the Tower of London to see the Crown Jewels. On it is a photo of a boy who looks to be Black (perhaps mixed heritage) staring in awe at the Imperial State Crown, a crown part of a collection which not only includes the Koh-i-Noor diamond from India, 'given' to the British colonisers 'lawfully', but also two of the world's largest diamonds, the Great Star of Africa and the Second Star of Africa, both cut from the same diamond mined in South Africa. In the poster, the Second Star of Africa takes pride of place on the state crown itself. There is no irony here. Instead, what we have is the reflection of a reality many observe to be true; we in and from the Global South live to serve, and our lands exist to provide for the West™. We are meant to idolise its power and status. Those of us living in the West are here due to its benevolence and its willingness to help the less fortunate seek better lives. We are not the same as its native people. How can we be when our dehumanisation is what feeds its supremacy?

The horrific killings of George Floyd, Breonna Taylor, Ahmaud Arbery and countless others at the hands of the US police rightfully sparked global protests, giving renewed momentum to the Black Lives Matter movement. These unjust killings are emblematic of centuries of systemic de-humanisation. Police brutality, the prison-industrial complex, inequality in the criminal justice system (as seen in the Belly Mujinga and Shukri Abdi cases in the UK), inequality in healthcare services and the cycle of poverty are not things that exist in a vacuum. They are all symptoms of the world we live in today. A world whose survival depends on racial superiority and places Black bodies at the bottom of this racial hierarchy.

School is often the first and most damaging institution to embed this concept in our young minds. It is the way we psychologically prepare each new generation to submissively take their *innate* place in society. While I was at school, I never really thought too deeply about how and why we study the history and culture of Africans and the descendants of Africa in the way that we do. I never questioned the un-nuanced, monolithic nature of what I was learning. Searching my memories, I can remember a term in which, during history classes, we covered the civil rights movement and apartheid. I can recall the two terms we spent reading *Things Fall Apart* and *To Kill a Mockingbird* in English Lit. I even remember, in geography class, learning about how, when the British left Ghana, development of the railway ceased and the country fell into disarray. It would seem our history is intrinsically about struggle and European arrival. We are simply there to contextualise Europe's rise to prominence; Europe's economic might, a stepping stone in someone else's history. The existence of Africa is viewed only as an exhibition through a gravely distorted, macabre, anglicised lens.

Ask yourself why it is that European history goes back thousands of years, but African history starts with the scramble for Africa. What happens when the only history you learn about yourself is one of degradation, humiliation and dehumanisation? What happens when the only history you learn about Europeans is one of power, status and enlightenment? Do you feel equal? What does a child learning this in a British school subconsciously internalise? Particularly when the concepts of these power structures are being physically and emotionally compounded as often the first memorable incidents of racism also occur within schools.

This child's world view is centered around the accomplishments of Europeans and the 'failures' of their own ancestors. What status do they then give themselves? If from childhood you are taught the history of your second-class-citizen people, this will be the lens you look through. This is the battle facing us African descendants in the West; descendants who have watched the culture and history of our diverse peoples be erased and reconfigured by European 'intellectuals'.

When the Italians colonised southern Somalia, every classroom had two geographical maps: a map of Somalia and a map of Italy. They were juxtaposed, with the drawing of Italy twice the size of that of Somalia. In reality, of course, Somalia is geographically far larger than Italy, but such is the privilege of the coloniser. Today, though we may use different maps, not much has changed. Modern-day maps most commonly use the Mercator projection, which makes the northern – wealthier – countries look bigger. Even though India is three times larger than the Scandinavian countries combined, it is depicted as smaller than each one. Even though Greenland is fourteen times smaller than Africa, they are depicted as the same size. Even though Russia is smaller than the continent of Africa, it is depicted as being larger. We have come to accept this projection of ideology as an accurate representation of our world.

In 1973, the Gall–Peters projection came out. This was an area-accurate map that was first presented in Germany. Its depiction of Africa is radically different to the conventional maps we find. According to German software designer, Kai Krause, you can fit the USA, China, all of Europe, India and Japan combined into the continent of Africa. This should come as no surprise because it is a continent. So why is it only really in the last decade that the Gall–Peters projection has become more widely accepted? Why was it considered controversial for so long and by so many? Those who cannot admit that this is about ideologies hide behind the argument that it is very difficult to depict a spherical image onto a flat surface. Although this is technically true, it does not acceptably account for the vast discrepancy in size.

So why does this matter? Since the days of Imperialism, the West has maintained control over global decision-making. Countries in the West profit from their supervision of the world's political, economical, educational, and societal structures. If we imagine this system as a massive Jenga tower and then take each structural issue as a block, we can remove the pieces in one of two ways. Either we remove them one by one, slowly, to ensure the tower stays as stable as possible for as long as possible, or we go about the game swiftly and without grace, knowing that at any moment the removal of just one block could lead to its collapse. At the moment, I feel we are not progressing as we should in dismantling these power structures because we are treading carefully and, worse still, we are putting blocks back and the tower is continually growing taller. In this way, a map is more than just an image of the world; it is political capital, entrenching in us the belief that this prestige the Western countries have ordained for themselves is irrefutable. They will continue to reign supreme while Africa will remain as it is: defined by its poverty and corruption. Were we to change the world map as we know it, thereby removing but one Jenga piece, what effect would this have on the next generation of Africans, and indeed on anyone living anywhere in the Third World™? It may seem small, but to some it may be that one piece that instigates the fall of the tower.

To regain control over your own history is to have control over your own identity. We underestimate the effect this has on self-esteem, self-worth and self-confidence. Many countries in Africa are in a turmoil, caused by colonialism, continual exploitation, humanitarian crises, African volun-tourism, Western aid's sustainment of poverty and the eco-nomic hold Western powers still have in many regions. That they do not allow their turmoil to be their defining character is not a profoundly 'African' nature as stereotypes have us constantly believe, but a human one. After all, turmoil is not a culture but a circumstance. Among African descendants there are questions to be asked in terms of identity and the long-lasting effects of colonialism but these issues will only continue to grow so long as we are not in control of the very tongues used to speak our stories.

So what happens when we lose this control? In 2015, the *Somaliland Journal of African Studies* (itself a revival of British colonialism) released its first issue. This journal, despite its given name, had chosen not to include any papers written by Somalis. Furthermore, not one Somali was present on the journal's editorial board nor on its board of directors. Worse still, the boards comprised nine European- and US-based academics, and the only Africans consulted were three Ethiopians (because, you know, *Africa is a country*). This all came to light when Somali-Canadian Dr Safia Aidid (at the time a PhD candidate at Harvard University) took to Facebook to call out the journal, closing the post with #cadaan-studies, meaning 'white studies'. The post quickly became a thread, with other Somalis weighing in on the bizarre, albeit predictable, turn of events. The post received so much attention, it soon reached Dr Markus Hoehne, a German anthropologist and member of the journal's board of directors. Hoehne entered the thread to defend the journal's decision, explaining in his lengthy and disturbing comment the 'unacademic' nature of the Somali people. Hoehne claimed he had not come across many young Somalis he would qualify as 'serious scholars', adding, 'I guess you would have to first find all the young Somalis willing to sit on their butt for 8 hours a day and read and write to get one piece of text out'.

Though this was mainly received with derision and humour (and even prompted Dr Safia Aidid to write an article for the online publication *Africa is a Country* titled 'Can the Somali Speak?') the truly insidious and unsurprising part of all this is that it showcased, yet again, the staggering arrogance with which these Western academics assert themselves into any and every space they see fit to do so.

The sense of superiority, entitlement and privilege it takes to believe with such confidence that you can speak for a people simply because you feel they do not have the inclination to do so is truly astounding. Not taking into consideration the wars and political crises dominating the region, nor the fact that the previous generation was too focused on survival to think too deeply about contributing to the *Western* academic world, to make assertions that levels of 'academic-ness' are linked to intelligence and race screams eugenics. Let's ignore then that what it is to be an academic or a scholar is defined by Europeans, and let's ignore that much of Africa records its history and culture through oral transmission. Speaking for a culture you are not a part of without consulting said culture is neither academic nor intelligent, and reveals the hubristic short-sightedness of the academic world today.

This is the flip side of the hidden curriculum. It breeds thoughtlessness and an internalised supremacy on behalf of those of European descent who are more interested in preserving the memory of the advancements and achievements of their ancestors to bother to delve beyond a two-dimensional understanding of the lived experiences of an 'Othered' people, pre-subjugation. What the journal and Hoehne's subsequent comments also highlighted is the ongoing problematic nature of anthropologists and the field of anthropology itself. It is an undeniable fact that the vast majority of anthropologists are of European descent. It is also an inescapable fact that this field is inextricable from colonialism. We are stuck between a rock and a hard place. How can we decolonise the mind if we then become a part of the very structures which oppress us? Yet if we refuse to take part, how can we ever gain full control of our own truths if the outsider is constantly and illegitimately 'whitesplaining' and homogenising our cultures?

The longer we spend in the West, the more susceptible we become to the hidden curriculum that upholds the archaic, imperial system we live under. The less we are exposed to the other side of the coin, the more we adopt damaging ideas about ourselves, knowingly or unknowingly. No matter how far removed you are generationally from Africa, if you identify as Black, you cannot divorce yourself fully from this continent. Undeniably, how it is viewed will have an impact on how you are viewed and how you view yourself.

In Chinua Achebe's *Things Fall Apart* we spend over two hundred pages getting to know the protagonist Okonkwo and following the complex emotional and structural changes he and his people go through as colonialists change the face of everything they know. On the last page, a commissioner, in other words a coloniser, is looking at Okonkwo and the tree from which he hangs and remarks how the protagonist's story could make interesting reading, 'perhaps not a whole chapter, but a paragraph at any rate'. Okonkwo, this powerful, problematic, complicated human being, will be reduced to nothing more than a footnote in someone else's story. It was in studying the Haitian Revolution, on which I chose to write my final-year dissertation, that I found a real-life parallel of this in Toussaint L'Ouverture. I pored over contemporary historiographies based on Toussaint's life and found over thirty letters between British generals discussing Toussaint as a formidable figure. I came across countless contemporary newspaper articles naming him and discussing the revolt. I read excerpts of letters sent between himself and Napoleon after he became the de facto leader of the revolution. I learned about the expeditions the French embarked upon to the island in an attempt to regain control, how Napoleon himself took part in one of them. I read the Black Jacobins and Aimé Césaire's detailed studies. Imagine then, after reading all this, after reading of how Toussaint was 'one of the most remarkable men in an age rich in remarkable men' (a quote attributed to Beauchamp) imagine how I felt when upon reading Napoleon's memoir, the only reference to Toussaint I could find was one footnote in the entire four-hundred-page book? History is usually written by the winners; the interpretation of the Haitian Revolution is what happens when the losers wield the pen. It is precisely due to this that we have minimised the impact of the revolution and all but erased it from our history books.

Much like how the commissioner in *Things Fall Apart* looks at the people around him as 'primitive tribes', the French historians began to craft a narrative of the rebels as ungrateful, uncivilised brutes and reduced Toussaint to a power-hungry dictator who did not care about the freeing of his people. The historiography of the revolution and the analysis of Toussaint began to change when historians of Haitian descent started to write about it. This is why it is imperative to control your story, especially when living at the heart of an empire that not only looks nothing like you but refuses to represent you.

What we need is an eradication of the destructive, toxic, colonial-minded hidden curriculum. This can only be done with the restructuring of the syllabus so that it no longer serves the purpose of exporting lies and maintaining the supremacy of the colonisers while surreptitiously invading the minds of the Other. We need to see a dismantling of the illusion of the distribution of power that exists today. We cannot go on uplifting one group of people while degrading another and wonder why the world is the way it is. We need to see more discourse among ourselves and seize the pen from the outsiders looking in. By writing our own history we can change the narrative to reflect the three-dimensional nature of reality. Think about any historical, anthropological or sociological fact you know – where is it from? Who carried out the research? Who penned the words? Why are all our history books written by European descendants? How authentic can an account be if it's written by someone peeking through a window?

It really is all about education. To change how a people are perceived, the people must first change how they perceive themselves. If you ask a Muslim to recite the first verse of the Qur'an to be sent down, they will say 'Iqra' ('read'). Seeking knowledge is a protection, a vaccination for the mind. When certain aspects of our history are omitted or changed, it creates confusion and opens the door for those lacking in knowledge to create narratives that, with context, would never be able to exist. It leaves room for some to state confidently that 'slavery was a choice'. It is context that we are missing. Kanye West, in his controversial TMZ interview, did, however, make a point I have to agree with: we are still mentally enslaved. Of course Kanye is not the pioneer of such philosophical thought. We have Ngũgĩ wa Thiong'o telling us to 'secure the base, decolonise the mind', Malcolm X asking 'who taught you to hate yourself?', Frantz Fanon examining our place within a Eurocentric world in *Black Skin, White Mask*. Where are *these* discussions in the curriculum?

This mental enslavement is not by choice. How can it be when decisions are being made on our behalf by those whose understanding of us is incomplete? Even the limited amount of history we are taught about our people is problematic. There is no reason why in the UK we are taught only the 'wins' of the Empire. Even its break-up is taught as a win. We are taught that Britain 'gave up' the colonies, reached agreements with the countries involved and created a Commonwealth. How much is said about the countries that expelled Britain? Even the way we're taught about slavery tastes like a win. We are taught how Black people were *given* their freedom. History either glosses over or minimises the stories of those who fought back and rebelled. If module after module about slavery and colonialism are crammed down our throats at school, why must we wait until university to choose an independent study topic to learn about the largest slave insurrection in history? Why do I need to take it upon myself to find out about Thomas Sankara and why Burkina Faso was named Burkina Faso? Let it be clear, there is no shame in being oppressed, only in being an oppressor. I am not claiming that those that rebelled 'deserve' to be heard more than the stories of those that were freed, but that agendas show themselves in the brightest of light when we cherry-pick a particular narrative. In the words of Albert Maysles, *'Tyranny is the deliberate removal of nuance'*.

It is difficult to put into words how emotionally exhausting it is trying to unpack centuries of the oppression and suppression of Africa when, as you can see even in these discussions, our ideas are not our own; even in these historical writings the recollections have been revised, changed and reinvented. How has struggle come to be our identifying character when those pushing the narrative cannot explain the depth of our trauma? Can we really claim that discussing these issues will help us achieve psychological closure when even physical decolonisation is an illusion?

This is why it's so important to reject the hidden curriculum, to reject this false image of ourselves draped over us by those in power. Education is one of the biggest imports of our identity crisis. It's not a rare thing that a country reshapes and redesigns its history so it is seen as the victor, the hero, the pinnacle of moral judgement. Yet the emergence of nationhood (as well as the consequences of 'decolonisation') has meant Western countries now have within them citizens whose ancestors suffered greatly at the hands of the ancestors of the indigenous population. When you have multiple ethnicities and races (as is currently understood today) in your land, it becomes imperative to set aside propaganda and have instead a multifaceted approach to historiography if unity is the objective. This conversation would look very different if it so happened that all advancements, achievements, enlightenment, philosophy, art and culture sprang from the hands of the Europeans (and the Far Eastern cultures Europeans seem to revere so much). This in part is a reason we of African descent are not often seen to have a universal human experience, because so much of our ancestors' contributions to humanity has been removed from the history books. So many examples of our ancestors acting with agency and living full, complex, great as well as problematic lives are not part of the conversation, because the curriculum serves the interest of the nation, and the nations in the West are predominantly of white European descent. It is their contributions we observe and centre and morph in ways that place them, their culture and their ancestors on a fraudulent pedestal.

As is human nature, we of African descent too look to 'history' to define our past, to show us where we came from. Unfortunately, those of us in the diaspora are at the mercy of the Western academic system as we tend not to take into consideration what modern-day Africa calls history. We do not place great stock in oral transmission because that is not the way we were taught to study history here. Even the education systems in much of Africa are guided and controlled by Western ideals and Western interpretations thanks to Western cultural imperialism. Nowhere in the world, arguably not even on the continent itself, are we taught to consider the contributions of Africa's people in a real, non-Eurocentric way. We are taught they offer little – outside of labour and resources – to the progression of humanity, a progression dependent on the regression of Africa. If we continue to ignore the complex, wide-ranging history of Africa (country by country), and we continue to ignore its importance and the priceless value of its thinkers and how its manipulation past and present informs its – and our – place in the world, then we in the diaspora start on the road to becoming nothing but a moving mass of whitewashed Black bodies unwittingly complicit in our own subjugation.

A very real reason we need to re-evaluate what we are learning is that we need to understand our place and our role as Black people within racial capitalism. It seems racial disharmony benefits those at the top, those making decisions and hoarding wealth. The hierarchy and ranking of races and ethnicities is how the means of production and resource theft and exploitation occur in the Global South by and for the profit of the West. Not much has changed since the days of imperialism and colonialism. In the words of Ruth Wilson Gilmore, 'capitalism requires inequality and racism enshrines it.'

Though those profiting and exploiting in meaningful ways are those in the 1 per cent, it has to be admitted that anyone living in the West does, to some degree, profit off the exploitation of the Global South. When it comes to those of us who are Black and live in the West, it has to be kept in mind that, oftentimes, we are neither seen nor see ourselves as equals in attaining power compared to our European-descended fellow citizens. The consequence of us not having real power nor seeing ourselves as having much of any power to contribute effectively to the ending of exploitation in invaluable ways is that we unwittingly allow ourselves to be tools maintaining the power structure oppressing our fellow people in the Global South. We see freedom and success as achieving the power, status and wealth our oppressors have held. A power, status and wealth that is to the detriment of so many that look like us. This is what we are taught is success. The current lament of 'we were kings and queens' shows how deeply we have internalised a 'truth' that is harmful – that this is the space we have been excluded from for too long, a space we deserve to occupy like so many of our fellow citizens with their family lineages and monarchies and empires. It is as though the form of power we ache for is beneficial to our well-being. We shouldn't want seats at broken tables.

We can't keep waiting to be handed the keys to our freedom and power, as it is a fragmented and distorted version of *real* freedom and power. If we want to effect real change in the world as well as in our own lives, we need to start centering ourselves as the protagonists of our lives and take responsibility for educating ourselves in what we actually are longing for. Why do we want what we want? Does it reflect what we need? We know we're dehumanised. It's all we're told we are. It's humanisation we want, a humanisation which, according to Paulo Freire, is 'affirmed by the yearning of the oppressed for freedom and justice, and by their struggle to recover their lost humanity'. That has been the focus before and should remain the focus now, no matter how alluring the lives of the wealthy and corrupted powerful. They have never been the face of humanisation but of the policing of it.

This is our journey to unlearning with new knowledge the toxicity we have ingested for so long. We need to organise so we ensure our children understand that what they are taught in school and in society is but a fragment of the truth, and we need to organise so we can make the changes we can. In the places we can't, we create, in the meantime, spaces of our own – spaces for knowledge-seeking that may one day become a road of sorts for those that can. We can't solve the world's problems in one day. We might feel helpless watching the ransacking of Africa and the Global South from the comfort of our rooms here, while trying not to drown in the everyday struggle of overcoming and succumbing to otherness and life-threatening oppression in the place we call home, but we can work on what we *can* control and have the power to change. The education of 'the other' is certainly an issue we can collectively move to resolve. We have to know what we need to know, and let go of what does not and will never benefit us in the long run, so we can protect our minds as well as the minds of those of us to come.

It is up to us as Africans and descendants of Africans to create a shift in historical perspective and assert ourselves in the conversations that continue to impact our lives. It's up to us to craft our own alternative paths to true liberation outside of the one defined for us, because, in the words of Audre Lorde, 'The master's tools will never dismantle the master's house' – no matter how much they convince us they could.

ON THERAPY

Sophie Williams

My therapist is a skinny middle-aged white lady. I've taken off my niqab, rather than flipping it back, because I want to skip past the bit where she's distracted by what I'm wearing; we only have an hour. She asks me what I hope to achieve. My therapy goals. I tell her I want to learn how to re-associate after I dissociate, and I want to reduce my insomnia.

She seems a little confused as to what PTSD actually is. She wants me to elaborate. I talk about dissociation, flash-backs, and the sheer exhaustion of always being ready to fight for my life, of being permanently hardwired for danger. She asks for examples of how it manifests in my daily life.

I think about it. 'OK, so for example if a large angry-looking man is staring at me, my brain goes into fight-or-flight mode and I start processing dozens of possible reactions in the event that he physically attacks me. Like in a milli-second I'll be flooded with adrenaline and decide that kicking him in the nuts then running away is probably my best option.'

She stiffens. My stomach lurches. I've said the Wrong Thing already.

'Well, you're in Britain now. This isn't appropriate behaviour in Britain. This kind of violence goes against British Values,' she says.

'Do you even know what PTSD is?' I ask, before remembering that arrogance is only OK when you're fully white, not treacherous Muslim-tainted off-white. 'I'm English,' I add more quietly, hoping to stem a lecture on British Values.

'You don't look English,' she mutters, meaning my clothes don't look English.

I can't believe that I'm having to explain my clothes to my therapist. I pick my niqab off the table. 'I wear this because I like it. I feel comfortable in it.'

'But it's part of your religion,' she corrects me.

'It's also part of who I am. I wear it for spiritual reasons, sure, but I also derive psychological benefit from it too. It's like sunglasses, but better. I value the privacy.'

She leans back, looking pleased. 'So maybe one measure of the success of our sessions might be that you'll be comfortable taking it off in public,' she says, making a note.

I take a deep breath, and decide to justify my hypothetical response to the hypothetical angry man on the street. Even though I'm here of my own free will, saying I have PTSD, which means I know perfectly well that things in my brain are permanently broken. It's the first session, and I'm already trying to reassure my therapist that I'm not dangerous.

'Islamophobic attacks on Muslim women are a thing,' I begin. I gesture at my belly. 'Being visibly pregnant makes me feel more vulnerable. It's pretty common for Muslim women to feel threatened if a large angry white man glares at them for any length of time.'

'What's your evidence for that?' she counters. 'In CBT, we examine the evidence for our fears. What's your evidence for your fear of being attacked by an angry man?'

I start telling her about all the times I've been verbally and physically assaulted in this country, but I'm on autopilot now. I'm already dissociating, my mind retreating down to the bottom of the ocean where it's calm and dreamy and safe. She's somewhere up on the surface, muffled and distant. My animal brain has identified her as a threat. It's clear that I have to be careful what I say to her. I remember, too late, that NHS therapists have Prevent training, and it's left to their 'better judgement' as to whether a patient is at risk of radicalisation.

I have eleven sessions left to convince her that I'm not at risk of radicalisation. That, I realise, is my true therapy goal now.

It's a few weeks after the birth of my third child, and I'm not in a good place. I've been crying a lot, secretly, in the bathroom. I feel overwhelmed. I repeatedly get the urge to walk out of my own life. I can't cope. I'm exhausted.

'How are you feeling?' the GP asks.

'A little tired,' I say, and realise to my horror that my face and neck are suddenly flooded with tears. I wave my hand dismissively, force a laugh. 'Tired and hormonal. But, *really* happy.'

I have to convince her that I don't have postnatal depression. I can't face another round of therapy, of pointlessly lying to another stranger about how sane and serene I am.

'Do you have thoughts of hurting yourself or others?' she asks.

'Oh my God of course not!' I lie, thinking of all the times I've fantasised about jumping off the balcony, just to get some sleep.

'Does your husband . . . support you?' she asks.

I see us through her eyes. Weeping Muslim woman with bearded husband. I can't tell if she's stereotyping us or genuinely concerned.

'He's amazing,' I say truthfully.

'Your medical history mentions PTSD,' the GP continues. 'Pre-existing mental-health conditions may increase the risk of postnatal depression. I'd like to put you in touch with a local organisation that can offer you extra support.'

'I'm fine!' I insist brightly, blowing my nose. 'Just sleep-deprived. Thank you for your concern.'

She looks unconvinced, but lets me go. I feel like I've dodged a bullet.

*

'Ummi, that woman is looking at you and making weird noises,' says my daughter.

I know. I've seen. An elderly white middle-class woman is miming explosions at me, making explosion sounds, presumably her way of telling me I'm a terrorist in a way that I'll understand no matter what my native language is.

'Ignore her,' I murmur, hugging my child into my chest so she can't see the woman. She wriggles free.

'She's making explosion sounds,' my daughter realises. 'Why is she making explosion sounds and doing that thing with her hands?'

'I don't know,' I lie.

I want to march over to the woman and yell at her. I long to slap her stupid face because how fucking dare she. I know I can't. Gone are the days when I could react aggressively to stranger abuse. I imagine the *Daily Mail* headlines: 'Burka Brutality!' 'Muslim Rage!'

I can't yell at the woman because I have to keep proving that I'm not a terrorist, that women who wear niqab aren't inherently violent.

'Let's get you a Kinder Surprise egg,' I suggest, and we break away from the queue. I don't look back at the woman because I'm too ashamed by my own lack of reaction. I feel like a wuss.

A man glares at me in the chocolate aisle. 'Jesus FUCK-ING Christ,' he snarls. A woman waits until she's abreast with me before she mutters, 'Fucking ISIS.'

I keep glancing at my daughter. Has she heard? She looks confused.

'You know what we forgot to get? Ketchup! For the hot dogs!' I say loudly, and my daughter brightens.

My daughter throws herself into my arms and cries into my neck. 'I hate school, I want to be homeschooled, please please please don't send me back to school tomorrow.'

I hug her and say soothing things like 'inshaAllah' and 'we're thinking about it' and 'I'll talk to your teachers again.'

'That's what you said last time and the time before and the time before that!' she wails.

It's true. Whenever she comes home complaining about Islamophobic or racist bullying, begging to be homeschooled, my husband and I email or call the school, sometimes arrange a meeting, and get brushed off with assurances that the school is very inclusive and has a zero-tolerance policy towards bullying and discrimination. The implication is always that my daughter is making things up, or being oversensitive.

'WHY can't you homeschool me?' she demands desperately as children with the correct levels of sensitivity hurtle past us laughing and shrieking.

'Well, because we have to, we need to, I'll explain later,' I say lamely. 'I'm not saying no, I'm just saying, not this term.'

It's like Batman told a kid that he couldn't rescue her today, maybe some other day, it was complicated, she'd understand one day. She's devastated, and I hate myself.

But I'm remembering the *Guardian* headline – 'Home-school families face potential investigation over "radicalisation risk"'– and I feel physically unwell at the thought of being investigated for potential radicalisation.

Because, as a Muslim, how do you prove that you're not a radicalisation risk? Once upon a time someone persuaded the UK government that Islam is a spectrum, from casual to practising to extremist. The more practising you are, the more red flags you wave. Everyday Muslim words like veil, madrassah, salafi, sharia law, Allahu Akbar and Islamic marriage – put them together in one paragraph and you have a tabloid editor's wet dream of a front-page story. Or an anonymous tip to the anti-terrorist hotline. Or a social worker's safeguarding report.

There are fresh images out of Yemen, ones of starving children and desperate mothers. My heart hurts. My stomach hurts. I don't know how to be detached from another mother's pain. I don't know how to not empathise.

My husband walks in to see me crying. He glances at the screen and understands. He's seen me react to news about families separated at the US border, and children's detention facilities. He's seen me react to news about babies around the world getting raped, bombed, drowned, gassed, shot, abducted and orphaned.

He hugs me and I pull away after a few seconds to scrub my face with tissues because I hate it when people see me cry.

I rant. About how awful it must be to not have the luxury of feeding your children when they're hungry and begging you for food. About the general situation in Yemen. And then I mention Syria. The Rohingya. Palestine. The refugees trying to cross the Mediterranean. Back to the families separated at the US border. I rant about yet another police officer shooting yet another Black boy in America. Yet another British man getting a ridiculously short sentence for raping yet another newborn baby. Donald Trump, Theresa May, Katie Hopkins, the far right.

So much pain and injustice in the world, and I can't do anything about it, and I can't unfeel it. I don't know what to do with all this horrifying information so I just rant about it.

My husband glances over my shoulder and he nudges my foot. I turn to see my daughter standing in the doorway.

'I had a nightmare,' she says dramatically.

I get up to hug her.

'Why were you crying?' she asks, fascinated. My apparent lack of emotion is a family joke. She can't remember seeing me cry before.

'It was a really sad movie,' I lie smoothly.

'You were talking about Katie Hopkins and Theresa May, I heard you.'

'Oi!' I tickle her and she giggles. 'How long were you listening for?'

'I wasn't, I just heard you say Katie Hopkins and also Theresa May. Did they do something on Twitter?'

Relieved, I put her back to bed and read Ayatul Kursi over her and kiss her forehead and tell her I love her. I sit next to her in the dark for a while, silently thanking Allah for our physical safety, for an abundance of food, for the colour of our passports.

I ask Him to protect us and to keep us together as a family. My demons are lurking on the fringe of our private conversation. I add a prayer for protection from ignorant authorities. I want to wake my daughter up and warn her not to mention to anyone at school that her mother was ranting about Katie Hopkins and Theresa May last night. I tell myself I'm being paranoid.

There was a video on Twitter earlier, of a woman wearing niqab talking about how she was raided in her birthing room, 'blood on the sheets, blood on my legs'. I can hear her voice now: 'They're taking away our babies!' I can't remember what her alleged crime was. Being too political, I think she said. I want desperately to believe that she made mistakes that I won't make.

That I'm safe because I'm careful.

I'm wearing pink, because I think it's a nice, non-extremisty colour to wear. It feels massively important to reassure my child's teachers that we're a nice, non-extremisty, non-terroristy family. Her teachers praise her kindness and good manners and progress. They ask if I have any concerns.

I do. I'm concerned about the fact that in the three years she's been at this school, there's been no mention of Islam, whereas all the other major religions have been covered several times. I'm concerned about the fact that my child is made to do this Just Dance thing several times a week, coming home singing sexually suggestive lyrics. More than anything else, I'm concerned about the fact that she's been bullied for wearing hijab and the school has done very little about it.

In a millisecond, I've already imagined bringing up my concerns, and how this might be viewed through the Prevent lens. Niqab-wearing woman and her big-bearded husband have problems with 'not enough Islam' at school, with music and dance, and are demanding that more is done to accommodate their daughter's hijab. I imagine an investigation being opened, my daughter taken into a room and interrogated about her family life.

'Do your parents talk about politics?' they would ask.

'All the time,' she'd reply. 'They think Theresa May is mean. Also my mum thinks the Queen is useless. And sometimes she cries because they bomb babies, she thinks I don't know but I wake up at night and creep into the corridor to listen to my parents. She gets very angry with the bad men who bomb babies.'

'Are you angry at the bad men?'

'Yes. Killing is haram,' my child might say, because this is how I explained to her that ISIS aren't good Muslims. 'Allah doesn't like people killing babies.' And then social workers would take her into care and my other babies would be taken away from me too and the pain of separation would surpass any pain I'd ever experienced and my mind splinters just imagining all this.

'None spring to mind,' I lie.

The support group is a safe space, we're told. But I haven't really allowed myself to relax until today. It's now the fifth session and these women are starting to feel like my sisters; our shared trauma is a powerful bond. There are three Hindu women, a Sikh woman, three women with crucifixes around their neck and one with a crucifix tattoo. And for once, our faith is irrelevant.

My niqab is pooled on the carpet next to me. I don't mind the lack of facial privacy today. We're all women. We're all vulnerable here.

We're talking about safety. We all have things to share. Experiences, tips, questions, plans. Someone makes me a mug of tea. Someone else laughs at one of my jokes. I feel safe, which is so rare that it's unfamiliar. I think how apt it is that today's topic is Safety.

'Another thing is, don't be afraid to share your concerns about your children, other children,' the group leader insists. 'If a child starts talking about the world, about wars, about politics, about God. Be vigilant. Take action. Radicalisation is a real threat.'

All heads swivel to glance at me.

'Just make a call and social services will investigate. Don't be afraid to make that call.'

I know it's just a knee-jerk reaction after years of media conditioning, the fact that it was me they all looked at. Nothing personal, nothing to worry about. But it feels like a punch to the gut. It hurts. They're not my sisters, I realise. The shared bond is superficial. No amount of hugs and mugs of tea can erase deeply entrenched prejudice.

Or Prevent training. For the first time, I notice that the group leaders have name tags proclaiming their primary roles as council and NHS employees.

I feel the urge to say something.

'Excuse me, yes, hi, as the token Muslim of the group I'd like to point out that talking about God doesn't make someone a terrorist. And also that I personally know three different women whose abusive exes used the whole "radicalisation risk" thing to win custody of their children, I know someone whose children were taken into care. And there was no radicalisation. They were just –' I gesture at my hijab – 'Muslim.'

An awkward silence falls over the group. I'm pretty sure I've said the Wrong Thing again. The two group leaders exchange glances.

I look at their name tags again.

I wonder what my child is saying in the kids' support group next door.

The irony is that when people ask me what I miss about my pre-Muslim life, they assume it'll be something that I 'sacrificed' for Islam, like bacon or beer or bikinis.

But the only thing I miss was not snatched from me by my new faith. It was seized from me by Prevent, by years of Islamophobic headlines, by British politicians who use anti-Muslim fearmongering to bolster public support, by the widespread belief among people in positions of power that the more Muslim you are, the more extremist you are. By radicalisation checklists circulated among doctors and midwives and teachers and therapists, listing warning signs like criticism of UK foreign policy and mistrust of authority. By news items about Muslim women getting kicked in the stomach and losing their unborn babies, or a Muslim woman getting run over twice by a car and losing her ability to walk, for no reason other than they were wearing hijab. By the first-hand accounts pouring out of social media from Muslim women who've had their children taken away for vague crimes like being too political or non-conformist or being related to the wrong person.

My love for my babies is my Achilles heel, my kryptonite. Anyone with the power to take away or hurt my children has me by the neck.

I'm surrounded by vague threats I can neither kick nor run away from, which is hard for someone whose signature moves are fight or flight.

What I miss is the freedom to navigate my life without constantly worrying that the assumptions of strangers or the state might destroy it.

DIRTY MELANIN, PRECIOUS MELANIN: BILAL WAS BLACK

Negla Abdalla

Apparently, it could not be a better time for Muslim women. You turn on your TV screens, you log into your social media, you step out onto the busy London streets and you are met by a range of strong independent Muslim women. Women who have a presence about them, women who are ready to 'make a change', women who always have a welcoming smile plastered across their faces.

Our society around us in the UK has changed, our cultural mentalities have changed, our mindsets have changed. Families are raising us to be queens. Empowering us to own our talents, to be leaders in our fields, to be innovative in what we create. Educational systems are putting everything they can into making women believe that they can do whatever their male counterparts can do. More and more girls and women are engaging in subjects like Engineering, Accounting and IT.

Instagram alone is flooded by Muslim women owning what they do. You have Muslim female fashion bloggers, Muslim female creatives and even Muslim female boxers. Everything around us is pushing us to be that 'vehicle for change', empowering us to reclaim our identities as women and show the world around us that we are a force to be reckoned with.

But is this really empowerment? And if so – why are domestic abuse rates still so high? Why are so many women still putting up with judgements – especially from our Muslim brothers? Why, in some households, are we still expected to get up and serve the men in our families regardless of how tired or sick we may be? Why are we still at the epicentre of debates regarding what we wear – mostly from our Muslim brothers and non-Muslims? When will we be allowed the chance to fully breathe without being told we should be independent and empowered just to be hit with reality in the same breath? Mentally are we Muslim women completely free? It seems that some elements of the community are not. It seems that a portion of our mind has internalised the notion of being inferior counterparts that people have labelled us with. We're at risk of falling into a self-fulfilling prophecy; sadly some of us have already fallen, taking the reductive exceptionalism outlined above as gospel.

If we really believe that we are not and never have been inferior, why do we remain in abusive marriages? There are, of course, any number of social, psychological and economic factors why women might stay in abusive relationships. But is some small part of it because we feel inferior and dependent on our husbands or is it because we've convinced ourselves that we need to be the glue to keep the broken fragments of the family together? Is it because we worry that our individual hardships will be used to vilify the community as a whole? Regardless, why is society still quick to blame us when we finally do speak out? Why is it that a woman can never just be a victim? Whether we are beaten or raped, our morality is always questioned. We are always faced with comments like, 'You must have angered him,' or, 'You must have deserved it.' When will this change? When will we change and stop centring men?

However, while many Muslim women are creating and offered platforms for their work, Black Muslim women are notably absent from 'mainstream representation' of Muslim women. When will Black women be seen as part of the recognisable face of Islam? When will we celebrate their cultural and creative output without sidelining or subjecting them to ignorant comments? At what point can a Black Muslim woman be appreciated without being victim to insults and structural bias because of the melanin in her skin? When will the Muslim community acknowledge the blatant racism pouring out of the comments they so confidently make in the presence of our Black community? How much longer will our daughters and sons be fighting to marry the ones they love, trying to break down their parents' ignorant stereotypes only to be able to overcome those barriers when the parents realise the potential spouses 'aren't that dark'?

The number of times I have seen this happen is worrying. It subconsciously started affecting me; I used to wonder if my in-laws would only accept me after seeing me and classing my skin tone as acceptable. Despite neither my husband nor they ever making me feel as if my skin colour was an issue nor making any remarks that could be deemed insulting or racist, I still had this worry, because I had seen it happen so many times. A Lebanese daughter tells her mother and father she wants to marry a brother from Kenya, and the parents go absolutely ballistic, only ever referring to the brother as 'that Black man', insulting his features and his hair, wearing the young woman down with questions about how she will cope when her daughter has 'unruly African hair', and who will marry that granddaughter? All of this before they even lay eyes on the brother, before they ask about his Deen, his manners, his education and work, his family and his hobbies. The moment they catch a glimpse of his picture or the daughter manages to convince them to simply meet the brother, all that anger disappears, all the barriers come down and the parents are now overjoyed. Why? Because they now realise that the Kenyan brother's skin tone is an acceptable level of Black to them. That is the reality of the Ummah we live in today.

As a Black African Muslim woman I have almost always been made aware of the fact that I belonged to groups which were deemed inferior, that were viewed stereotypically and that were feared due to the Islamophobia that continuously swept the nation and the globe. But any negative comments about my Muslim or female identity did not upset or provoke me. Rather they made me more proud to be a Muslim woman, they taught me how to merge the two and wear both identities with pride, they made me more determined. However, I was very sensitive and protective about my Black African identity. I never stood for any comments about my skin colour, or any other person's skin colour. All my life the 'lightness' of my skin has been a topic of discussion. Although I do not consider myself as 'light-skinned', I am very much aware that I am closer to the lighter end of the spectrum than my darker-skinned sisters and brothers, something I became more aware of when I began to wear make-up. I realised that I was wearing shades with names like 'Golden Honey', 'Cool Golden' and 'Honey' while my younger sister was wearing shades called 'Cocoa', 'Mocha' and 'Espresso'.

Constantly feeling as if discussing my skin colour was necessary made me angry and self-conscious, but the older I got the more I began to understand that these conversations were actually a much deeper issue. Since childhood, I was made to believe by almost everybody around me that my beauty lay simply in the fact that my skin was 'not that dark', or that I was 'not Black but brown'. As a child my skin colour was almost close to that of someone from North Africa or the Middle East, and as I grew my melanin levels began to increase. This did not go unnoticed by the society around me, and many people used to subject me to comments about how white I used to be and how

I needed to use face masks and scrubs to get rid of the 'dirt' and return to that skin colour.

I was baffled; I still am baffled. Why, in 2020 and with far more complicated and worrying problems, are our Black brothers and sisters still fighting against racism and colourism? Why did it take having Instagram pages for people to finally appreciate the different tones of Black skin we have in this world? Why does the BLM movement have to be trending for us to be noticed? Why is it only when graphic videos of Black people being murdered go viral that people listen and question their own complicity? Ask yourself what action you took personally after listening. Did you act or did you belittle years of pain and struggle to a mere social-media trend? Black people, whether they be Christians, Jews, Muslims or Atheists, single or married, straight or gay, are still facing ignorant comments on top of structural racism. Comments by people who curse other racists but who with those same lips say the most appalling things. Or sometimes, in the face of racism, say nothing at all.

Message to the world – it is not OK under any circumstances to say to anybody any of the following statements:

'You're not Black, you're brown.'

'You're not that dark.'

'Do not use that foundation shade; try to make yourself look brighter,' followed by suggesting a shade ten times lighter than our actual skin colour.

'Your sister/brother is much blacker than you.'

'You should use a mix of honey, lemon and sugar scrub – it will make your face so white.'

'I'm Muslim, I cannot be racist. Bilal the first muezzin was Black.'

These are just a few to give you an idea. But how dare you! How dare you still assume white skin is what we should all aim for! How dare you try and belittle Black people and teach them that the melanin that shades their skin is nothing but dirt that needs to be washed off!

Most young girls dream about their wedding day. I was no different. Even with all the excitement of being spoilt and having my hair, nails and make-up done, celebrating with all those I love and care about and spending the rest of my life with the one I love, I still could not escape the ignorance. Every woman who visited our house in the weeks and days before my wedding seemed to have a home-made remedy that I had to use to make sure I would look 'white and pretty' on my special day.

To my non-Black Muslim community. It angers me that so many of you are happy to sit among us in mosques and invite us into your homes quoting the hadith of the Prophet Muhammad (SAW) which states that 'There is no superiority for an Arab over a non-Arab, nor for a non-Arab over an Arab. Neither is white superior over Black, nor is Black superior over white – except by piety.' Yet the moment one of my Black brothers comes and asks for your daughter's hand in marriage you react as if Satan himself has asked for your daughter. Or when one of your sons decides he would like to marry one of our Black sisters he is stopped in his tracks and told horrible things like, 'Your child will come out Black like her and who will marry them?'

To my Black community. Is there really a need to add to the segregation and isolate our brothers and sisters by using terms such as light-skinned and dark-skinned? Can we not all just be Black? Black lives matter is not restricted to one group of Black people, it's inclusive of ALL Black people. We need to sort these issues out within our own community. The hashtags #teamlightskin and #teamdarkskin formed one of the worst trends I have ever encountered. I saw more and more Black people glamorise being lighter skinned, and more and more Black people loathing their darker skin. Ponder on the connotations of light and dark, and think what the result of labelling people, human beings, with such terms can be. This trend made dark-skinned people feel like they did not even belong in their own race – was it not bad enough they already felt isolated by other races? Trends and ignorant comments such as these are what cause many Black people to self-loathe and even self-harm. The bullying can push them to suicide. Mothers are having to listen to their child beg them to buy them bleaching creams. Can you even begin to imagine the torture and the turmoil your actions put people through?

*

To my Muslim Black community. Mainly to our grandparents, mothers and fathers, stop discriminating against other Black people. Do not internalise the anti-Blackness. Why is it such a bad thing if your Somali daughter marries a Nigerian brother? Their children will be blessed to get double the dosage of melanin, their children will be blessed to get those full lips, their children will be blessed to get those curls falling from their head. Do you not see how every other race that made us feel inferior for our skin colours and our features invests their hard-earned money in achieving our natural looks? Do you see how hard they work to get that tan in the few days of English summer we have? Do you see how they pour into clinics looking for lip fillers or a bigger bum? Why are you still insistent on plaguing the young generation with this detrimental mindset? Arabs, why is your TV, especially during Ramadhan, full of shows that mock other Black Africans/Arabs such as Sudanese people? Egyptians, why is it OK to use blackface when you have a sizeable Black population? Could you not find Black actors or actresses among them or is it just to mock and belittle us? My Sudanese people, you are on the receiving end of so much racism from your white Arab neighbours in Africa and across the waters in the Middle East, why are you then taking the role of the oppressor and the superior over our darker-skinned population? I am perplexed as to how Muslims today can think it is OK to treat people from their own community this way simply because of their skin colour. I once read that whenever a non-Black Muslim exercises racism, you do so to reach a proximity of whiteness. Doing so could mean that you are trying to replace white supremacists, that you now want to be the oppressors and hold that power. To me, sadly, that makes a lot of sense. I will leave you, the reader, to make your own decision.

To my Black women. As with most things in life we are definitely at the receiving end of a lot more than our brothers – which it is not to say that they are not battling stereotypes and ignorance in their own way. We have lived through the music that always seemed to romanticise the 'light-skinned girl', we have had to deal with picking up foundations that look like our shades only to see a range of different names for black coffee, while our lighter-skinned sisters have the honey shades and the tan shades. But we never let it break us. We live with the daily realities of misogynoir.

Thankfully, we have mostly left behind the days where we were focused on bleaching our skin. We reclaimed our identities and told the world with such a gleaming confidence that we accept ourselves and we do not need that acceptance from you. We went ahead and shone on YouTube, created our own brands and dedicated many different Instagram pages to celebrating darker skin.

To my non-Black Muslim community. The fight is not a burden for Black people. It is your duty to call out racism in your homes, in your communities and wherever else it may occur, especially when the Black community is not present to defend themselves. Do not run away from the issue and choose to believe that racism does not exist within the Ummah simply to satisfy yourselves. Do not be afraid to discuss these issues out of fear that the non-Muslim community may judge us or speak negatively of us more than it already does. Our honour does not lie with mankind, it lies with Allah and thus we must remember His rulings and the teachings given to us through the Qur'an, hadith and the Prophets throughout time. Do not silence a part of our Muslim community just to please others. Do not prioritise society's views of Muslims over the treatment of your own brothers and sisters. Remember the Ummah has been likened to one body, and if one joint is afflicted then so is the whole. Recognise your responsibility to your brothers and sisters in Islam.

Tackling racism means we need to tackle the oppressive systems that are prevalent in societies globally. People feed off having power over those they consider beneath them. Without eradicating these systems we will not be able to eradicate racism. But the first step is to recognise and admit that there is an issue to begin with.

Our religion's main doctrine is one of equality for all regardless of religion, sex, race or age. As Muslims we are a representation of the religion we follow, and yes, that is a big responsibility, especially for the women who wear Islam so visibly through their hijab, abaya or niqab. Once upon a time the sahabah used to say, 'Look at the Muslims and you will know Islam'; and now we run from this and say, 'Islam is unflawed, look at Islam, do not look at us.' While it is true that Islam is unflawed and as human beings we will always have our flaws, that does not mean that we should take a passive approach and submit to those flaws. No! We should rather identify our individual flaws and our shortcomings as a group and take an active and progressive approach to changing them.

The hierarchy of belonging to Islam is one of the most ridiculous notions I have ever come across. As a child I was always taught that Islam was inclusive, that anybody could be a Muslim. However, as I grew up, that teaching I held so dear to my heart became a distant memory as that was not what I saw being practised. What I saw being practised was that Islam belongs to Arabs. They were at the top of the hierarchy, Black people were at the bottom and everybody else was slotted in the middle. This notion made it hard for people to understand that there were Nigerian, Kenyan, Rwandan, Gambian Muslims to name just a few, or to put it more bluntly, that Black people were Muslims. Born Muslims and not reverts. That they understood and practised Islam, that in fact they had received Islam before many other parts of the world.

Worryingly, this is an idea we are allowing to take root, between us and also in the non-Muslim community. This is one of the reasons that brands that are trying to cater to modest fashion and be more 'inclusive' only contact our Arab or white Muslim community, when there is a plethora of stunning Black and Asian women who would also make good brand ambassadors. Time and time again I see my Black and Asian sisters talking on platforms such as Instagram or YouTube about how they find it much harder than the white/white-passing Muslim community to land collaborations and brand deals. The same sentiment has been expressed by the white Muslim community on social media – they have recognised the lack of collaborations with and event invitations offered to their Black Muslim sisters. This is partly because our actions have made non-Muslims believe that Islam and Arab are the same. The sad reality is that when non-Muslims think of terrorism they think of Pakistani Muslims, and when they think of modest fashion they think of Arab Muslims. As Muslims we are aware of this, but what are we going to do to change it?

We are going to fight. We are going to follow the progressive lead our non-Muslim Black community has taken and keep pushing. Not for recognition, not for acceptance, not for money or deals, but for our generation and every generation to come to love themselves and their skin colour. We are going to push to create our own brands, our own platforms and our own successes. We will work collectively as a team. You are either with us and our progression, or you are not – if you fall in the latter camp, step aside and watch how real kings and queens shine.

*

To my Black Muslims, I see you shining. I see the way you have been marginalised within the Muslim community.

To my Black non-Muslims, I see you shining. Thank you for accepting your fellow Black Muslims and not focusing your energies on isolating them because they do not share the same faith as you. Your struggle is our struggle, our fight is your fight. Let us be one community always. Let us show the world the worst decision they made was marginalising us. Let us be the kings and queens our ancestors were.

Self-love is key. Love yourselves, love each other, our melanin is something to be so proud of. It will forever live on through our children, grandchildren and great-grandchildren.

Melanin is not dirt, it is the most precious gift bequeathed to me by my parents, by my ancestors and by my ruler.

COVID-19 AND RECALIBRATING MY RAMADHAN REALITY

Khadijah Elshayyal

It was an unremarkable morning in Sha'ban/April, and I was scrolling through Twitter as I prepared breakfast for my sons, while they completed their morning 'PE with Joe' workout. We were gradually adjusting to our new lockdown routine – or to put it more accurately, our lockdown lack of routine. Like many busy families with young children, we had previously been coping with life's demands and pressures by chasing an illusory ideal – the ideal of being 'organised'. This entailed compartmentalising our days in such a way as to optimise efficiency and productivity. There was the morning rush of getting everyone out on time, armed with the requisite tools for the day ahead. Bags, coats, lunches, equipment all at the ready, as we headed our separate ways with familiar precision. At the end of the day, a timetable of homework, sports or extra-curricular activities was followed by family time in the evening, then bedtime for the children, after which my husband and I would cram in unfinished work and household duties, and prepare for more of the same the following day. Functionally speaking, it certainly meant we were getting by. But how much pause for thought or contemplation did such a hectic routine afford us?

As a mother in this man's world, I often get asked how I balance the various obligations that I have. My first response is always that it is more a case of juggling than balancing – and that balls are very often dropped in the process. But I also find myself asking – what is this coveted equilibrium that we are expected to strive for?

When lockdown came into force, the fragility of this intricate system became abundantly clear to us. Still, we worked out ways to be organised and efficient, trying to understand the uncertainty – or, more importantly, trying to have patience and faith as we accepted what we *could not* understand. We were all missing our family and friends, and though frequent Zoom calls certainly helped, they also underlined to us all the huge imperative and the real challenges of developing a much more flexible and open-minded approach to life. We were realising that deliberate efforts were required to actively appreciate the smaller details, to slow down and allow for more flexibility and spontaneity. This was in itself an exercise in patience and fortitude.

And I thought about all this, as I scrolled through Twitter and wondered absently whether I was going to intervene to diffuse the latest row that was erupting between my sons. Sibling squabbles had become ever-present as the boys were now spending 24/7 with one another, and the usual intermittent cry of 'he pushed me!' had been joined by the COVID-19-specific protestations of 'he coughed at me!' and 'he breathed on me!'

I thought about how instinctively absorbent a child's mind is. Its capacity to take in new realities and incorporate them into everyday existence with so much ease presented such a contrast to the anxiety and second-guessing that characterised adult conversations in this moment. While I was fretting with my family, friends and colleagues about how we were going to 'cope', how soon or easily we would get back to 'normal', my sons demonstrated how they effortlessly took new challenges into their stride, to the point of incorporating them into their bickering.

As I did all of this, some exchanges on what we affectionately refer to as MT (Muslim Twitter) caught my eye. I noticed several influential commentators – preachers and public figures – discussing how the forthcoming month of Ramadhan was going to present us with exceptional challenges. People were expressing apprehension around what a Ramadhan under lockdown would look and feel like. The practical aspect of mosque closures and public gatherings being forbidden meant that this month would, unusually, be a much quieter and less eventful affair than many people were used to.

There was an unmistakable poignancy to this realisation. After all, iftar gatherings with family and friends traditionally constitute a staple of Ramadhan – with diary dates being strategically coordinated in such a way as to allow as many households as possible to access the honour and anticipated rewards of hosting one another. Another hallmark of the month that was having to be called off was congregational taraweeh. These communal gatherings for nightly worship hold huge significance for many, bringing together as they do communities in their numbers to stand in straight, tightly packed rows for prayer, filling up mosques and overspilling onto courtyards and pavements. But there is also so much more to the place of taraweeh – it radiates a palpable and unique vitality. It acts as a vibrant community hub for the month, where charity collections are made, news is shared, and where you can be sure to catch up with everyone that you haven't had a chance to break fast with. In many congregations, children variously enjoy joining in intermittently with the adults, or the unbridled glee of being left to their own devices as adults are engaged in prayer. For little ones opting to go with the latter, all manner of adventures can be patched together from the makeshift resources at their disposal – games are devised as children explore nooks and crannies within the mosque grounds, often with the older children intuitively keeping an eye on those younger than them. In this way, relationships are forged, fond memories are made and lessons learned in a wholesome and affirming environment.

The mosque can also offer a safe space for individuals to find companionship and support as they observe Ramadhan. As a result, those with no family nearby as well as converts, whose families may not be observing the month, would now be facing the prospect of a very solitary month ahead of them, as communal worship and gatherings were called off.

It was very sad indeed to realise that this Ramadhan there would be no access to these spaces. But I couldn't help noticing that it was male teachers and preachers, in particular, who were writing extensive Twitter threads, recording talks and sharing elaborate bullet-point plans with ideas about how to make the most of this different and difficult Ramadhan. Suggestions were being shared that people should focus more on coming closer to their families during this month by worshipping together at home. We were being encouraged to think about how our home lives could be adapted so that they could create an atmosphere that was conducive to the intense worship, self-reflection and fasting of our whole selves from desire and temptation. But even as helpful tips were being shared, there was a mournful tinge to these conversations. As some commentators expressed despair at the prospect of their first-ever Ramadhan as adults without attending nightly taraweeh at the mosque, it fascinated me that the difficult Ramadhan they were describing was not so different to my own Ramadhan experience for the best part of the past decade – as a mother. The striking difference was that as a mother I, and many others like me, had to come to terms with the challenges of a Ramadhan in solitude on my own, with little or no support, or even acknowledgment, from our communities, as we navigated this difficulty.

I thought back to my first Ramadhan as a mother. My first child arrived in early Ramadhan 1431 and, needless to say, no Ramadhan has ever been the same since. Of course, for that first year, there are obvious reasons why being postpartum would detract from a 'typical' Ramadhan experience. For a start, I was not fasting, nor was I praying for the duration of the entire month. The immediate whirlwind of emotions, and the physical demands on my body and my attention, are difficult to adequately put into words. It is cliché to say that becoming a mother turns your life upside down, but giving birth during Ramadhan acutely highlighted this reality to me. Here was a month which, throughout my life, had been associated with certain constants. Constants in how my day was structured, in my focus, my priorities and my personal goals. The arrival of a baby that Ramadhan threw all of this into disarray as he became my overriding priority, and my entire existence, particularly during that first Ramadhan as a mother, revolved around catering to his every need.

It is most common for a mother's Ramadhan in isolation to be bracketed away, conveniently categorised as a 'women's issue', and for mothers to be sagaciously counselled with that other cliché: that looking after their homes and their children is their 'ibadah. I cannot count the times I and women I know have felt slighted and excluded by the implied tone of such 'advice'. We see statements 'reassuring' mothers that they shouldn't worry if they are unable to complete a reading of the entire Qur'an over the course of the month, or if their caring duties make it impossible to attend taraweeh at the mosque, since the hours they spend in the kitchen cooking and washing up are regarded as praiseworthy and rewardable sacrifices. Yet despite the pervasiveness of these platitudes, we still find resourceful ways to make our Ramadhans meaningful, even if we do this in the context of a community that, more often than not, has made clear to us that our struggles in this area are not worth much more than a passing thought.

So I will be honest and admit that there was something distasteful and insensitive about seeing Muslim men now using their platforms to express inconsolable despair about the sense of loss they felt, as they realised that the impending Ramadhan would be lacking in the communal experiences to which they were so accustomed. Many of these men held positions of leadership and guidance in their communities, and I wondered how aware they were of the Ramadhan realities that mothers had to navigate – the struggles and sacrifices we contended with simply to be able to stand a chance of focusing – even a little – on our own spiritual growth for that month. I also wondered how *they* might respond to advice that their reward for looking after the home and family would compensate for their exclusion from communal spaces, or from fasting and worshipping in community.

It then struck me how the discourse around 'COVID Ramadhan' *still* came from a place of privilege. It still spoke to those who were always fortunate enough to be at the centre of the communal hub during this most precious month of the year. Those who had consistently occupied spaces at the periphery – by virtue of our caring obligations, or by aspects of identity: our sex, our age, ethnicity, disabilities and perhaps also those of us who were converts to the faith – we *remained* at the periphery of this conversation, even during this frenetic time of unparalleled stress and uncertainty. Where had these conversations been in previous years? Where had our concern and empathy been for those in our communities for whom Ramadhan was by default a lonely and isolating experience? People for whom access to support and upliftment from others was little more than a distant dream or a nostalgic memory from times gone by? There was something bemusing in the fact that it was only when men in our communities were confronted with the unappealing reality of a Ramadhan in isolation that it became a subject deemed worthy of mainstream conversation, compared with previous years when it had been relegated to the realm of 'women's issues'. I wondered what this told us about what we took for granted about ourselves and our communities, and our relationships with one another – as women and men, sisters and brothers, wives and husbands.

Pondering this then took my thoughts to what Ramadhan signified to me on a strictly individual level. Though it encompasses many collective experiences, an important aspect of this sacred month is the focus on the individual – their independent agency and their personal connection with God. In the hadith qudsi, we are informed that, in the eyes of God, fasting stands apart from other acts of worship. It is depicted as the most intimate act of worship, a pure act of devotion – placing each fasting person in direct connection with God:

'Every deed of the son of Adam is for him except fasting; it is for Me, and I shall reward (the fasting person) for it.'

In recognition of the limitlessness of sacrifice and adversity that a fasting person can potentially endure, and how, indeed, it is a uniquely personal experience, this hadith tells us that the reward for our fasting is at God's own discretion. Ultimately, I thought, everyone's Ramadhan was truly their own. Do we lose sight of this reality, as we worry and seek to mitigate for the challenges of a Ramadhan in isolation?

The long days of a summer Ramadhan are physically and emotionally taxing at the best of times. They can pose specific challenges and conflicting demands to me, as a parent of young children. On one hand, I experience the urge to slow down and focus on my spiritual development, but on the other, I want to focus on creating a wholesome and enjoyable Ramadhan experience for my children. Often the juggling act that I described earlier makes it difficult to devote energy and enthusiasm to the latter, while also giving the attention that I would like to the former.

By the time Ramadhan arrived, we had been in lockdown for around one month already. If you will forgive me one final cliché, I am pleased to report that for me, it was without a doubt, the most enriching Ramadhan I have had since becoming a mother. One month into lockdown, my family and I were confidently coming to terms with our newfound flexibility. Rather than fit our Ramadhan around our pre-existing routine, we had the freedom to come up with a model that suited us and our needs – both as a unit and as individuals. Lockdown had meant that our home environment was so much calmer – albeit as a result of circumstance rather than by design . . . and we reaped the rewards of this calm by centring our spiritual growth. We still sought community wherever we could get it, and to some extent, my years of semi-isolated Ramadhans as a mother placed me in good stead in thinking outside the box about how to connect with others as we invested in making our home a space of spiritual growth, connecting with others as we strove to connect with God and His revelation.

People often refer to Ramadhan as a 'training ground' for the rest of the year. A chance to focus on spiritual and self-development, to build up good habits, to focus on bettering our characters and our relationships. My Ramadhan in COVID lockdown underlined to me how beneficial it is for us to see this month not just as an opportunity to build ourselves up, but also as an opportunity to pause and reflect. This aspect, I feel, has often been lost in the familiar drive that we see in our communities to 'make the most' of our month – a drive which can still rely quite strongly on the ubiquitous, capitalistic obsession with productivity. I don't want to take away from the communal features which are so central to Ramadhan – it is undeniable that we draw strength and inspiration from fasting and breaking fast with others, from praying, reciting and learning with one another, from struggling together to keep our desires in check and from the huge amount of charitable giving that takes place.

But ultimately, if we focus too much on meticulously coordinating iftar gatherings, if we find that we are unable to maintain focus in taraweeh except when it is at the mosque, then maybe we need to ask ourselves questions about how we approach this month, and what we are *really* taking away from it.

What I am suggesting here is that it is worth pondering and perhaps recalibrating what we perceive to be a maximisation of the month's benefits. To what extent is our focus on productivity influenced by the systems and structures that surround us in the societies that we inhabit? To what extent is this conception of productivity and efficiency aligned with our own natural disposition, or fitrah. To what extent is our productivity-obsessed approach to Ramadhan actually offering true nourishment to our souls?

As lockdown is eased, but also reintroduced in various forms, and as this pandemic remains with us for the foreseeable future, it is worth pausing to ask ourselves how much we have learned and how much we have we changed. Perhaps many of us have tended to measure our fulfilment during this month against a somewhat socially determined notion of 'tick boxes', the absence or disruption of which causes existential panic and anxiety. Maybe the capitalist context within which we live has pervaded even our search for spirituality during our most sacred time of the year, such that we have yet to consciously decouple ourselves from the impulse to focus on the form and quantity of an idealised 'output' that we have been able to produce. An output that is measured by norms and conventions which might assume a uniformity of social conditions, rather than one which appreciates and values the range of commitments, experiences and situations we bring with us – from the mundane to the exceptional.

Ramadhan provided me and my family with a salutary case study in this regard. I won't pretend that, in our home, we now live blissfully unstructured and spontaneous lives. What I can say is that we are trying to be more mindful – not only of ourselves and our positionality, but also of consciously being more humble and awake to the reality of the spaces we occupy in this universe. Ramadhan during a pandemic has enriched my and my family's self-awareness and our understandings of productivity.

For this, I thank the Muslim men on Twitter for their comments – unwittingly insensitive as they were – as without seeing them, perhaps I would not have been prompted to take this contemplative journey towards recalibrating my Ramadhan reality.

THE QUEST FOR MODESTY IN THE DIGITAL AGE

Ruqaiya Haris

Social media makes it clear that interpretations of Muslim women's modesty are hugely varied across cultures, communities and individuals. Without delving into the complexity of modesty within our character, through the concealment of our sins and humility of our speech, the physical aspect of modesty is in itself a major topic of contention. While most of our acts of faith remain private and deeply personal, the highly visible nature of our appearance opens us up to public scrutiny in a unique way. This has resulted in a microscopic focus on Muslim women's bodies that often reproduces much of the same toxic obsession with women's looks that we criticise in our secular counterparts.

The explosion of the modest fashion industry in the West generated media interest from those whose perception of Muslims seemed to be shaped by television dramas and provocative newspaper headlines and were thus surprised to see Muslim women wearing anything other than burqas. It also sparked heated debates within the Muslim community about whether the commoditisation of 'modesty' was in fact a positive thing at all. Numerous modest-fashion bloggers, hijab-wearing models and major fashion brands curating 'modest' collections were suddenly catering to Muslim consumers, and while some women were delighted at the prospect of being able to find modest clothes on the high street, many Muslims questioned whether this would undermine and ultimately dilute the notion of modesty in Islam.

The idea of corporate giants such as Dolce & Gabbana or laypeople such as bloggers setting the boundaries of modest dress was unsettling for some. Others felt that a fashion industry largely built on harmful beauty ideals and labour exploitation now catering to Muslims was hardly something to celebrate. It seemed that 'championing diversity' was often just another way of expressing a desire to profit from the global Muslim consumer market worth billions, with the prices of many modest clothing items being affordable only by the ultra-rich.

But a world away from wealthy Gulf women looking at designer abayas in Harrods, the average teenage Muslim girl may have been scrolling through her social-media feeds discovering glamorous women wearing hijab and flowing, modest outfits – and for the first time felt empowered enough to hold her head up high amid all the Islamophobia and far-right rhetoric young people are exposed to, and wear her hijab with pride. And those are the girls I'm concerned about: the Gen-Z Muslimahs who have grown up online and who may not be given the room to continue to evolve and learn as they embark upon their individual spiritual journey with the impossible scrutiny and religious policing that will be inevitably thrust upon them.

It is a historical reality that as religion grows in popularity and spreads across lands, it adapts to new climates and will ultimately be interpreted and practised in different ways. It seems impossible to separate our ideas around modesty from our individual perspectives, and such varying perspectives rarely speak to an objective, uniform conception of modesty in Islam. One woman's turban hijab is another woman's not-quite-authentic-hijab; one woman's modest fashion ensemble is another woman's immodest fashion ensemble. Of course, we do have sharia rulings to guide us, but I wonder how many people can *truly* say they embody what Surah an-Noor instructs us to do by way of 'not displaying' our beauty? A woman with no hijab and loose clothing may be quick to demean another woman in no hijab and more reveal-ing clothing. Of course, to the self-proclaimed traditionalist internet troll, both women have fallen short of observing proper hijab and will be insulted and degraded in the same way, so perhaps we should attempt to find some unity in that. Our willingness to draw attention to flaws in other women without reflecting upon our own may be a desperate tool to regain some power we feel we have lost in a sexist society where notions of modesty can vary so greatly.

Flawless make-up, brows on fleek and even cosmetic enhancements such as fillers and Botox have become somewhat normalised among many Muslim women, including those in Muslim-majority countries governed by hard-line Islamic law. We even see them on women who otherwise adhere to the requirements of hijab and modest dress in their clothing. The boundaries of modesty have become blurred in many contexts, as has our understanding of what it is to 'hide' our beauty in a world that seems to pressure us to be beautiful at all costs.

I remember one of my Islamic teachers telling me years ago that 'beauty is a test'; it certainly gave me something to think about over the years as I struggled between wearing hijab in order to fulfil a religious act of worship, and taking it off to feel prettier. As a twenty-six-year-old woman, it's hard for me to remember a time when Brazilian-butt-lift surgery and the homogeneous 'Kardashian look' reproduced a thousand times on social media weren't part of the mainstream, and didn't subconsciously permeate the walls of my mind.

In my adolescence, we used our mobile phones to painstakingly send texts on a keypad made of numbers, and used our computers to play Microsoft Solitaire and maybe visit Wikipedia to help with our homework. Our social conditioning was largely restricted to the school playground and of course a limited selection of television programmes and films.

It's different for teenagers now. The advent of the smartphone brought with it largely unfiltered access to the digital sphere as well as social-media addiction and the need to be constantly plugged in. Checking our phones every few minutes has become the norm, and the digital world has become, in some ways, more real than the world around us. Through algorithms and targeted advertising, we can be sure that it is shaping the way many of us think.

We aren't too sure of the long-term effects just yet, but it's safe to assume that it's difficult for young women to stare at screens all day and see images of beautiful, airbrushed women enhanced with make-up and cosmetic surgery without it impacting their psyche. Since the dawn of advertising, women's bodies have been used to sell every product imaginable, and influencers today also use their beauty, monetising it to sell products and build a following. The difference between being sexualised and sexualising ourselves is one that cannot be denied, but often the outcome can be the same: the overwhelming sentiment that beauty is something that is rewarded. People seem to forget that Muslim women existing in these societies are growing up exposed to largely the same conditioning as everyone else.

It's worth noting that Muslim societies are no different in the quest for beauty – whether it's Fair & Lovely adverts telling women to loathe their dark skin, or the bitter vitriol spewed by aunties who fat-shame the young girls in their family, the social conditioning that encourages women to spend their time worrying about their looks is ever-present. The idea that you have to be beautiful in order to get a husband, to please your in-laws, to be accepted in society and loved by your peers is in some ways a universal expectation thrust upon women. Beauty is also weaponised in combination with some kind of deeply subjective concept of modesty; you must be beautiful, but not show it off too much. Attractive, but not sexy. It is, in essence, brainwashing women to understand that they must live their lives attempting to fulfil unreasonable cultural expectations in relation to their personal choices, their body shape, their clothing and their presentation with or without make-up. All of this in order to win the affections of a man who probably uses the same shower gel to wash his face, hair and body, and whose personal shortcomings will likely have been excused throughout his life in a way that yours may never be.

The virtue of modesty in men is rarely spoken about, and when it is spoken about it isn't generally met with debate or scathing commentary that relentlessly attack the character of the individual in question. Whether in cases of Muslim sportsmen showing their awrah (the parts of their body that are impermissible to show in public) or male Muslim public figures exposed for sex scandals, the entire notion of modesty seems more malleable and forgiving for men. While allegations of male Muslim scholars abusing their power and conducting unlawful, predatory relationships with female students was met with some outrage in the community, it still inspired statements from many other notable figures encouraging us to 'cover the sins of our brothers', which felt like a cop-out that only served to facilitate the silencing of abuse victims. When compared with the public reaction and vilification of female Muslim public figures who simply failed to adhere to sharia requirements of hijab or modesty in their personal practice, the contrast is evident. The lengths that the Muslim community will go to in order to cover the sins of men is rarely extended to women.

Misogyny will always find a way to adapt to new contexts, and reinvent itself to fit within the parameters of social acceptability in different communities and historical periods. As such, the microscopic focus on women's appearances within our community seems to operate in close proximity to the focus on the hijab that comes from society at large, which reproduces Islamophobic tropes about veils and hijab-wearing women. It is generally understood by Muslims today that Western media is utterly obsessed with the hijab, often presented implicitly or explicitly as a symbol of regression and all the perceived ills of Islam as well as foreignness. Statistics show that visibly Muslim women face greater job discrimination and are more likely to be exposed to Islamophobic abuse. And where we are given less hostile representation, it can feel a little bit like David Attenborough narrating the lives of frogs. It treats us as strange creatures that need to be examined, ultimately still 'others' us in a way that reduces us to our faith and feels tokenistic. You may be seen as nothing more than a hijab spokesperson or Islam advocate rather than as a multi-faceted person. The reality is that the hijab becomes our selling point, our defining feature, and the only aspect of us deemed interesting.

This obsession seems mirrored within the Muslim community, where hijab or our perceived modesty is what defines us and gives weight to our words. Women who don't wear the hijab are often dismissed and deemed less knowledgeable about Islam or less authentically Muslim. This can often present a conundrum for a Muslim woman struggling with her faith – do we present a version of ourselves that appears more outwardly religious for the approval of our community? Do we present a less religious version of ourselves to avoid backlash and prejudice in a climate that feels hostile towards our religiosity? While we should make these decisions for ourselves and for God, our subconscious need to 'fit in' or avoid public shaming may contribute towards these decisions, even in 'free' societies that claim to value individual liberty while perpetuating sexist, xenophobic bigotry.

Given that the fixation with modesty largely centres women, it is perhaps unsurprising that many men fail to really empathise or connect with the way in which women today are under immense scrutiny to live up to beauty ideals that are amplified through social media. It is always more surprising, however, when women fail to extend this empathy to one another. In a sexist society it can be easier to embrace internalised misogyny than to unlearn it, and women can be quick to turn on each other in order to divert the unwanted attention and judgement we receive ourselves. There is an underlying sentiment that suggests if we join in with entry-level sexism perpetuated by bigoted men, we will cease to become victims of it. Yet the reality of this is that you are assisting in your own oppression.

The vast majority of us are tested by beauty ideals and the quest for modesty as well as battling a disrupted sense of peace in our own self-image in a way that men, frankly, are not. It is true that men may feel an urgency to become muscular and 'ripped' or handsome enough to get the girl, as demonstrated in the recent 'incel' movement that saw men who felt unattractive directing their anger towards the women who did not want to sleep with them. However, the expectation for women to look a certain way is something uniquely insidious and almost impossible to escape. Whether it is in advertising, the entertainment industry, corporate workplaces or retail environments, there is an onus placed upon women to be desirable and conventionally attractive that is highly gendered.

I remember being acutely aware of the way in which society rewards women's beauty from a young age, when I would be complimented for being 'cute'. I also remember the damage to my self-esteem when I was teased for having facial hair and being 'ugly' during those painful pubescent years before I discovered the gruelling yet transformative world of waxing, shaving and make-up. The self-love movements online tell us (through pretty drawings and lettering) to unlearn our child-hood trauma and 'live in the now!' But it's difficult to put it fully behind me when I'm still very much holding on to the same insecurities I grew up with, and also still paying direct debit payments each month for my laser hair-removal treat-ment. The quest for beauty was and still is something that exists in the forefront of my mind.

As I grew up, I experienced through trial and error that pandering to mainstream beauty ideals made people treat me better. Although I was often told I was funny and bright, looking 'pretty' is what made people want to spend time with me, made boys want to talk to me and what made me start to be able to value myself.

So, upon rediscovering Islam properly in my late teenage years, the narrations and commentary surrounding modesty spoke to me immediately. I had unearthed an entire belief system that attempted to remove the pressure for women to conform to beauty standards by making much of a woman's beauty private, reserved only for those she chooses to show it to rather than leering strangers ready to value or dismiss her for superficial reasons. I had found a reason not to spend hun-dreds of pounds on fake hair and beauty treatments just to be deemed worthy of anyone's time. I had finally unplugged from the matrix!

It didn't take long after I started practising Islam for me to start wearing a hijab and dressing more modestly, and I can say wholeheartedly that I genuinely loved wearing it. It changed my relationship with my body and mind. It affected how I interacted with people, as I was aware that I was in some ways an ambassador for my religion. It coincided with a greater sense of spirituality that saw me lose interest in clubbing and the drinking culture I had grown up around in London. When I suddenly found myself in the club, sober, covered from head to toe and uninterested in talking to men, I really couldn't help but realise how smelly and tacky it actually was. I was surrounded by sweaty foreheads, bad breath and girls in minuscule outfits despite below-freezing temperatures outside, and it became hard to ignore how much of British youth culture centres self-destructive behaviour and the hyper-sexualisation of women.

Observing hijab wasn't exactly a fix-all solution for all of life's problems, but it was a constant reminder of Allah, and I was able to stop seeing myself as somebody who needed to be a 'hot girl' and to connect with my true, intellectual and spiritual self in a way that I hadn't really expected to. It's remarkable how much of your personality can be suppressed when you place such a strong emphasis on your looks. I was able to appreciate different parts of myself that I hadn't connected with since I was a child, such as my strong ability to empathise with others, my passion for writing and other hobbies like art that I had forgotten I enjoyed so much. I had discovered a sense of purity and true peace that I have been chasing ever since. I believe that I experienced what al-Ghazali referred to as tasting 'the sweetness of faith' which could only be felt rather than explained, and, like a born-again Christian, I felt I had found a new sense of purpose.

It changed my whole outlook on romantic relationships too. I didn't want to date anyone who saw me as nothing more than somebody they were physically attracted to, and who didn't appreciate any of the complexities of my character. I found myself drawn to entirely different types of men – instead of Muslim-by-name bad boys, it was the nerdy religious types that caught my eye, those who would have previously not crossed my radar. Once I got past their social awkwardness around women and inability to hold a conversation without calling me 'sister' at the end of each sentence, it was uplifting to experience deeper connections with people who also centred their lives around God. The novelty of practising religious men wore off a little as I realised that they were often still just as emotionally unavailable as non-religious men, with the added cultural baggage of projecting their own ideal of a religious Muslim woman onto me. Still, they had nice beards and were polite, and it felt fulfilling to be able to have religious discussions with somebody on a similar wavelength.

The wider Muslim community were also welcoming to me both at university and online. I was surprised to find that conservative people I worried would be judgemental towards me were quick to encourage me to put my past behind me, look forward and continue making strides in my faith.

After all, everybody loves the story of a reformed sinner who left a life of sin to strive on the path of righteousness. It is often heralded as an example of the transformative nature of faith and leaves people with a feeling of warmth and hope – but what happens when that journey isn't linear? Or when it isn't quite the fairy-tale ending where somebody 'found the light' and lived happily ever after? The painful back-and-forth of losing one's grounding, battling weakened faith and navigating difficult experiences that affect our ability to practise are all harsh realities that many striving Muslims are faced with.

As the trials and tribulations of my life played out, I experienced battles with mental health and emotional abuse that impacted my religious observance. I would have deep low periods and unstable highs that left little room for the serenity of faith. I wanted quick fixes, and ended up revisiting a lot of my old destructive behaviours, which included relying on attention for the way I looked to give me a boost. Modesty was just about the last thing on my mind, but it added to the sense of guilt and shame I felt about who I was and how I had let things spiral out of control.

How could I explain my actions to my community and to those I felt accountable to in my daily life, as well as on my online platform, in which I had developed a following sharing my journey towards faith? I had been given media opportunities to speak about my religion, my hijab and sensitive issues like Islamophobia. It seemed impossible to explain in any coherent way how I was able to go from a kind of reluctant role model to some younger Muslim girls, due to my visibility and discussions of faith, to somebody having a destructive meltdown and a spiritual crisis.

I really just wanted to let my hair down (excuse the pun) and have fun to distract myself from the way I was feeling, and so I decided, quite impulsively, to take off my hijab.

In doing so, I experienced a lot of backlash online. This wasn't a new phenomenon to me, but it was surprising to see a lot of religious folk distance themselves. But as much as I wanted to still be seen as an outwardly religious person and respected as such, it began to feel fraudulent when I really just didn't feel like that person any more.

My self-image would fluctuate so frequently that I would try to put my hijab back on for periods of time, eventually start to feel that it was inauthentic and then would take it off again. Then after some time, I would feel that showing my body and not feeling like my true 'religious' self was depressing and a betrayal to my fitrah or natural state, so I would try to adopt hijab again. Then sometimes I would have my convertible 'half-hijab' on, with a bit of carefully styled hair showing at the front. I was trying to figure out what actually felt authentic to me, but my identity was pretty much changing with the wind.

All the while, the quest for beauty seemed to occupy more and more of my time. Seeking religious knowledge like I had spent my early twenties doing took a backseat to the all-consuming, brain-cell-destroying hobby of surfing Instagram for hours and saving images of women with beautiful faces –

which eventually contributed towards me deciding to get lip fillers to change the way my own face looked. I did like the outcome, but as they were temporary and would change shape over time, it was sort of like chasing a big-lipped mirage in the desert and I was left never quite feeling satisfied.

I have since had ups and downs with both faith and my outer sense of modesty, and found some peace in recognising that my relationship with my 'self' is a work in progress and isn't necessarily always going to be fixed or stable. While our religion sets the boundaries of hijab, modesty itself is much more than that and far from a binary. It is a journey, just like many other aspects of our faith, that requires commitment and may not always be straightforward. It's important for us all to look at modesty in a holistic way, and take into consideration all the different factors that contribute to a person's sense of spiritual well-being.

There is a unique type of pressure that many Muslim women face, as we may navigate the line between not feeling beautiful enough and not feeling modest enough, battling sexism from within and outside our communities as many attempt to reduce us to our appearances. I've found that sometimes, while it is virtually impossible to detox completely from some of the damaging scrutiny we receive in our communities, we yield more power than we think in choosing who we give our time to, and whose opinions we attach importance to. Often those leading the witch hunt against others are projecting their own sense of discontentment in regard to their spiritual journey or personal circumstances.

It can be quite therapeutic to strip our faith back to basics, unburdening ourselves from much of the cultural stigma and shame we carry around subconsciously, and focus instead on the simplicity of our private acts of worship with our Lord. It is important to be kind but firm with ourselves, and internalise the notion that we deserve to be valued for more than our looks and to be able to practise our faith, flaws and all, without being berated for trying.

'ARABIC-SPEAKING': LIBERAL RACISM AND TRANSLATING TRAUMA IN THE HUMAN-RIGHTS SECTOR

Fatima Ahdash

The Human-Rights World, Justice and Disillusion

The 1990s were difficult years for Libya. The Gaddafi regime had instigated an aggressive and ultimately lethal crackdown on political activists that culminated in the infamous Abu-Salim massacre of June 1996, when 1,200 political prisoners were ruthlessly killed within the space of a few, unforgiving hours. I grew up haunted by the spectre of the Abu-Salim massacre, which my father, a political dissident, luckily escaped but which tragically claimed the lives of many of his activist friends and colleagues. Overhearing my parents whisper, in easily decipherable code, about the gruesome details of the massacre and the dawn raids, public executions and forced disappearances that both preceded and succeeded the massacre made me acutely aware of the injustice and pain that can be inflicted by the state on those it deems a threat or even just a nuisance.

In hindsight it is no surprise that I decided, from a relatively young age, that I wanted to be a lawyer. I used to daydream, rather naively, about becoming an international lawyer and finally bringing Gaddafi and his regime to justice. Of course at that age I did not really know what that justice would look like, how it could be achieved or even where it could be demanded. But I was still motivated by a vague and perhaps elusive notion of justice. And although this childhood dream was quickly abandoned once I became acquainted with realpolitik – that miserable adult concept forcing us to compromise with injustice *just because* it is reality – I never gave up on the idea of using the law to fight power and to demand accountability.

I therefore spent most of my late teens and early twenties dedicated to the human-rights cause. I studied law for my undergraduate degree and specialised in human-rights law for my master's degree. But despite the fact that I had excelled academically, achieving distinctions and winning prizes, I found it extremely difficult, if not near impossible, to land a job in the human-rights sector. I eventually discovered that the only way I could 'get in', as it were, was by emphasising my Arabic language skills. In fact, the only positions that I succeeded in getting were 'Arabic-speaking' positions. So for two and a half years, I worked, successively, as an 'Arabic-speaking' intern, an 'Arabic-speaking' researcher and an 'Arabic-speaking' paralegal in a number of human-rights organisations, focusing primarily on the Middle East and North Africa, commonly and somewhat reductively abbreviated to 'MENA'.

A part of me did resent being limited to only the 'Arabic-speaking' roles. It made me question my own legal and academic credentials: I worried that *all* I had to offer the human-rights world was my Arabic and nothing more. I also resented the fact that these roles were either unpaid 'voluntary internships' or minimum-wage research and paralegal positions. Yet another part of me was confident and at times even optimistic about working in the human-rights sector. I told myself that I was finally going to fulfil my childhood ambition of using the law in order to seek justice for people whose human rights have been and are being violated. What's more, since I was working in Arabic, these people would be *my people*.

But I quickly became disillusioned, and here I want to tell the story of this disillusionment. The human-rights movement is currently experiencing a long-overdue moment of reckoning as its failures and abuses are brought to light. A common and unwavering belief in their inherent goodness has meant that, for too long, human-rights organisations have escaped serious scrutiny and criticism for the harms that they have perpetuated and for their mistreatment of their (usually non-white) staff, associates and beneficiaries. But the conversation around the human-rights sector has finally begun to shift.

Liberal Racism and Woke Orientalism

Everyone who works in the human-rights sector is a good, left-leaning liberal. Everyone who works in the human-rights sector is also very keen to let you know (especially if *you* look like a minority) that they are a good, perhaps even 'woke' liberal. So you quickly learn, through no real effort on your part, that your colleagues all vote Labour (or Liberal Democrat if they are a bit rogue), fervently abhor racism, are constantly shocked at the Brexit vote and all the racism and xenophobia that it unleashed, and love diversity, inclusion and London Mayor Sadiq Khan.

But all this rather performative liberal 'wokeness' did not prevent me from experiencing the human-rights sector as a deeply alienating and at times even hostile work environment. Firstly, and on a rudimentary level, very few people actually *looked* like me. The different organisations that I worked for were predominantly, overwhelmingly, stiflingly white spaces in terms of the staff they employed and paid well. Secondly, the other non-whites, including Arabs, tended to be very junior members of staff, primarily tasked with translation and interpretation work, despite being – for the most part – more academically and legally qualified than the rest.

Of course our knowledge, skills and expertise as the 'Arabic-speaking' members of staff were absolutely vital to the work of the different organisations that I was part of. Without our ability to conduct detailed research in both

Arabic and English, translate complex legal documents, interpret client testimonies and turn them from harrowing personal stories into clear, accurate and legally workable witness statements, these organisations would not have been able to work in or on MENA. And it wasn't just our Arabic language skills that they depended on. Our close cultural knowledge regarding the people and places being worked on and with was often heavily relied upon and, I would say, *mined* to ensure the smooth working and success of various projects. For example, had my Iraqi colleague not mentioned to a project supervisor that the approaching month of Ramadhan would necessitate a different, more accommodating work timetable, the Iraq project we were working on would have been seriously derailed and might even have collapsed. And had I not shared my personal media contacts with the press team, a project in Libya would not have had the wide local reach and impact that made it so successful.

Yet none of this was reflected in the pay that we received or the positions that we occupied within office hierarchies. For we, the 'Arabic-speaking' employees, were invariably among the lowest-paid members of staff, usually on precarious temporary and sometimes even zero-hours contracts, highlighting – I often felt – our disposability. Our efforts towards career progression, for example our attempts to develop our legal skills and to diversify our work by requesting tasks that did not just involve translation or interpretation, were consistently met with evasion and sometimes outright refusal. Our demands for permanent contracts or promotions were almost always rejected. We were excluded, on account of our junior positions, from decision-making processes, even when the decisions required our expert input and directly affected our work. Those who complained or in any way refused to accept the status quo were labelled 'difficult' in probation meetings and subjected to close and stifling micro-management.

This systematic and institutional form of marginalisation occurred despite the fact that the 'Arabic-speaking' staff were often required, and at times even pressured, to travel to dangerous, dictatorial and/or politically unstable countries and to undertake work that put their lives and livelihoods at risk. I will never forget that unbearably warm and humid afternoon in July 2016 when I was asked, in all seriousness, by the director of a reputable human-rights organisation to travel to a war-torn area in Libya to spearhead a covert project that would have placed my life and the lives of my family members in immediate danger. Remarkably, this was presented to me as a 'unique opportunity' to advance myself professionally and perhaps even, with time, become a project leader. I remember that I gasped slightly in response, not quite able to contain my disbelief. Only by showing a willingness to sacrifice, quite literally, my life would I be considered for a more senior position. It was at that moment that I fully grasped my *dispensability* to the organisation. For the sake of advancing the human-rights cause in MENA, it appeared that actual Arab humans could be sacrificed.

More pervasive, and therefore more damaging, were the subtle and insidious forms of racism that characterised the everyday workings of the human-rights sector: the racism of assumptions, expectations and imaginations. Here it is worth noting that the figure of the shifty, untrustworthy native that, as we all know, underpins the colonial imagination loomed large within and was reproduced by the human-rights sector. At one team meeting I attended, the 'Arabic-speaking' staff were encouraged to approach the clients giving us their testimonies on some of the most brutal human-rights violations with caution and even suspicion. We were to probe their stories, looking for holes that could suggest that they were lying. Although our supervisors conceded that the passage of time and memory lapses might explain some of the discrepancies in the testimonies that we were collating, we were reminded time and time again that our clients were mostly poor Arabs who would be financially motivated to fabricate stories. We needed, therefore, to root out any potential discrepancies through rigorous questioning that bordered on interrogation, regardless of the trauma that we might be triggering through the re-creation of the very abusive and violent dynamics of power that the clients had endured and that we were, ironically, supposed to vindicate.

Many other orientalist tropes underlined and indeed guided the approach of these human-rights organisations to both the clients and the organisations and associates that they worked with. My supervisors designed most of their projects around the expectation that their partner organisations and associates in MENA would be producing delayed, poor-quality work that would need to be rectified and improved. Even though, from my experience, the work that was produced by the local organisations and associates was rarely ever submitted later than the work produced by the partners, consultants and associates based in the UK and Europe, for example, nor was it of distinctly inferior quality, these expectations and assumptions persisted. And while partner organisations and associates often possessed a degree of local knowledge and expertise that was unparalleled and that was invaluable to the work of human-rights organisations, their judgement was routinely questioned, second-guessed and ignored.

They were also often the butt of crude and overtly racist jokes. One particularly disturbing instance of this was recently relayed to me by a close former colleague. She informed me that during a high-level staff meeting in preparation for a trip to an Arab country, a senior member of her team joked that he would be bringing with him a 'pack of condoms' so that an Arab member of staff in a Middle Eastern branch of the organisation 'would stop having so many children'. The eugen-icist streak to this cruel and humourless joke was either lost on or simply did not faze most of the staff who, according to my former colleague, laughed hysterically in response. Another less blatantly racist but equally disrespectful remark that I heard during my time working in the human-rights world pertained to the holy month of Ramadhan. After my colleague alerted the project supervisor to the fact that Ramadhan was soon approaching, our supervisor began to talk, during meetings and in emails, of the need for the team to 'deal with the *problem* of Ramadhan'.

I cannot quite convey how deeply upsetting it was to have to hear, on a daily basis, your people being spoken about in such a demeaning and, dare I say, dehumanising manner. For although these jokes, comments and remarks were not, of course, directed at us the 'Arabic-speaking' staff, it was enough to know that this is what our supervisors and colleagues in the human-rights sector thought of Arabs *like us*: as incompetent breeders whose sacred rituals and spiritual lives amounted to nothing more than a nuisance to be dealt with.

Translating Trauma

It wasn't just through the insults and pejorative comments that we, the 'Arabic-speaking' employees, identified with and related to the MENA clients and partners with whom these human-rights organisations worked. The act of translation itself, which formed the bulk of the work assigned to Arabic-speaking team members, allowed us to develop a strong (albeit complicated) affinity with the people being worked with from 'back home'.

Translation work within human-rights organisations can be divided into two main categories. The first type involved translating handwritten letters from prisoners alleging illegal detention and/or torture, inhuman treatment and punishment. The Arabic here was exceptionally difficult to decipher, for the authors of these letters were determined to cram in as much harrowing detail of their conditions, thoughts and feelings as they could. But that was not the reason why I came to dread translating the handwritten letters. What I found particularly gruelling was having to translate highly emotional, heart-breaking and at times even lyrical letters, which often read more like Arabic poetry – such was the linguistic proficiency and desperation of their authors – into cold, pristine and legally workable English prose. Here the act of translation felt akin to betrayal.

Even more excruciating was the second type of work that I was required to undertake: translating the oral testimonies of the victims of human-rights violations. This kind of translation work involved hours-long conversations with victims, who we referred to as clients, either in person or (more commonly) over the phone. My job was to ask clients to recall, in detail, their stories of abuse and suffering at the hands of governments, corporations or armed groups and to type these out in English for the lawyers and advocates when they drafted witness statements and other legal and advocacy documents. But how does one translate a sigh or an intonation? How does one translate a changing cadence, whose meaning is familiar only to those who think and feel in Arabic? How does one make *that* legally intelligible?

The difficulties I faced, as I attempted to translate trauma, were exacerbated by the fact that I did not receive any specific training by any of the organisations I worked for in how to take and process the testimonies and accounts of victims who have seen and who were relaying some of the most serious human-rights violations. I was overwhelmed by the stories I was hearing and translating. The violent, visceral stories of death and torture I heard, translated and documented during the day often came back to visit me in my sleep during the night. At one point I was having vivid nightmares every single night of the working week. Yet there was no one at work I could openly and confidently speak to about this; there was no system in place to deal with the trauma that came with trans-lating trauma. The few senior colleagues I spoke to did nothing more than simply advise me to 'leave work at work' and to remember to deal with the clients and their stories 'as cases'. But, of course, that was easier said than done. You cannot help but become attached to and emotionally invested in the people who have so openly and generously shared with you, in your own mother tongue, their grief and anguish. So I could not leave work at work; I could not approach the clients and their testimonies as cases. Instead, I cried passionately for and with them. I prayed desperately to God that He might ease their pain and redress their suffering.

This lack of training was, however, probably more damag-ing to the clients. Many of those I interviewed were clearly extremely vulnerable people who needed to be interviewed by someone with mental-health training to ensure their psychological and emotional well-being. But the emotional and psychological vulnerability of the Arab, forever presumed to be an austere and harsh member of the human race, is rarely ever contemplated or accounted for, not even by human-rights organisations.

For these and many reasons, I found that I could no longer work in the human-rights sector. In late 2016 I left, feeling marginalised, disillusioned and, above all else, profoundly guilty for being complicit in enabling a sector that held Arab people, *my people*, in such contempt.

Not much has changed since I decided to leave the human-rights world. Even though I and many other Arab colleagues have repeatedly challenged, publicly and privately, the racist assumptions and practices, the orientalist tropes, the systematic marginalisation and exclusion that have plagued the human-rights sector, the racism, orientalism and marginalisation persist. Friends and former colleagues remain unsupported and vulnerable to traumatisation as they translate and document trauma. While critique might be superficially heard, it is never listened to, acted upon or earnestly taken on board. Nothing short of a total overhaul and a complete restructuring of the human-rights sector that centres Arab voices and perspectives can begin to address its deeply ingrained, systemic and institutional failings.

THE GIFT OF SECOND-SIGHT

Sofia Rehman

If you are never to see yourself depicted . . . Not in story, nor song, nor poem, nor painting, nor prose . . . No shred of a tale by some distant kindred soul who saw and knew and felt then as you do now, and else another who loved and bore witness . . . Never see yourself except as crude caricature, mythical beast, or Magdalene penitent . . . You believe no other like you ever existed. Unquiet women, defiant women – we live invisible lives, and if we are seen and seen by strangers, we are reduced to monsters. Vampires, who have no reflection in a looking glass. Mermaids, who die and become seafood, blown away by the wind. We will take up and take back the tools to tell our stories as our own. Civilisations may rise and fall and rewrite the history of the dead, as is often they do. But we are here . . . and we lived, and loved, and mattered.

– Marguerite Bennett, InSEXts Vol 2

So, an opportunity presents itself; a platform is raised, a mic is switched on, and I am invited to speak. But where to begin? Let me start with a story of the man with whom it all began – the Prophet Muhammad (SAW) – and his encounter with a woman who, nevertheless, persisted.

Aisha (RA), wife of the Prophet Muhammad, relates the circumstances in which the Qur'an's 58th chapter, al-Mujadilah, 'She Who Disputes', was revealed. She recounts the story of Khawla bint Khuwaylid who came to the Prophet, distressed that her husband of many years, 'Aws ibn al-Samit, had invoked the worst type of divorce, that left a woman socially suspended: neither the responsibility nor recognised partner of her husband, nor able to remarry. Essentially, Khawla was left a social pariah. Not only had 'Aws invoked this divorce, he then attempted to be intimate with her, but she refused, instead turning to the Prophet, anxious for support. Sadly for her, the Prophet had no reason to abrogate this customary practice, and informed her that she was now unlawful to her husband. Feeling destitute and unsupported, she did not accept that she could be left in such an unjust position. Despite the severity of the situation, and the force of 'Aws' words, she continued to plead, to dispute with the Prophet. 'Oh Allah's Messenger!' she cried. 'He spent my wealth, he exhausted my youth, and my womb bore abundantly for him. When I have become old, unable to bear children, he pronounced this divorce to me!' The Prophet professed his inability to comment on her situation, for prevailing customs were to be considered accepted unless specifically reformed through revelation. The custom of the Arabs remained victorious. But she continued to adjure him to action, exclaiming, 'He is the father of my children and the most beloved person to me, I will continue to dispute this! I will continue to complain!' And she implored both the Prophet and his Lord, until finally, Allah revealed what became the first few verses of the 58th chapter of the Qur'an, announcing, 'God has indeed heard the statement of she who disputes with you and complains to God . . .'

And with the complaints of this lone woman, and the response of her Lord, both she and all believing women to come are emancipated from this misogynistic practice that left a woman neither free to move on, nor entitled to make demands of her husband.

As a believing woman, this whole chapter and its principal motivation for revelation are a source of comfort. Khawla's lived experience caused her to feel acutely the full brunt of this unjust customary pre-Islamic practice. When the chips were down and this practice was executed against her, she was stripped of the protection she was provided by the institution of marriage, and exposed to the injustice of its implications. The precise words said by a husband to his wife to invoke this sort of divorce were, 'You are to me like my mother's back', meaning, she no longer held the status of wife but remained bound to the man in such a way as to prevent her physical or emotional movement beyond him. She could not remarry, but she could make no claims upon him either. What interests me further, though, is that in Fakhr al-Din al-Razi's exegetical commentary on these verses, he recounts that Khawla was beautiful and that 'Aws was 'unstable'. Al-Razi goes on to say that this instability of 'Aws was not in fact a mental incapacity, for if that was the case his provocation of divorce would not have been held against him nor his wife, but that this mental instability was in fact an 'instability towards and dislike of women, and a deep cowardice/insecurity [regarding them]'. 'Aws was a misogynistic man, and his misogyny was his insta-bility. It is empowering to know that the voice of a Muslim woman standing up and beseeching our Lord against the misogyny of her husband, and indeed her people and ances-tors who endorsed this practice which even the Prophet seems to have had no remedy for at first, is heard and responded to at last. That push, that change, that persistence means that all of us are free from that possibility now. We find in the practice of this Companion of the Prophet an example of noble per-sistence in the face of injustice, standing up to the tradition of her people, and the response of God to her invocations and the eternal memorialisation of her bravery and insistence in no less than the Holy Book of the Muslims.

We find in her the audacity to question and the courage to call out, to remain steadfast and to be optimistic of change, even when conditions seem severely restricted. She gives birth, in that moment of turmoil, to the possibility that allows Muslim women to imagine themselves as capable and entitled to legitimately question tradition, and not only to question it, but to petition for its change. Indeed, her example also gives us the strength to imagine that changes can be enacted. Are we really to presume that her experience, eternalised into Muslim memory by its place in the Qur'an, has no bearing beyond sixth-century Arabia? That Allah sent verses to resolve the matter instead of inspiring His Prophet by other means to rectify the situation, to respond only and specifically to this sixth-century Medinan practice and that the verses were made instantly redundant the moment they were revealed? Was this manner of divorce really the only gendered injustice that needed resolution? Surely not. Surely one can see the gendered injustices that continue to plague society in general and from which Muslim communities are not immune. We still have domestic abuse; an ongoing heated debate on women Imams; the growing #MosqueMeToo movement documenting the sexual harassment of women in Makkah and Madinah, the holiest places on earth for Muslims; the apparent inability to deal maturely and adequately with sexual predators lurking among us especially if they have attained celebrity-speaker status; women becoming 'un-mosqued' for lack of mosques' satisfactory accommodation of Muslim women; the fight for girls' education – to name but a few of the ongoing challenges which are gendered injustices and which Muslims have yet to address. How then can we not see that in the preservation of Khawla's story in the Qur'an, we have the establishment of a practice, a path beaten for Muslims to tread down, not to gate off?

The chapter of al-Mujadilah is testimony to the Muslim responsibility to rectify gender injustices, and the acknowledgement that this mantle will most likely be taken up by its womenfolk. The women will raise the issues, challenge established tradition; the men may struggle with it but their allyship is not only essential but in keeping with the Prophetic example. Indeed, once Allah had revealed that the words of Khawla had reached Them, and that those who utter such proclamations of divorce, as her husband had, have erred despicably, Allah then laid out the various means of expiation and seeking God's forgiveness. Allah says, 'Those who commit *dhihār* then wish to go back on their words, should free an enslaved person before they touch each other ... however, he who cannot do so, should fast two consecutive months before they may touch each other; and he who is unable to do that shall feed sixty needy people ...' Khawla was not confident her old man was capable of fulfilling any of these tasks in order to exonerate him of his foul utterance. She petitioned the Prophet once more, informing him that 'Aws was too poor to manumit an enslaved person, nor could he afford to pay for the feeding of sixty poor people. As for fasting two consecutive months, old age had enfeebled him beyond possibility! The Prophet had been given a chance by Allah to show solidarity with Khawla, so asked her if she was able to afford to feed thirty people. She said she could, and so he put his money behind his support and committed to paying for the other thirty. Between the two of them they achieved what only moments earlier had seemed impossible. Indeed, when Aisha recounted the whole event, she recalls feeling so acutely Khawla's desperation that she and all the women of the Prophet's family who were present began to weep. The women sat in solidarity with Khawla's pain, they did not move to silence her, nor did they move to ameliorate or defend the initial incapacity of the Prophet to resolve her situation.

The contemporary Muslim woman is emboldened by such narrations, and the Muslim man is ready to align himself to the effort of achieving full self-actualisation for the Muslim woman – but something is amiss. Generations have passed since this incident occurred. Civilisations have risen and fallen, empires have expanded and contracted, colonisation, wars, mass migrations, new mutations of patriarchy and sexism, racism and xenophobia have all afflicted this world, and each has left its indelible scars. Today's Muslim woman and man, living in Britain, children of these various legacies, do not find the story of Khawla told to them, even while it sits so conspicuously in the Qur'an. And if a Muslim woman finds herself spurred into action against an injustice she has perceived that is practised in her community and legitimised by so-called religious authority, she is faced with a conundrum: does she speak out against the injustice she has witnessed and risk having her voice co-opted by the racist Islamophobes who would love nothing more than to make her their brown Muslim woman poster-girl? Or does she remain silent and not condemn her community to more unfair bigoted scrutiny, and so restrain her tongue, muffle her voice and submit to unjust patriarchal practices?

In 1903, W. E. B. Du Bois wrote *The Souls of Black Folk*, in which he coined two essential metaphors for the condition of the Black community in America, thirty-eight years after slavery had been abolished, but freedom was yet to be realised. He wrote:

After the Egyptian and the Indian, the Greek and the Roman, then Teuton and Mongolian, the Negro is a sort of seventh son, born with a veil, and gifted with second-sight in this American world – a world which yields him no true self-consciousness, but only lets him see himself through the revelation of the other world. It is a peculiar sensation, this double-consciousness, this sense of always looking at one's self through the eyes of others, of measuring one's soul by the tape of a world that looks on in amused contempt and pity. One ever feels his two-ness – an American, a Negro; two souls, two thoughts, two unreconciled strivings; two warring ideas in one dark body, whose dogged strength alone keeps it from being torn asunder.

In this short paragraph, Du Bois managed to capture much of the experience of the Black individual born into American society in his time, but the power of the metaphors he coined retain their relevance in a world that still has much left to wrest from the same power structures instituted by white supremacy, that still has much left to do to decolonise society and its pillars that uphold its oppressive structures.

First there is the concept of 'double-consciousness'. While the name indicates a dualistic approach to psycho-social identity, that of being both African and American, Du Bois acknowledges other fragments of identity too that are thoroughly scattered and in need of merging in order to achieve full self-actualisation. It refers to the complex feeling of 'two-ness'; of the disparate and sometimes conflicting thoughts of the Black person in a white supremacist world, built and contingent upon their dehumanisation. It is the imposition of a racist society upon the individual Black person that causes them to view themselves both from the perspective of that white supremacist society, and from their own unique perspective. This rending asunder of aspects of the Black person's identity makes its unification and, as such, full self-actualisation difficult to achieve. Crucially, though, this is not a bio-racial trait, but one that has been constructed in a particular socio-cultural context. In other words, it can be overcome –there is every reason to believe things can change. Additionally, Du Bois argued, this double-consciousness, while the product of undesirable contexts, bears two more phenomena: the 'veil' and the 'gift' of 'second-sight'. The 'veil' represents an invisible barrier between white and Black people, behind which a 'Black world' exists, one which white people are wilfully ignorant of and which structures of power maintain so as to uphold racial separation and a limit to the progress of Black folk. The second-sight which Du Bois termed a 'gift' was the ability to see the true bloody face of, in his case, America. On this Du Bois wrote: 'Once in a while through all of us there flashes some clairvoyance, some clear idea of what America really is. We who are dark can see America in a way that white Americans cannot.'

That position as an insider–outsider, American and yet not, allowed the Black American an insight into the society they lived in; an insight that white America would deliberately ignore at the cost of its own betterment and prosperity. As Du Bois warned in words that now appear prophetic, 'Either America will destroy ignorance, or ignorance will destroy America'.

The brilliance with which Du Bois captures this experience is evidenced by the longevity of its usage in critical race theory and in the many ways in which it has been developed and enhanced as a framework for understanding the experiences of subjugated minorities. One of the ways this has been developed is by Black feminists who have talked of triple-consciousness; all the trappings of double-consciousness with the additional complexity of womanhood and the sexism a woman has to navigate. For the Muslim reader the relevance of this theory is most likely self-evident. In modern Britain, the non-white Muslim man too experiences the bind of double-consciousness; hyper-aware of the white gaze and how he is constructed in it, and of his experiences as a Muslim. The Muslim woman experiences the triple-consciousness of being

Muslim, Brit*ish* and woman; all of the experiences of the Muslim man, with the additional double-bind of the pressure to perform to both a white supremacist patriarchy and a Muslim one too.

Under the scrutiny of the white gaze, the Muslim is constructed repeatedly as a problem. Who can forget the *Sun* newspaper's infamous 'Muslim Problem' article by Trevor Kavanagh, for which he was cleared of any misconduct by the press watchdog, which was a blatant manifestation of this, but there's the constant drip-dripping of Islamophobic imagery and discussion that daily reifies this perception of Muslims in the popular psyche. The Muslim woman is presented as both uniquely oppressed by Muslim men, while also being the gatekeeper to the community and the nefarious secrets its men hold. She is cast even as an enabler to their plots – the BBC drama *Bodyguard* triumphed in its ability to reinforce both of these stereotypes in one single Muslim female character. The Muslim woman is at once the walking embodiment of a number of contradictory tropes thrust upon her, and she in turn is always hyper-aware of the ways in which she is perceived as she moves through the world. Among her own community, she is burdened with the 'status of women in Islam'; expected to be a paragon of piety, a dutiful daughter, a supportive wife and a nurturing mother, but always balancing delicately on the precipice of honour, teetering over the pits of shame. But all the while she is able to see the realities too. The lived experience of this triple-consciousness gives birth to her gift of second-sight. She can see the ills in society at large and she can see those of her own community too.

Furthermore, it is through second-sight that women are able to envision a future that allows more freedom to the womenfolk from the constraints of gendered oppressions, and freedom to the menfolk from the burdens of its toxicity. It is also in this moment of foreseeing such a future for the Muslim Ummah that a way towards it is also conjured. It is true that in our high-speed, globally connected world, information can be condensed and repurposed and weaponised in unintended ways, but that should not mean that truths can be silenced and injustices left unchecked. So many brilliant Muslim women have spent decades of their lives dedicated to the service of the Muslim Ummah through a variety of means. Some of these women include scholars, but their names are seldom mentioned, except occasionally to revile or refute them; 'critiques' that are often at best infantile and at worst scholastically dishonest and disingenuous. We are told repeatedly that Islam has a rich history of women scholars, but why the apparent dearth now? Occasionally, a few Muslim women who have the seal of patriarchal approval slip through or are tokenised, but what do we make of those who have contributed something new to the understanding of our Deen? What happens when Kecia Ali writes about sexual ethics and Islam, when Asma Sayeed writes about the history of women's scholarship in Islam and maps its ebbs and flows? Why are the shelves of Islamic bookstores bereft of the titles by Asma

Barlas, Amina Wadud, Ziba Mir-Hosseini? Muslim women who have argued against patriarchy in all its guises and Islamophobia, and have called for gender justice and decolonisation enacted through Islamic principles. I spent over a decade studying Islam through traditional learning, travelling to teaching centres and teachers around the world, and while the learning I gained was foundational and important for my development and understanding, there was always that deafening silence where one hoped for honest, empathetic resolution on issues pertaining to Muslim women in the contemporary world and navigating the space that was often hostile towards them. I marvelled, then, when I re-entered academia to complete my Master's in Middle Eastern and Islamic Studies before pursuing my PhD, where I was introduced for the first time to these female Muslim scholars in terms that didn't couch them as controversial flashpoints but as rigorous scholars with valuable contributions, whose work warranted engagement. But what astounded me further was that none of what we read was written recently; much of it was decades old but had been constrained to the realm of academia. The ideas and scholarship had not traversed the divide between the ivory tower of the academy and the grassroots community because of the barriers to entry created, in one direction, by elite institutions of higher education pulling up the bridges, and in the other by the constant vilification and scaremongering against these women in the community. As always, the women's voices are there; they are just very effectively put on mute.

It is in our hands as Muslim women to unmute these voices. To do so, we must use our agency to seek out the answers that we are worthy of receiving instead of being placated by promises of Paradise and calls to patience; especially when God's reply to the Angels after being asked why humankind was created – to establish vicegerents on earth – deputies and overseers for God. Part of that role is to seek to be an agent for the establishment of justice. We unmute the voices of our sisters by giving ear to their words, by taking the time and energy to seek them out and read their works for ourselves, and then to start talking with one another; and then, finally, to embody the practice of Islam we wish to see manifested. And all of this takes courage, because nothing is more resisted than change.

I wonder, then, if we could move towards a position of maturity and trust; a position whereby the works of Muslim women scholars could also be made more accessible. Could a Muslim woman be free to experiment with her understanding of Islam, question certain tenets and perform her Islam freely, without being trolled or harassed back into silence? I hope for a movement of the Muslim community away from attacking the Muslim woman who speaks, and towards listening to her as the Prophet listened to Khawla: a movement that, when the Muslim woman hurts, has fellow Muslim women empathise with her pain and feel it with her, as Aisha and all the women of the Prophet's family did for Khawla; a movement that, when a Muslim woman moves to action, our brothers meet us halfway, like the Prophet did Khawla.

For the British Muslim community and all its members to be able to move forward and find harmony, it is important that all its members be afforded a voice, especially a critical one, so that we can poke in the dark recesses of the margins we have long ignored in our collective consciousness and address the shortcomings and wrongs that lurk there. And, once again, we must be brave, for courage is the only way to acknowledge those dark recesses. Rather than worrying that speaking up will cause outsiders who seek to discredit Islam and vilify Muslims to be vindicated, we must worry that, by not speaking up, it is our own community members who bleed first, whereas Islamophobic trolls will always find fodder for their bigoted hate, whatever we do. We must find our individual voices; that voice the Prophet urged us to find when he told his Companions three times 'seek counsel from your heart', and let it be unleashed without fear of the clamour that may ensue to muffle it once more. For through the turmoil we have lived, we have been given the gift of second-sight.

YOUTH IN THE TIME OF MADRASSAHS

Mariam Ansar

A madrassah in a neighbour's home on some suburban street doesn't have a dome, or a minaret, or anything to declare it as holy.

There might be square-shaped cushions on a well-vacuumed floor. A mithai collection left to spoil on a nearby kitchen island. A Bollywood song on a passing ice-cream van's techno-logical interface. But no single honeyed voice uttering the call to prayer properly. No dome, or minaret, or any large swathe of bearded men and pious women passing along the shadows this holy architecture draws on the ground.

In the predominantly Asian madrassahs of some very distant childhoods at least, there were only cushions, mithai, the stiff, shiny sound a colour-coded qaida makes when it's peeled from the inside of an overheating bag, and a bunch of kids doing their best to feel, under the watchful eye of that neighbour – an Apa, or an Ustaadji – at least a little bit closer to God.

With small fingers tracing over an alif, baa, taa, thinking this isn't as hard as it looks. Mouths opening to recite a memorised verse a little while later, and realising, just a few minutes in, they've messed up. Who's laughing already? Who's got Apa or Ustaadji shaking their heads? Foregoing the ruler in their hand to tell them to go stand facing the wall, and not lick the paint the way a Halima, or a Ruqaiya or an Aisha did last week? Laughter again. A too-smart teacher's pet uttering a sigh of disgust at such childish ineptitude. Apa or Ustaadji without words, and everyone needing a reminder, amidst the chaos of a quickly catching laughing hysteria – and the softening of some once-hard after-school hours – to go back to their quiet recitations.

The funny things in those hours were never holy. A girl in trouble for talking or drawing unflattering pictures of Apa or Ustaadji beneath their very nose; a parent tossing a shoe at them for using a ruler against their child's fingertips; someone singing a nasheed that ended with a Nelly Furtado chorus; a whole class sitting with their back to Apa or Ustaadji on an uncancelled snow day; the partition between the girls and boys in the later years, breached by a throwing of mosque hats over the barrier, and them being thrown back.

They were simply human, before the pressure to prove as much, the one that, with ageing and arriving at the fact of a politicised identity, could chip away at our innocence.

This state, marked by finding news channels boring, and not knowing how to respond to sectarian questions, and fumbling over phrases related to Wahhabis, Sunnis, Shias, when all you wanted was to warn somebody about the tidal wave on the floor of the wudhu area, was easy. Like inside jokes, or the way any kid heading anywhere in the world chooses not to walk, but always – with their feet pounding, their heart racing – breaks out into a run.

I think that if there's anything God must appreciate, in the quiet holiness of house madrassahs, the ones in hollowed-out, shut-down schools, cousins' houses and rickety buildings on busy roads, it's the way the youngest of us get to be – without political projection, and therefore human in them.

The articles, reports and speeches which accuse madrassahs of radicalisation take up most of the internet search results for the word. Page after page of criticisms loaded with words like *extremism* and *intolerance*. Word after word which carries the spirit of media speculation: an ambiguous shape, a racialised fear and little substantiated claim, but a swaying persuasion anyway. Like being taught that to greet guests with your right hand possesses the threat of imminent danger. Sharing excess food with a neighbour becomes a truly criminal act. Covering another's flaws instead of taking the option to expose them? Why, only the most barbaric of them all. Still, the image of so many closed doors, the space around them echoing with the sound of Arabic recitation, undulating to a rhythm of countless rocking bodies, and how they provoke the image of a disloyal Other behind the grain isn't wholly perplexing.

Places closed for public consumption, and made comfortable for the needs of a confident minority, invite some degree of suspicion from those so unused to difference they demonise it. Sometimes they even seek to destroy it.

What would those suspicious pairs of eyes have seen in the Victorian architecture of the school-turned-madrassah I went to once?

It was almost grand, with high ceilings, a propensity to whistling cold draughts, and equipped with a dozen different classrooms, an assembly hall, a shoe-rack, a sweet shop on the way to the exit which always had a bunch of eleven-year-olds in the line, counting the change in the pockets of the hoodies they wore over their abayas, asking one another for an extra 5p or 10p because that was the difference between a small bag of blue bonbons and a big one.

On the Fridays when everyone rushed home, quick to save their shoes from a pair of particularly greedy hands, slipping on pairs of strappy sandals, slip-on loafers, faintly luminescent Nikes, ballet pumps, large combat boots, for a weekend unbothered by the demands of all kinds of education, that line was quite short. Shorter still when the frenzy of freedom around the corner carried another violent energy. 'Hurry up,' someone older than all of us would yell over the din, 'You lot don't wanna miss the fight, do ya? Fahmida Sharif's gonna bang Humaira Khan out!'

And there, along the crest of a quickly moving wave, spilling out onto a street jammed with our parents' cars, the girls'

YOUTH IN THE TIME OF MADRASSAHS

side and the boys' side would come to a standstill, every few weeks, while two well-liked girls yelled profanities at one another. Why? One of them was a bitch, the other would say, and then the other would ask who she thought she was calling a bitch, and any explanation would end there, even though it seemed obvious both were simply caught in the animosity of being intimidated by another who wore the same lip gloss and pinned their hijab the same way. They'd land punches, take breathers, ask their friends to hold their scarves with all the gum-popping drama that we usually saw in made-for-TV movies. And the way we'd laugh and chant 'fight' by the wayside was always condemned by our parents; deemed improper, by those Apas and Ustaadjis who demanded answers the following Monday; damningly hilarious when brought up in our exaggerated recounts of the only real violence we knew, and encouraged, in sensational hearsay: 'Don't you know so-and-so said this about you?' and 'Well, what are you gonna do about it?'

All of it so regular and ridiculous that no one thought it boast-worthy.

The writers of all those articles, and the white supremacists planning and scheming and hell-bent on a mosque massacre, never considered it at all.

Well, maybe they did, and carried on with their plans anyway. You can't convince someone to care if they don't. You can't give them your blinking eyes, your beating heart, if they're proud of their own. If they can't see those organs as the same as theirs, anyway.

On the evenings that the friends I made at madrassah were as bored as I was of memorising the correct adhaab on Muslim womanhood, conducting ourselves with politeness and propriety as representatives of our faith, and ways to maintain our identities as doting daughters, sisters and students, we made paper chatterboxes, and drew spirals for ongoing MASH games, and talked about boys. Famous ones, and infamous ones: baby-faced heartthrobs who sang songs for eleven-year-olds like us, footballers our siblings liked, actors in sugary teen magazines, neighbours and strangers, and the ones each of us bestowed with private nicknames, ears pricking when they passed by the corridors of our different schools, minds reeling with another story to tell when the opportunity presented itself.

They all started in the same vein: 'Red Backpack smiled at me today', or 'Did I tell you lot Hamster got a haircut? I think we need to change his nickname', or 'Sandwich got to pick who he wanted to sit next to at form-time, and it might have been because there was only one chair empty, but anyway, he sat next to me . . .'

There was always a great deal of whispering, snickering and demands for stories to be told again when they were finished. The girls I once knew like the back of my hand would sigh, feigning irritation, tossing the loose ends of their hijabs over their shoulders and shutting their blue adhaab textbooks over their wooden desks before they got to it; and Apa, watching from the front of the classroom, would break the ease with which we lounged over the carpet with a very sharp tongue. Something about a madrassah being no place for a mothers' meeting. Or was it a frustrated complaint that we weren't sitting in the comfort of our individual homes?

But the freedom that came with being separate from our parents' chore-chasing whims was addictive, and the intimacy of our shared space, only encouraged by the space heater breathing hot air in the corner, the vacuum cleaners in the cupboard down the hall, and the way in which all of us took the opportunity to compare the patterns on our socks when we stood up to pray together, wasn't deceiving. The empathy contained in so many of our conversations, which made the listening walls and our listening bodies safe for secret-keeping, only grew stronger with each passing day; all of this, in a way, an accidental predecessor of the psychological safe space which entered popular culture a decade later and in other ways, a thing too raw and complicated to be classified in the same way.

After all, feeling at home doesn't necessarily translate into feeling at peace. Just the pursuit of it.

'Have you ever had a deep dark secret?' the first-ever friend I remember making asked me once.

She made me laugh a lot, knew more about football than I did, and was a few years older than me: in my eyes, a teenager conversing with a partial one, and never mind the fact that truthfully we were both children, thirteen and eleven.

Our class was almost at the end of our two madrassah hours. Her question was a welcome distraction from the fact of my unpractised tongue tripping over so many unfamiliar Arabic words at Apa's request. I hadn't done so well with my recitation that day and struggled towards the end of an ayah with teeth-clenching determination before I placed the red ribbon page marker, fraying at the bottom, between the pages of my Qur'an and closed it shut.

'What do you mean?' I said.

The wooden desk – one of those we set across the carpet every day, engraved with so many ink pens, carrying allegiances to football teams, song lyrics and some very detailed doodles – creaked at my leaning on it.

'A deep dark secret,' my first friend said. 'You know what I mean.'

I met the seriousness of her dark eyes, saw the perpetual dimples in her cheeks, and nodded.

'One time,' I told her, voice lower than necessary, 'in Ramadhan, my school was having this party, and no one told me about it, so I was the only one fasting that day, and my mum said I shouldn't, but I didn't listen to her, so anyway, when everyone was cleaning up the crisp packets and their drinks and stuff, I stole a Jammie Dodger, and I ate it under the table—'

'Mariam,' my first friend laughed, 'that's not what I meant.'

And I frowned, feeling more than a little out of my depth as she went on to say that a deep dark secret was a terrible one that offered little joy, and had the potential to haunt you for the rest of your life. It was something hard, and scary, like a shadow that didn't flee when the morning came, but merged with your own in the daylight. It chose never to disappear. It couldn't.

'Do you have one?' I said, in the forthcoming silence, and over the lump in my throat. 'A deep dark secret like that?'

My first friend nodded. 'I'll write it down for you. I can't say it out loud.'

I didn't understand them though. The words she wrote down. I was too young, and eventually, with her pen discarded over her exercise book, her dark eyes so still and unblinking, I listened in silence as she told me a story a lot like the ones I'd heard the girls in my class tell – in hushed whispers – before.

There was a sliding scale of serious to unserious subjects we were taught to avoid, which aligned with the sins we were taught to suppress in our formative years: smoking, sex, yet more unwelcome ways of tainting the human body ... My first friend told the story of a relative touching her in a place where she didn't want to be touched like she knew this wasn't her fault. Like it was something that went beyond the way we thought of sins. And with the detached sadness of someone who simply wanted to confess something to someone she trusted.

'Don't tell anyone,' she said, like the prospect of seeing her as she was, a child wronged by more people than I can collect in my mind, was better than someone doing something about it.

I said I wouldn't, because I didn't know how to tell anyone anything, and she made me promise, and friends are supposed to keep the promises they make.

I cried when I found out, weeks later – my whole body hurting with a wrongness that crept all the way into my heart – that she no longer attended madrassah. She left without saying goodbye. She never told anyone she was leaving. It wasn't this betrayal which hurt so much. I think I cried because I knew I'd betrayed her. Failed her, in some way I couldn't articulate. Me, not so different to a misplaced article, or report, or speech; an education system too broken to be able to pay attention; a tactless Apa; the hazy aggression of a potential police call; a parent apologising for their own dumbstruck ignorance somewhere far away . . .

Sometimes I still hear her, asking me that question, all these years later.

It comes back to me every time. We were just little kids.

There is only ever one mirror in the wudhu area. It's usually a half-smeared, water-splattered thing that you have to stand on your tiptoes to look into, but it does the job. It lets you wash your face, pin your hijab to a neater messiness than usual, adjust your mosque hat over your growing head. It provides you with a reflection for what you are when you're not being asked to figure it out.

Still, sociology states that asking a fully-grown someone with a racialised identity to describe their reflection results in an answer comprised of labels: 'I see a brown Muslim boy', 'I see a Black Muslim girl.' Sometimes, it results in simply a name: Hasan, Laiba, Tariq, Muna, Shuaib, Aisha . . .

Can the space where both of these answers combine – identity and personality, how we're perceived and who we are, the fact of our humanity and nothing else – exist without empathy? The construction of caring places we know so well that we take them for granted? The homes we create for our own humanity? The truths we teach of our own existence? And all that we rightfully deserve?

The eight-year-olds in my family are at the right age to be learning their kalimahs at the local madrassah.

At our get-togethers, they saunter in, shy with childish bravado, offering their salaams – the long phrasing of course – to sounds of impressed adoration. They combine all the Arabic they know into a gasping paragraph of holy conjugation, and everyone offers their mashAllahs, their SubhanAllahs, their alhamdulillahs in response, because everyone recognises a past they left behind in these representatives of the present. Everyone remembers their introduction to God.

When dinner has been served, and the TV switches to something sweet and kid-friendly, the eight-year-olds tell us what they think we should know: like how we can't celebrate Halloween because they heard it's the devil's birthday. They sit with the poise of people already in the midst of prayer; graceful without intention, grinning at the newness of their favourite religious rumours. It isn't the stuff we heard at their age: not what Coca-Cola supposedly says backwards, and if Michael Jackson was the true-star of the too-real illuminati, and whether 'mosque' is an abbreviation for the word mosquito. But sometimes, over their reticence to say the word *pig* aloud, and the way they yell it anyway, we catch eyes, fall into split-second silence and try not to laugh.

We, at least, see the things they want us to see: the droplets of some half-truth, cupped in the palms of their hands, brought to us in the hope that we can carry it better, coax it to something much more carefully considered because we're not kids any more and age demands such responsibility.

Sometimes it feels like I can't fulfil it. But then I look into eyes that want to meet mine, and how accustomed they are to Apas, and Ustaadjis, and sweet shops, and childish fights, and bathroom mirrors, and brown wooden benches. I remember the ease with which a mouth will talk about them, and more, if given the chance. I remember the way the past gives way to a present once considered the future with demonstrable, imitable ease. I think, in the space of humanity attempting holiness, I can.

Even if so many others can't.

4,091 MILES AWAY FROM HOME

Aisha Rimi

The year is 1982. Three young Nigerian girls arrive in the UK for the first time to attend a boarding school on the England–Wales border. Excited and bright-eyed, they don't know what to expect as they begin this new chapter in their lives. Their names are Hauwa, Sa'ada and Aisha, or, as I like to call them, Mama, Aunty Saa and Ai. My mother and two of her sisters came from the bustling city of Kaduna, Nigeria, to the scenic English town of Malvern, Worcestershire, to continue their education, which was also where they made their first home in the UK.

You would think being both a Black and Muslim teenager in a foreign country, where barely anyone looks like you or practises the same faith as you, would have made the initial experience of moving to England a difficult one. Yet surprisingly my mother did not face as many challenges as I would have expected at that time. 'Everyone was really nice and friendly when we arrived. Of course, there were some questions, but I think it was just out of curiosity,' my mother tells me. Before coming to the UK, her race and religion were not aspects of her identity that she felt would cause many difficulties in England. Spending much of her childhood and the majority of her adolescence in Nigeria meant that my mother was never Othered; she didn't grow up around racism, or that kind of discrimination. She was never made to feel less-than due to her race and religion. It was this sense of always belonging to the society that she was in that made her quite comfortable and excited about the prospect of moving to England, rather than anxious about becoming a minority.

Fast-forward over thirty years later, and you would hope her children would be feeling the same way. Well, it's somewhat the contrary. I'm living in a time when Black people are risking their lives to tread the streets during a pandemic, shouting 'Black Lives Matter' in an effort to justify our right to peaceful existence. Despite the constant visual reminders of the denigration of Black bodies circulated on the news and on social media, there are still people out there responding with 'All Lives Matter'. When it comes to race and ethnicity, verses of the Qur'an and hadiths remind us that we are all seen as equal in the eyes of Allah. However, the Black Lives Matter movement has emphasised the anti-Blackness that exists in the Muslim community today. I've seen non-Black Muslims on social media use the movement as a time to talk about the atrocities happening in Muslim-majority countries, such as

Palestine and Syria, in an attempt to belittle and derail the conversation around Black lives, which only contributes further to the alienation Black Muslims feel within the Muslim community. While these, of course, are issues that need to be highlighted, bringing them up in this opportunistic manner, as a sort of rebuttal to the discrimination that Black people face, only serves to undermine these very causes by putting them at odds with anti-Black racism.

I've grown more conscious of how my race and the visible acknowledgement of my faith (my headscarf) will affect my experiences and the way I'm treated in society, particularly when I leave the comfort of multicultural London. Travelling is easier than it's ever been, yet as a Black and Muslim woman living in today's world, I feel as though I have to be more cautious than ever. Is that particular country known for racist or Islamophobic tendencies? Will I be forced to remove my hijab at airport security? Will I be stopped and searched unnecessarily – as I once was – upon arrival at my destination? There's just so much I have to think about these days, while my white counterparts have the privilege of travelling without having to think of such risks that could pose a threat to their well-being or safety.

This feeling of being cautious also feeds into the spaces that I enter. Whether it be social or professional, I have to remember I am seen first as a Black woman, regardless of the fact that I cover my hair, and I may be perceived in a particular way. Most images of Muslim women are those of Asian or

Arab women, which feeds into the stereotype that Muslim women come in only one shade. Although the hijab seems, to me, like an obvious display of my religion, this continuous misrepresentation of the diversity of Muslim women means that my faith is still questioned by non-Muslims and non-Black Muslims alike. As advanced, globalised and connected as the world is today, racism, Islamophobia and general prejudice against anything or anyone that's different to what is considered the 'norm' are so much more visible and prevalent, and almost more accepted and tolerated in the name of free speech. Yet for my mother, it's as though she grew up in a different world to the one I am experiencing.

We had similar, but at the same time very different, upbringings. Many of her formative years were spent in northern Nigeria, but on arrival in the UK, she spent her first couple of years in small English towns, very much like my upbringing. When I was seven years old, my parents made the decision to move our family from west London to a small Cambridgeshire village. We uprooted our lives from a very diverse area in London, where we were inconspicuous within our community, to the countryside, where we would stick out like a sore thumb. Surely making such a big move with two young children would cause my parents some sort of apprehension about how our lives would change? Of course, my mother, ever the optimist, had no worries. While being a minority didn't concern her, it's become something of a second nature to me. Growing up, I was one of a handful of Black girls in my school, and one of an even smaller number of Muslims. Whether I wanted to be or not, I was very much a representative of both communities to my predominantly white, middle-class peers. Was it a burden? Looking back, it was not so much among my friends, but I definitely felt it as I got older, especially with teachers. As Black people in today's society, we are all too familiar with the notion that we have to work twice as hard to be seen as half as good as our white counterparts. So yes, the pressure was there.

My mum has worked in secondary schools in rural Cambridgeshire for almost twenty years now and has never really had any issues. There's been the odd comment here and there, but only in the last few years has she encountered more racially driven remarks from students. I asked her why she thought students were more brazen and felt they could get away with making such comments towards her. Brexit was one of the first reasons that sprang to mind. After all, it has dominated British politics since 2016. Brexit opened up a whole new perspective for many to see how British people felt about issues facing the nation, particularly around immigration. The Leave campaign was primarily fuelled by fearmongering about the number of immigrants coming into the country. With the majority of those who voted opting to leave the European Union, albeit by a very narrow margin, it opened up a whole new avenue, where people who held negative views against those from different backgrounds felt at liberty to confidently express them, no matter how offensive. In the wake of Brexit and the election of Boris Johnson as prime minister, despite his derogatory comments about Muslim women and others of ethnic minorities, and Donald Trump causing political chaos further afield, I question if we have really progressed as a society since my mother first arrived in this country.

I may not have experienced direct racism and Islamophobia, but I've known since I was younger that my race and religion would always make me stand out, and potentially make me a target of unwarranted attention. My mother, on the other hand, was not really aware of the racism and prejudice she could have endured until her move to England, where she became more knowledgeable about it; it was a gradual realisation. We in the diaspora are made all too aware from an early age that the world will judge us due to the colour of our skin or our religion. I think of my younger sister and cousin, who were born into a post-9/11 world and don't know of a time when followers of their faith were neither judged nor discriminated against. Furthermore, it seems that Black and brown children are experiencing these feelings of discrimination from an earlier age. While I went through my entire education experiencing only some micro-aggressions, my youngest sister experienced her first racist incident at school, at just fifteen years old. Reflecting upon our experiences, my mother finds a type of solace in the fact she was able to grow up unaware of the challenges that might face her, sheltered at boarding school where she was in her own little world.

I'll admit, I was surprised by my mother's experiences and sentiments of her time growing up in 1980s England. The first two years were spent in Malvern and Exeter, which are hardly hotspots for diversity, yet she was welcomed and embraced with open arms by a host family and by others within the community. Everything seemed fine. However, during the 1985 Brixton riots in south London, she was living in west London, and racial issues became a little more real for her. Despite living in the same city, the riot was something she was able to distance herself from. 'I had never been to Brixton at the time. I didn't live in an area with a lot of different ethnic minorities, so the whole thing felt very far away from me although it was happening in London,' my mother tells me. What strikes me is how it contrasts with the way I and others of my generation often feel so connected by the impact and severity of racist and Islamophobic incidents across the world. I find the power of social media and the speed with which we can access information and first-hand reports forces this feeling. Still, some of what my mum expressed about being able to distance herself from the riots resonates with me. Our capability to instantly connect and to be online also makes it easy for us to tap out and *dis*connect from atrocities happening both in our own countries and worldwide, especially when they don't touch our own communities.

My mother and I both approached the hijab in a similar way. My mother was in her early thirties when she first decided to cover her hair; I was twenty-two. I have grown up in a time where the hijab has become such a key signifier of the Muslim faith. Whether it's people assuming you are more pious or holding you to a higher standard than non-hijab wearing women, everyone has their assumptions about us, right or wrong (in most cases it's the latter). When I ask my mother why she didn't start wearing the hijab earlier, she tells me, 'When we were younger, we made sure we prayed, and fasted etc., but we were not really that deep in our faith. Even in Nigeria, my peers and I weren't really wearing the hijab, and it wasn't necessarily expected of us. I think it was similar in Muslim-majority countries too.' She's right – look at pictures of 1970s and '80s Afghanistan and you will see images of women with their hair out and wearing Western clothing. Would my mother have started wearing the hijab earlier if others around her were doing so? Perhaps, but even when she did start in 1998, she still wasn't seeing as many visibly Muslim women on the streets, nothing like the numbers in which we see them today. The hijab was something I had been thinking about for a few years leading up to the moment I actually decided to start wearing it. In those years I began to make some small changes here and there to my dress, trying to be more modest and more conscious of what I was wearing. Much like my mother's first time wearing the hijab on a day out with my dad, little sister and me, my first time was also nothing that special. I simply covered my hair to work one day and never looked back. It's been four years now.

The pressure to assimilate is greater now than ever. With restrictions placed in several Western countries on Muslim female dress and general societal pressure to act and think a certain way, it can be difficult for young Muslims to feel like a part of the society they have always lived in and reconcile their faith with the culture. As my mum tells me, 'I never felt a pressure to assimilate. I never wanted to. I felt I was able to just be myself over here.' It's different for me and my peers. We were born and raised here; this country is all we've known. Yet we're having to deal with a cultural dichotomy, stuck between holding on to our parents' culture and also embracing the culture of our homeland. I'm proud of my Nigerian heritage and hold the culture, my native language and customs close to my heart. Still, as a British-born Nigerian, it's hard to find my place in both societies; from both sides I'm never seen as 'enough' to claim either identity entirely. Nevertheless, as complex as identity can be, my faith helps me centre it all, as ultimately that is the most defining thing about me.

'I identify as Muslim more than anything else,' my mother explains when I ask her. 'As my faith takes precedence in how I identify myself, I feel free to be anywhere and do anything. I think once you have that strong sense of faith, you ultimately feel protected by Allah, so you're able to tolerate, accommodate and be friendly, and much more. It's my faith that teaches me to treat people the way I want to be treated. It's because of that, I have faith in people and so much hope for myself and people around me.' For both my mum and me, our faith is the biggest influence on our day-to-day life and shapes everything we do. However, in terms of nationality, that's where my mother and I understandably differ. My mother has spent the majority of her life in England, but still has a strong attachment to her Nigerian culture and heritage, so I was curious to find out how she identified. She holds both British and Nigerian citizenship, but does she align with one nationality more than the other? 'Nationality-wise, I identify as Nigerian. Nigeria is where I spent the formative years of my life. It shaped me and is my foundation. As a result, I will always be Nigerian,' she explained. As for me, it's a little more complicated. I think for many young Black British and Muslim people in the UK, there's a constant battle with how we identify. There are some things about me that are inherently British, and others that are very Nigerian, and I can't change that I am influenced by both.

From my conversation with my mother, you could almost say things have regressed in some respects for my fellow Black and Muslim women. However, it's not all negative. As challenging as things can be, I know I am privileged to live in a country where I can openly practise my religion. I know that not all my Muslim brothers and sisters around the world have the same freedom. Many, especially Muslim women, suffer from the over-policing of their bodies and how they choose to cover them. Nevertheless, the one thing Mama and I both share is hope. These are turbulent times, and just like in previous moments in history, we will get through them.

WAITING TO EXHALE: THE SCARCITY OF SAFE SPACES

Hodan Yusuf

This essay was originally written and submitted in 2018 before the COVID-19 pandemic, before the disturbing murder of George Floyd, a Black man, by the US police which sparked global Black Lives Matter protests against systemic racism. And before it became alarmingly clear that structural inequalities were leading to a disproportionate number of people from Black, Asian and other racially minoritised backgrounds in the UK, US, Brazil, etc., being affected by this virus. I'm particularly vulnerable to COVID-19 and have to be extra careful to avoid exposure as much as I possibly can. Since this is a virus which attacks the respiratory system, the title of this essay continued to be fitting, but the rest of it had to change with the times. I have a poem called '#BlackMuslim MamasPrayer', written in 2016, which is sadly more and more relevant with every passing year. It will be included in the prints for those people who pre-ordered this book at the reward level that included my poetry.

Every word is a will and testament. Every breath is not guaranteed.

I know the value of safety. I know what it feels like not to have it. The fear of the inevitable if you stay and the search for a place of safety. That desperate need to breathe and to exhale the distress. Sometimes that pursuit of safety is hidden from view, other times it is more obvious.

I am from so-called Generation X; post-Baby Boomers, pre-Millennials. We witnessed as breaking news things that children in school today learn about in history lessons. The Berlin Wall, Tiananmen Square, Nelson Mandela's release, the *first* Iraq War and a pre-civil war Somalia. At the beginning of that civil war, my parents, like many thousands of families, made the decision to pack up a few things from their cherished home, a house they had built from scratch, and take their children to safety.

I am the eldest and only girl and I distinctly remember a conversation my mother had with me, away from my brothers, when the war began to get closer to home. There were reports of girls and young women being raped and assaulted by soldiers entering homes in the middle of the night. My mother told me that she and my father wanted to keep me safe by sending me to distant relatives who lived away from the conflict zones, but the road there was too dangerous.

My parents' Plan B was to drain the water from an underground concrete reservoir in our garden. If the soldiers did come, I was to quietly climb into this dark chamber like a condemned Roman Vestal Virgin awaiting her fate in a crypt. I grew up *a lot* that year.

Privilege is a currency. And my family had privileges, including being able to secure visas and afford plane tickets. But if anyone asked we were to say our trip was to a nearby destination to visit family, so that we wouldn't arouse suspicion when packing and putting our affairs in order. The truth could get you killed. Only someone who has lived through political instability and the ever watchful 'eye' of state security can understand the kinds of measures people must take just to survive. Alhamdulillah we made it out, but it was not lost on me that so many others did not. Suddenly I was back in London, this time not as a tourist but to seek refuge, asylum. It was a little while before those terms became quite the politicised, loaded insults they are used as today. Or maybe I was just too young to notice.

I spoke English and, while it afforded me some privilege, it also exposed me to the full range of the racist and xenophobic language used against people like me. In one school, a male teacher, who was also a senior member of staff, often asked me to translate between him and other Somali students. His behaviour always felt uncomfortable, but there were never any guidelines on where to turn if a male teacher was asking to see you alone in his office, not respecting your personal space until he'd backed you into a wall an inch away from your face, regularly. Jimmy Savile was still on the TV in those days. There was no accessible internet, no social media, no #MeToo movement then; Tarana Burke was still in high school too.

I soon became fluent in Racist. And since I lived in east London, I learned all the racial slurs in the various languages of the Indian subcontinent too. I learned them because I heard them. Often directed at me or my friends, or dropped in casual conversations.

Later, as an adult, I found myself making a similar scramble to leave a home I'd established and find safety. This time not because of a civil war, but to escape the brutal actions of a repressive regime in a Middle Eastern country. Now *I* was the parent, packing children's clothes into suitcases, leaving loved ones, indefinitely locking up the door to my home with dua; just like my mother did years before. There was a moment when I stopped everything and looked around and wondered to myself if I was just born to be running my whole life from one unsafe place to another. Is this what my life is? Safe, unsafe, safe, unsafe. And asking myself, how does *this* story end?

So once again I boarded a plane destined for relative safety. Hiding tears as the plane ascended and the landscape disappeared behind me. No one near me could have guessed that I had to leave so that I wouldn't be taken and raped to extract a false confession from the member of my family they *had* arrested. Once again, the threat of sexual violence followed me, and was followed by an urgent need to escape. While I was consumed by sadness and uncertainty, the food trolley rolled up: 'Madam, the chicken or the fish?' Life has a funny way of going on.

I was back in London as a single mother of a toddler and a preschooler, and legally homeless. It was now post-9/11, the political climate had changed in the UK and it was palpable.

Previously on How to Get Away with Racism, the common racist abuses heard in east London ranged from 'n*gger' and 'Black Paki' from white racists, '*kaali*' (a racial slur used among Urdu/Hindi speaking South Asians), to 'You Black Iraqi'. That last one was a short-lived special edition courtesy of the first war in the Gulf. Now we could add 'fucking terrorist' to that list. Charming!

By now I was quite well versed in the impact of the lack of political safe spaces and the traumatic effect such displacement can have on people, often for years to come. What I had not banked on was the lack of safety *within* the communities and spaces I had assumed were havens from the hostilities around me.

I'm still paying for that naivety.

Safety is not just important physically but also emotionally and mentally. Social spaces can become homes from home, providing support where wider structures fail.

In Islamic tradition, masajid, or mosques, are meant to be community centres. They are places of prayer, sanctity, the metaphorical House of God, or Bayt ul Allah. But too often Black people are harassed or refused entry to mosques simply because they are Black. Sometimes non-Black Muslims ask them to prove they are Muslim by asking them to read from the Qur'an! I will never forget when I was refused entry to a mosque. An Asian man stood at the door and point-blank refused to allow me to enter and pray my maghrib salah. He said no women were allowed in, as he made way for Asian women dropping their kids to madrassah and stayed blocking the door to me. What does it mean when some of us cannot even enter the places that are meant to be sacred safe spaces? If I was a white racist Islamophobic far-right protester I believe that man might have let me in, and maybe even offered me tea and biscuits (as has happened in some mosques that have invited in EDL supporters)! It was becoming increasingly clear to me that this Muslim 'community' had gatekeepers and that they were very selective, often choosing in their own image.

Most Muslim people in the UK are from the Subcontinent, which means mosque committees, community centres, etc., are predominantly run by Asians. And while people love to quote the words from the Prophet Muhammad's (SAW) last sermon about racial equality, the practice on the ground is rather different. There is a blatantly anti-Black element within non-Black Muslim communities that functions to remove safe spaces from Black people in multiple ways.

The lived experiences of anti-Black racism from within the Muslim communities make it exceptionally difficult for Black Muslims to enjoy the religious and cultural spaces in already Islamophobic societies. These transgressions are sadly not limited to the streets of the UK or other Western countries but are also very apparent in the experiences of Black Muslims globally, even at the holy sites.

I went on hajj for the first time a few years ago. Moments after I first set eyes on the Kaaba the adhaan was made and people lined up in rows to perform the congregational prayer. My first salah at the Kaaba. I was so excited, in awe and grateful to Allah for bringing me all that way to fulfil one of the pillars of my faith, a once-in-a-lifetime opportunity. I went to stand next to a South Asian woman in a green salwar kameez. And what happened next is as bewildering for me to recount as it was to experience. This woman started shouting at me and gesturing for me to move away from her. I tried to be a 'good Muslim' and gave her the benefit of the doubt, assumed she was saving that space for a family member, so I made a little space between us. But it wasn't enough for her. She carried on shouting and then physically assaulted me. It was then that I realised it was *me* she didn't want anywhere near *her*. One of the conditions of hajj is that you do not fight or argue. It apparently nullifies the entire ritual. I had to make a very quick calculation, deduced I couldn't afford financially or practically to come back to perform another hajj, so I decided to resist her violence without succumbing to slapping her face from Mecca to Medina. I felt *really* tested by Allah in that moment. She pushed me, so I responded in broken Urdu and Hindi with gesticulation: 'Stop. NO! I'm praying here!' I joined the jama'a prayer, which had already started with millions of fellow worshippers in ihram while this racist in Makkah continued to hit and kick me. I defied her by praying exactly where I stood. She soon gave up and moved away. And when the prayer ended I saw her pull herself away from an unsuspecting Ghanaian woman who happened to sit next to her. Her foot had brushed against this racist, who wiped her clothes with disgust. On her other side was a non-Black woman and she showed no such disgust at their shared bodily proximity, because her repulsion was reserved for our Blackness.

Social, cultural and educational spaces like restaurants, iftar gatherings and even Muslim schools can be racism minefields for Black Muslim families to navigate on a regular basis. Some Black parents have had to withdraw their children from independent Muslim schools and place them in state schools due to unchecked racism at the hands of not only students but also teachers. Those of us who speak out against these abuses quickly collect labels that are often themselves racist and employ anti-Black tropes, such as 'angry Black woman', 'aggressive', 'over-sensitive'.

It is suffocating especially for Black or mixed-race Black Muslims who have non-Black family members who refuse to walk that walk with them, instead choosing to remain wilfully ignorant to the unique experience of being a Black Muslim in the UK. These people compound the oppressions by diminishing or denying the experiences of their spouses or children within their homes. Often, they don't check the casual racism of their own families, gaslighting their Black spouses and children into self-doubt, silence and isolation, until it feels like there are few places left to turn to.

Others expend much energy making excuses for the transgressors. Usually well-meaning Muslims offer (unsolicited) naseehah, that the aggrieved should forgive and be patient – affu and sabr at all costs. Abundant excuses are forthcoming for aggressors: 'they're just ignorant', 'maybe they didn't mean it'. The empathy and safety afforded to blatant racists is mind-boggling to me. Anyone doing mental gymnastics to exonerate racists holds the belief that our humanity is worth a lot less than that of the ones who harm us. Full stop. End of. Period.

Alongside holding people accountable for their actions, Black Muslim communities are creating their own solutions in the meantime. Many Black Muslims have grown tired of the macro- and micro-aggressions levelled against us and are increasingly creating events and activities designed especially for us. One of the most common obstacles to these Black Muslim events is the outcry and protestations from non-Black Muslims who accuse organisers of being racist. These are textbook workings of white supremacy, though it is harder to recognise or name it when one is experiencing it, especially when the perpetrators are fellow believers and (often) not white. Unpacking that last part would require a whole other essay!

Furthermore, the marginalised are told in no uncertain terms that the oppressions they speak of are a 'Western' problem. 'There is no racism in Islam,' some declare, ignoring the fact that the teachings of a faith are very different to the practice of those who claim it. To say you experienced racism at the hands of a fellow Muslim invokes indignant denials (cue the gaslighting), which leaves the victim of the racist abuse almost questioning their own sanity.

Some Black people are finding that non-religious Black cultural spaces honour their humanity by valuing and not shunning their Blackness. Many are only dipping into Islamic venues for the necessities. Hatch, match and dispatch, or Aqeeqah, Nikkah, Janazah, plus of course Jumuah, taraweeh and the Eids.

Even in women-only Eid gatherings, when we take our hijabs off, non-Black women are quick to comment on our hair and try to touch it without permission, even calling their friends over to come and have a feel. Making Black women feel like animals in a petting zoo is not the definition of a safe sisterly space. I have decided that the next time someone does this I will match the violation by grabbing a fistful of their own hair and commenting. Maybe it's the only way some people will start to understand just how disconcerting and inappropriate this behaviour is. It is exhausting doing martial-arts-level leaning back and ducking to stop people casually invading our personhood.

As a result of the issues around this scarcity of safe spaces, Black people are being more deliberate about how we navigate towards a safer and more healing existence. Self-care, and I don't mean that in the co-opted consumerist sense but in its original form, is an act of survival. It was Audre Lorde who said, 'Caring for myself is not self-indulgence, it is self-preservation, and that is an act of political warfare.'

Mental-health awareness is another area in which the scarcity of safe spaces becomes painfully apparent. Many Muslims, and I don't know how we got to this state, seem to have an aversion to seeking professional help because of an overwhelming belief that mental ill-health is mainly the work of the devils and jinn possession. I have been in rooms and in conversations where someone has said they or a loved one have depression and a Muslim has very self-assuredly proclaimed, 'We are Muslims, we have faith, we don't do depression.' The implications of these attitudes can cost lives.

This scarcity of safe spaces has a deeply alienating impact. Many women are pilloried if they post anything on social media which is deemed 'immodest' or 'un-Islamic' by the ever-ready, judgemental, misogynist keyboard warriors. Social media for Muslim women is a very unsafe space. I have received all manner of threats, abuse and trolling from far-right racists but also from Muslim men, for innocuous things like retweeting a news item. Friends of mine have received far worse. Many of us worry about the consequences of *anything* we post in a way that others don't have to. Even social media, which has (sort of) democratised access to global instant communication and information, comes with hidden hazard signs of gendered Islamophobia, misogynoir, etc.

There is a saying of the Prophet Muhammad (SAW):

The Muslim is the one from whose tongue and hand the people are safe, and the believer is the one who is trusted with the lives and wealth of the people.

– Sunan al-Nasā'ī 4998 sahih

No conversation about safety can be complete or sincere if I am not candid about the importance for others to feel safe from my actions and behaviours too. It is all well and good saying that as a visibly Muslim Black British Somali woman I am not made to feel safe in such and such places, but I must acknowledge *my* privileges (whether real or as perceived by others) which immerse me into the mainstream. People who have visibly different identities or needs to mine are often treated very differently.

Once again, privilege is a powerful currency. And I see it as my responsibility to use my currency wisely and to try not to reproduce oppressive structures. I don't get it right all the time – no one does – but we have to make it a daily practice. Making people feel safe begins with acknowledging, facing and dealing with the bigotry that has been fed to us all under white supremacist patriarchal hegemonic culture and society. While we cannot change our pasts, we can begin to actively unlearn the thinking. Then commit to doing better and to refusing to let the dehumanisation of other people take place on our watch. It is my view that any expressions of bigotry directly or indirectly contribute to the erosion of safety for somebody, somewhere, even if we are not aware of it. And it is both our individual and collective responsibility to do better.

Safety, for some of us, can be fleeting. What is a safe moment can very quickly become unsafe. It means having your wits about you almost all the time. That means being tired almost all of the time too.

Sometimes leaving a place that is not safe is simply not possible. That is not a weakness, it's circumstance. Sometimes safety is not saying that thing you want to say, because the harm from it will outweigh any good you seek. Sometimes safety is exhaling with one friend or two. One meal. One prayer. One cup of tea. Sometimes safety is prioritising your own survival in that moment. It is ironic that in an essay about safety I have decided to self-censor so much of what I wanted and needed to write about, but I've had to consider all possible repercussions. And we are not there yet. At least for now.

The search for truly safe spaces still continues. So, while we wait to exhale, we work and hope that all oppressive structures fall before us, like the statues of slavers being brought down across the world. Things cannot go back to 'normal', because exploitative capitalism, climate change, structural racism, violent misogyny, etc. should never be normal. They are destructive to the vast majority of the people, creatures and resources of this Earth.

Our every word is a will and testament. Our breaths are not guaranteed. But soon we will exhale, inshaAllah.

A CARTOGRAPHY OF MOTHERHOOD

Suma Din

You have arrived on my map. A map in motion; stretching in one place and shrinking in another; you may find my nadir in the clouds, and my zenith below.

Adjust.

I am still here, standing on the axis where the clear blue line crossed the highway of youth; once a mother, always a mother. This is the anomaly of this space, that you venture forward and stand still at the same time. I have stood here for over two decades. By the end of this jaunt, you may move some distance, or you may not.

Isn't that why you read, to travel?

Within the confines of these lines, I will introduce you to two regions: the experience of raising Muslim children, and how I, as a mother, have grown on this terrain. Sink-holes, landmines, marshes and the odd lavender field line our path.

Distorted and contradictory? Yes. This is the lie of the land when you mother as a Muslim woman; there are clashes, there are contradictions, there are soul-splitting challenges.

Adapt.

Take the first right.

My roots in this land were anchored young, at twenty-three. Somewhere in between the pastel tones, sweet fragrances and serenity of a newborn's world the explanations of clarifying who you are begin . . .

'Your surname and the baby's are different . . .'

I replied, I have my own name, while our daughter has my husband's surname. The warm-eyed health visitor looked up from the beaming red baby book at me with a polite frown in the shape of a question mark. Rigid with the after-birth pains, I shuffled around after putting our firstborn in her cot to address the searching frown and said:

'I didn't change my name when I got married. No need to. We can keep our own names.'

'Well, I thought about that too . . . back then, about keeping my maiden name. But when we got married everyone changed names. What did your husband think?'

'He was fine with it, because –' and now the 'explaining me' took over to regurgitate parts of past discussions – 'a woman keeping her identity is normal. Things like inheriting, keeping your own finances separate, keeping your own name . . . all that's part of a Muslim woman's right – if they're aware of their rights.' I added the last part as I read the expression on her face, which looked incredulous. In all the houses she visits and clinic appointments she handles in this part of west London, 'Muslim women' and 'rights' are not always partners. I was well aware of this incongruity.

'Now, how's the feeding going since you've been back home?'

Thankfully we returned to the comfort of baby talk and left my identity and my community's chequered identities on the page with my details.

I've wondered about this small exchange at random times since, questioning why I felt the need to say anything. There are surely enough people in the world, especially with marriage going out of fashion, who don't share the same surname as their partners and children. The difference between myself and other women who keep their own name and identity is that there are no assumptions made about them; they don't have to labour at establishing who they are. Over here, we do. Had time permitted, there is more I would have liked to say to this tender health visitor. Her role sits in the heart of the community, among women and their babies; a community in which restrictive cultural practices have become so entwined with the faith that it is difficult to separate them out from within, and so much more difficult to comprehend from the outside.

This thing we call identity has within it multiple layers: the babushka doll. All these identities – faith, familial, cultural, local and global – co-exist and enrich each other when all's going well. But when it's not, when one identity is being dissected and no longer fits easily within another, then there is work to be done. While I had the luxury of growing up in less troubled times, I know that's not the case for my children. As my experience of mothering went from one child, to a second and then a third, I felt the season change; they would have to flourish in the frosts of fear, suspicion and misinformation around their inner identity; their faith. And so the challenge surfaced, how was I going to protect, support and nurture their balanced selves to develop?

Welcome to mothering Muslim children: watch out for the quicksand.

Take a left here.

My mother's generation dealt with the school lunches, figuring out what to do on Eid in a new country, tackling parents' evenings and getting used to a foreign neighbourhood, often with little support. The changes in the landscape over the last forty years have certainly made the nuts and bolts of having a Muslim child in school logistically easier for most. Their basic struggles are all but absent now, so the baton handed to us, the next generation of parents, is to deal with the inner.

What do I mean by the inner? It's knowing how to handle the climate of public opinion, world and local news that incessantly feature your faith in a negative light. It's knowing how to navigate this to cause your child's sense of self the least harm. In short, we aim for damage limitation. How can I raise positive, enthused children amidst the negativity out there?

In an everyday sense, it can look like this. One moment your mind is trying to reinvent itself to adjust to the latest phase that one of your children is going through. At the same time, you're out concentrating on conquering the family shopping list. And then – bang! You walk past a Sky News kiosk in the shopping centre, and there's another 'terror suspect' crime investigation underway. Like any passer-by, your instinct is to stop and watch the headlines unfold on the screen. And then as you swallow the news for yourself, the details, the victims, the place . . . you stop. The atrocity is shocking. You take in the effect on the victims, and then your mind switches to your children and whether this information has reached them yet. The elder two were in that blessed time when mobile phones were not treated like oxygen masks, and they only had the basic 'brick' when they finally did own one. With six years' difference between the eldest and youngest, we have to deal with the seismic shift in technology and its implications. With the youngest in secondary school, I always wonder how *much* he knows, not *if* he knows.

Repeated incidents bring about long-term weariness, accumulate like plastic in landfill; it doesn't go anywhere. No schooling experience can be ideal, and I count our family's good fortune to have gone through it positively with much good to draw on; from the songwriter teaching in reception to the brilliantly inspiring history teacher in Year Ten and several remarkable educators in between. Periodically though, through my own children and through interacting with families in the community, I learn of things that should never happen to young people – they are insidious, they are not easily definable '-isms', they are far-reaching patches of black ice. When teenage girls are singled out by teachers and questioned about the failures of their community; when they are questioned about why their uniform, regulation trousers are all so similar; when a mother is phoned at home and quizzed because her infant-school child said they attended a fundraising bazaar at the weekend for refugees; this is when you smell something new in the air.

Can you smell it?

Personally, my nadir was a school day organised around a particular RE theme. Our second daughter, then in the sixth form, came home from school quietly distressed. And before long, out spilled the cause of her unrest, at speed, as though the brakes had failed on a steep downward gradient. As she relayed what had happened, it transpired that the day's theme was Muslims and current affairs. One wall display had factually incorrect information about Muslim marriages and divorce; another room displayed a shocking, violent video of a South Asian cult group's crimes, with another part of the day featuring a right-wing leader.

I was taken to a new location I wasn't prepared for. As with all the other public problems that find their way into our dinner-time conversations, I talked this one through with her. Asking more than answering. I wanted to know exactly what she understood – and more importantly, what she felt. I reassured her with concrete examples that the information her fellow sixth-formers looked shocked by was inaccurate and, as far as the video was concerned, completely irrelevant. We talked for at least a couple of hours before we both needed a break.

I thought long and hard about a response and penned an email. A few parts of it read:

Dear Mr Y,

I understand the RE day was held yesterday. I'm writing because I have some questions about the learning objectives which my daughter didn't understand.

In the spirit of parents being partners in their children's education, I need to share how distressing and in her own words 'disturbing and traumatic' she found some of the content of the day. In particular, the two-hour documentary about genocide was definitely not understood.

Having looked at the trailer and read the documentary-maker's rationale, I realise it may have been shown to the girls to demonstrate how artistic methods can be used as a tool to present alternative perspectives and deal with horrific events, which ultimately led the perpetrators to having some remorse. I gleaned this much from a quick glance at the website; however this was TOTALLY lost on my daughter and I guess the majority of girls – if indeed this was the objective.

What has remained, however, is a feeling of confusion and disgust. Reviews of the documentary have stated it is 'more terrifying than any horror film'.

Marry the above to the first part of the day, which was all about the Woolwich atrocity, misinformation about the rules on divorce and Muslim women, and it all begins to take a different shape – in the eyes of students, there is one common thread, one faith, here, that ties the Woolwich murder to inequalities for Muslim women, to their dress (not sure how this came up, too), and to Southeast Asian criminals guilty of a genocide.

If critical thinking was the objective, are all faiths subject to the same style of study, planned around criminals and their horrific acts?

Regarding the misinformation about women and divorce law . . . I am not going to even begin to offer any answers as the subject is not my speciality, even though I know that what came home was incorrect.

. . . If girls' well-being is a consideration, how do you suggest I undo the damage of feeling humiliated and demoralised from the first half of the day's content?

However my communication comes across to you, I can assure you I'm not complaining for the sake of it. I'm actually not complaining. I'm trying to understand what the intentions and educational benefits are of a day that chips away at the identity of a minority, while misleading the majority.

Kind regards,

Suma Din.

I mention this letter to my daughter with a mild 'Do you remember . . .'; she looks at me with a troubled expression: 'Yes, I remember – that was traumatic,' she says. It is now four years since that experience. And so, we mothers turn for inspiration to ourselves and our children.

Follow me into the ancient world. The ground beneath our feet turns to sand, and I am in the scorching barren desert of a strong mother: Hajar – mother to Prophet Ismail (AS). I draw from her strength, like the four million pilgrims each year who acknowledge her struggles as they retrace her footsteps as part of the hajj. This courageous mother sustained herself and her baby in a barren wilderness; established the foundations of a city, modern-day Makkah; and kept control of its most precious resource: water. For my daughter, there are personalities she encountered when younger in exhibitions, in books, in films – they need resurrecting periodically; like the ninth-century Tunisian Fatima Al-Fihri who founded the world's first university offering degrees, in the city of Fes, Morocco. From female astrolabe-makers in the tenth century to calligraphers, to physicians, to renowned educators in the nineteenth century, to the line-up of contemporary Muslim women thriving, every-where from sports to politics, here and now. They matter.

One more left turn.

I question times, when in the throes of parenting, with pre- to early teens, when there were issues to iron out; I wonder if the attention I gave, or we gave as parents, was somehow diluted because we were also dealing with nurturing and protecting their identity. Have I allowed wider margins as a gesture of empathy for the attitudes they face in general school life, rather than zoning in on the specifics? And I question, if none of the global attacks, none of the ideological 'clashes' had surfaced, and weren't visibly connected to our faith, would I have got a better grip on the parenting handle as I would only have the regular 'stuff' to do? Would I have had more space to focus on areas of their lives that needed addressing? I'll never know. At the same time I remind myself that mothers locally and globally have far more trying circumstances to contend with; poverty and socio-economic policies that don't support raising a family are the tip of that iceberg.

Look over here, an artefact for your perusal: my personal journal in which I made notes when researching and writing my book about the experiences of Muslim mothers educating their children. In the midst of raking over their interview themes, and reading related articles, I reflected on the raw reality of our collective situation, as mothers:

2015: Media-wise, my strategic avoidance of all things ISIS is no longer possible to sustain. Every day there are several newspaper articles. Either someone has gone, someone is analysing who has gone or others are taking a critical, thematic look at the bigger picture; about youth, about parents, about multicultural society, about government policies, about wars. The scale is gigantic. I don't have a degree in international politics or Middle Eastern history, nor have I read a lot of books on extremism. These are not my subject specialisms. They never were. Do I need knowledge of these now in order to understand the latest insults thrown around in the comments section of the Guardian? *How does the average mother deal with all this – she is implicated by association in some of the articles . . . do my mums even realise?*

I haven't kept track of the hours I've spent in the last two weeks reading all things CTS Bill-related, PVE and school-related and now Muslim youth and ISIS-related. I'm tired of hyperlinking and hyperlinking again in my 'References' document. I can't bear to look at another article.

Is this what our lives and identity have become – these hyperlinks? And from the same ink, on other weeks, flow articles about the difficulties facing mothers and their work/ life balance. How much would I love to have an unproblematic identity and the struggles of 'normal' parenthood like the work/life balance . . .

There was one ray of hope today; one academic's article is finally arguing for common sense in their piece about university surveillance. At last!

Our elder daughter is at university now and the second is to start imminently. My mind flits between conflicting images with that admission: 'the best days of her life' is framed in a hazy sun-kissed scene on a brochure, a blur of happy-looking undergraduates walking out of the gates, ready to make their mark on the world. And before this image can settle in my head for more than a few seconds, another scene crops up, and another ... and another: our 'debate' at 8 a.m. about her commuting on the train, wearing a hoodie with her name in Arabic on the back; the 'Charity Week' activities; the questions I ask about the speakers they book; the WhatsApp groups she's on; her Facebook statuses I skirt around before my transparency is exposed with 'I don't write anything political ... you're so paranoid!'

I move towards protection and invisibility while they forge ahead with assertion, with being themselves, without apology. Tread carefully here; these stresses cause the plates we stand on to move in different directions. Watch out for the fault-lines; some are invisible.

In our global village, when out for a scroll, articles on young Muslim women and self-defence; another viral clip of abuse on public transport; a personal account of airport body-searches, enter the same brain that mothers (the verb) – however vainly I attempt to disconnect from negativity when I'm browsing the newspapers. These news items seep into the very fabric of mothering and somewhere their relevance, or their caution, or their bleak landscape, greys the horizon you see for your children – if you allow it to. If it doesn't, if you are aware of the stories and the non-stories and haven't allowed these to permeate your parenting, then know that there has been significant work going on to put that internal border up. The Great Wall of China in length and the Sahara desert in width was constructed to ringfence 'a normality'. A normality, because 'normal' in parenting terms is not a shared experience.

The last left turn, here, up this wall.

So here we have it: the dilemma. The world questions parents, and specifically mothers, about how they raise their children; that's a given. Within this, Muslim women are characterised as lacking agency, as victims of misogyny and oppression, economically dependent and unable to 'break free' of their repressive cultures. There are grains of truth in this, just as the same can be said for women from a host of other communities, unfortunately. But Muslim mothers are also under suspicion of having children who are not integrated enough; they are not connected enough (*why don't they come to school discos . . . ?*). Have you tried standing on a smooth rock at the edge of the sea? As the waves push their way to the shore, vying to make you slip, destabilising, you shuffle to strengthen your foothold, arms flailing to keep your balance. Looking out, you see others in the same sea, swimming calmly. The best you can do is keep your balance.

I am at my son's school, at a meeting set up specifically for Muslim mothers. 'So, ladies,' the police officer says as he claps his hands together after tucking his protruding stomach into his belt, 'how much do you know about the way youngsters are radicalised online? How much do you know about the way extremists work?' It is a scene to behold: a classroom with mums sitting behind desks on a sliding scale: the ones who read the news regularly look uncomfortable, while the less informed just look bemused but happy; they will be grateful for everything – even this. They got changed out of their cooking clothes, especially. We are all polite.

I don't deny there are problems and I know these are important questions. I'm merely showing you the terrain on my map. And the difficulty is the cross-associations, the warped equation – and it has been said to me in different ways with varying degrees of 'politeness'; in the end, though, the equation is this:

Your community (as in any person of South Asian descent) is rife with social problems; just look at the women from deprived areas + look at the treatment of women in Middle Eastern & Asian countries (let's homogenise whole conti-nents) = Be silent, don't speak up, or leave.

Now, there are academic labels and theories to frame the coarse equation, but we're not travelling together for the high-brow stuff today. We are staying on the ground. Essentially, this way of thinking seeks to remove our experiences from the con-temporary narrative of what it means 'to mother'. It seeks to use the problems of the weakest in society to say, *Look at the mess you come from first, before you notice the way you are treated*, and most pointedly, it seeks to absolve the privileged, everyday, structural racism and anti-faith attitudes that pervade society. It's a whisper that is dressed in respectable language. It's pervasive.

Let's stop at this hill; there's a view to take in. The girls are adults now. They have each steered their own version of culture which prioritises their faith identity. It's not been without many a late-night walk into history, faith and geography. The eldest works, now, in a field she explicitly connects to her values as a Muslim and as a global citizen; this is seamless for her. She starts her first permanent job, with a postgrad, three contract jobs and a steely strong CV to her name. Have things changed, have people changed, or has she encountered good luck? She's respected and comfortable. No serious jibes. The occasional remarks 'go over my head, we're desensitised now,' she explains. We talk about projects, about the infrastructure in developing countries, and she tells me about mining and sanitation in these regions. Her grandmother, though, asks her where her colleagues come from in her office – and it amuses us. There is entertainment too, around this corner. The second is still in university, on a long-haul degree into a profession with automatic respect built in; I worry about her less as time goes on. She'll soon be able to contribute to society with one hand, and manoeuvre into a safe space with the other, I imagine. The youngest, the one I stared at in his cot when the Twin Towers came down and feared for the most, is in his last year at school. Not so far from where we stand, I taught him, aged three, to politely correct anyone who says his name wrong: 'tell them the three sounds'. His name remains intact.

His playful language at home crystallises how he finds his space in this world; Bangla words are thrown in with the odd Urdu phrase for entertainment, swirled in with some sociology terms on race and culture, encased in UCAS-style aspirational lingo of seeking a respectable career. He finds his own subculture, including various cultural 'influencers' online. We discuss balance and bias; mealtimes last for ages, so we can digest his observations. He flips between BBC headlines and news channels from other continents as his norm; he compares. He asks questions about who has it easy in society and who doesn't. If a programme taps his memory, he admits to feeling frustrated about the 'banter' of 'Allahu Akbar' jokes sprinkled over the race-related 'digs'. But the irritation dissipates quickly, he says, and he doesn't mention it again. I consciously savour his last year at school. I put off thinking about his university experience. I take nothing for granted. I 'mother' less nowadays, I observe more. We've come this far, so far.

Our lines diverge, I'll take your leave now.

Retrace your turns and you'll find yourself somewhere.

Disoriented?

You've arrived.

GROWING INTO HIJAB

Rumana Lasker Dawood

'Did your husband make you wear that?'

What a cliché. Can you see my eyes roll? It's the kind of thing that as a hijabi you expect to hear and have a stock answer for. Depending on your mood it could be an enlightening and informative spiel about the hijab and the reasons why women wear it, or it could be a straight-up 'no', with a face that says: 'I dare you to ask if I'm hot in this too.' But this time it caught me off guard and left me speechless.

I had been a doctor for nearly three years, and I had met with a consultant at work to discuss my application for the next stage of training. We had been going through my CV and he had even expressed an interest in the research I was doing. It was a professional conversation between colleagues . . . and yet he asked me this question as easily as asking if I wanted sugar in my tea.

I couldn't understand it. How was it that I was intelligent enough to work alongside him as a doctor, to discuss the diagnosis and management of patients in our care, but not have the intelligence or agency to make a choice about wrapping a scarf around my head every morning? No, apparently that was a decision for *my husband.*

The shock (maybe horror? Or was it revulsion?) must have been written across my face because he mumbled something inaudible and quickly moved on to a different topic. But that moment stayed with me: it was a rude awakening that, despite everything I do, some people would only ever see my hijab and, with that, whatever prejudiced picture of a Muslim woman they held. In that instant I was stripped of my autonomy and reduced to a demeaning stereotype.

I know this may seem obvious, but honestly it came as a surprise to me. I grew up in north London, where there were few Muslims at school but a strong community of Bangladeshi Muslims outside of it. All the children my age were boys and there were few women wearing the hijab in our circle at that time. It was always something I was aware of but thought of as something I might do 'in the future', if at all. As with most people, the transition from teenager to adulthood was a period of reflection and trying to find who I was. It wasn't until I went to university that I started to consider my religion on a personal basis – what these ritualistic acts of praying five times a day or fasting meant *to me.* I was never one to attend lectures or courses on Islam, preferring to absorb my understanding of my religion from my environment and those around me, and from reading up on my own. Perhaps I was stubborn, but I was no longer satisfied with just being told how to practise my religion by other people.

This stubbornness meant that I kept my thoughts around the hijab completely secret from nearly all my friends and family. It was such a personal decision. In fact the only person I discussed it with beforehand was one of my best friends, who isn't Muslim. I wanted to keep a critical head around the hijab and I didn't want to be influenced by blindly positive encouragement from the Muslim community. Nor did I want to be overly criticised by someone who couldn't understand acts of faith that make life 'harder'. But in this friend I found the perfect balance.

So one day, two years into my six-year course at university, I started wearing the hijab. There was no weaning process where I gradually wore it more and more: I just put it on one day and walked out of the house to go to university.

In the end my decision to wear it was as an act of devotion; it was something I was doing for my Lord. It was as simple as that.

The 'hijab' is actually a misnomer. Generally it is used to refer to the headscarf women wear, when it actually refers more broadly to the concept of modesty: modesty in how you dress, modesty in how you act, modesty in what you do. It wasn't until I started wearing the hijab that I truly understood this.

Over the years I had honed how to dress myself, apply make-up and tease my hair in a way that made me feel presentable to the world. It was my comfort zone. It really wasn't until I covered my hair that I realised how intertwined my inner confidence was with the way I looked. In a society where there is so much emphasis on our external appearances, I had naively thought I was immune to it all. Until then, I hadn't been aware of my own vanity. It's quite a startling experience: suddenly you feel like an awkward teenager – unsure of yourself, and uncomfortable in your own skin. And worst of all, it's all your own doing.

I find it hard to look at photos of myself from that period of my life. Yes, partly because of the questionable hijab-styling, but mainly because I don't see myself in the pictures. I can see the self-consciousness seeping out of every pore of my skin. I knew I still wanted to wear the hijab – my commitment to that hadn't changed; it wasn't my relationship with God up for questioning here. It was my relationship with myself.

At my lowest point this crash in self-confidence actually had me hiding behind a wall. Not in a philosophical sense . . . an actual wall. I was in central London on my way to university and walking towards me was a friend I had gone to school with. We hadn't seen each other in years. She looked exactly the same, and I . . . well, I didn't. My heart raced. I couldn't face her. I couldn't deal with the awkward look, or the explaining I may have to do. I was so embarrassed about myself that I hid behind a wall and waited for her to walk on by.

I was mortified. Why had I done that? How could I have let myself become so overwhelmed by self-consciousness? It was one of those moments that made me step back and think, 'What am I doing?' I was otherwise the same person: my sense of humour hadn't changed, my friends hadn't changed, the food I ate and the things I did hadn't changed. All that had happened was that I had started to wear a hijab. But that's just it; I couldn't simply think of the hijab as just the scarf on my head. It wasn't just about covering my hair in an act of worship. It was more than that, more than merely a symbol of my faith. It was a tool for me to use to better myself and to become the best version of the person I could be. I was forced to face my own vanity and consider the fragility of my ego. How could my inner confidence have its foundations based on the way I looked? I had never thought of myself as vain; the uncomfortable truth is that we are all vain – but it was the extent of this vanity and how it influenced my day-to-day being that I needed to be aware of.

Brick by brick I eventually built myself back up. As I became more content within myself, I found everything else fitted into place. I rediscovered my sense of style, and this time it was complementary to my being rather than at the core of it. As the years went by, the hijab became second nature. I know I look 'better' without it, but I no longer needed that external validation.

*

This internal battle took up so much of my mind-space that for a while I was blissfully unaware of how others would perceive me as a hijab-wearing woman.

When I first started wearing it, it had been such a personal decision I really hadn't considered how it would make the people around me feel. I could see the surprise on people's faces when I walked into a room. Some people would congratulate me (other hijabis in particular would suddenly notice me like I was now part of the private club), others would acknowledge it with an 'Oh OK' and move on, some would feel too awkward to bring it up at all, and then there was the group who would get so caught up in trying to treat me correctly that they would trip up over their own feet – 'Oh sorry! I didn't mean to swear in front of you!'

The hijab was so much a part of me that I no longer noticed it – that is, until it was pointed out to me. It's a bit like how you don't really think about the brownness of your skin until someone asks, 'Where are you from?' and they're not expecting the answer 'north London'. That's when you remember that you look 'different'.

Slowly I became more aware of the little comments that slid into conversation, ones that betrayed the person's prejudices. Be it the 'Did your husband make you wear that?' or the 'Are you allowed to work as a doctor?'

Some of it was more direct. There was the patient who shouted at me, 'I don't believe in *your* God,' before refusing to let me come near them. Or the patient who would aggressively shout for me to 'TAKE THAT OFF' as her relatives sat by in horror. In the end I had to swap patients with other doctors on the team as it became so difficult to care for them. But these things were easy to shake off. It was things like the ward clerks sitting in the shared clerk/doctor's office discussing loudly how 'if *they* don't like to eat bacon then *they* should go live somewhere else' as both I and a colleague – also a hijab-wearing woman – sat working in the room. That's what got under my skin. It was a reminder that even though they would smile at me and work with me as a colleague, or even ask me for advice, I was still the Other.

Would you believe me when I say I'm actually an introvert? I'd jump at the chance to stay at home on my own with a movie, book or my sewing machine. I'm naturally very quiet with new people. When I was younger this shyness was misinterpreted as being aloof. It's not in my nature to put myself out there onto centre stage. So how exactly did I end up applying for a sewing competition that aired on BBC2 to millions of viewers?

Well, in my journey of self-discovery I had found it impossible to find clothes on the high street that suited my needs and my style. Fed up of having to layer cardigans over dresses and dresses over trousers I took up sewing to create my own clothes. More than a hobby, sewing became a passion. It was my way to unwind after a stressful day; it was my way to get some creative juices flowing. This particular show was one of my favourites and I had followed it from the very first episode, after my mum discovered it while channel-hopping and called to tell me to run and put the TV on 'right now!' I had always joked with my family that it was my 'life's goal' to be in that sewing room one day – the reams of ribbons and bias tape, bottles of buttons and shelves flowing with fabric. Obviously, I never actually thought I'd be on it. I mean, I had only been sewing properly for a few years at that point and, besides that, I had a full-time job; there was no way I would have the time to do the show even if I was selected. But as you do when you harbour secret dreams, I quietly checked to see if they had opened up for applications after the third series.

When the applications for the fourth series finally opened I happened to be taking a year out of practising in the hospital and was teaching medicine at a university. Practically, this meant no night shifts; no weekends; no twelve-hour shifts. It was planned to be my year to enjoy life again, and if there was ever a year to apply, this was it.

With each stage of the audition process I would get more and more excited at the possibility of being chosen for the show, and when the phone call came I genuinely couldn't believe it. As they kept telling us, the final ten contestants had been chosen from tens of thousands of applicants. It was mind-blowing. The whole process was exhausting, but exhilarating and hands-down one of the best experiences of my life. I was so proud of what I had achieved, of all the things I had learned, and made an amazing group of friends. After the whirlwind of filming we waited anxiously for the line-up to be announced publicly. That was when I could finally come clean to all my family and friends about this huge secret I had been keeping.

When it came around at last there was so much excitement in the air – I got sent screenshots of newspapers in Australia featuring my face; messages of support from far and wide; my family took to stockpiling newspapers and magazines that had any mention of the show. You can imagine how surreal this felt. It was such a high, until I read the articles and comments.

I guess, unsurprisingly, the idea that there could be 'another' hijab-wearing woman on a televised contest was not one some people were happy with. Before the show had even been aired, these strangers were already making judgements about my worth, my merit to be on the show and my religion. All based on what? The 150-word bio that describes me as 'a junior doctor who enjoys sewing to unwind'? Or was it the accompanying photo of me in a hijab?

Apparently I was an obvious, tokenistic choice of contestant, just there to tick the politically correct diversity box. For some it was a conspiracy – after all, we had already reached the national quota for 'generic non-violent brown Muslim woman on TV' (for future reference, the quota is one per decade). My individuality was erased as sweeping comparisons were made with another hijab-wearing woman on a TV contest, because, don't you know, all hijab-wearing women are the same. My experience and sewing abilities were ignored, dismissed under the brazenly insulting assumption that all

Muslim women are 'well domesticated'. One national paper decided to use my headshot as the headlining photo, inviting more scorn: why had they chosen me over the other contestants?

As much as you expect all of this to come out, and prepare a barrier against it all, the self-doubt started to seep in. Was I really just chosen because of the way I look? Were the producers just playing diversity bingo and I happened to hit a few points in one go?

I hated that people who knew nothing about me stripped me down to this caricature of a Muslim woman. They didn't want to look beyond my hijab, they didn't want to wait to see what I could do or hear what I had to say. They weren't interested in my truth and my very being was enough to rile them.

Whatever the reasoning behind my selection, I tried my hardest to put those voices to the back of my mind. After all, the vast majority of people were supportive, and despite not feeling 'good enough', I had made it all the way to become a quarter-finalist. Not bad for just a quota-filler.

It's not the first time, nor will it be the last, that I find myself being gagged by these assumptions and opinions. Even if I say I'm not oppressed, I'm still treated with pity and told, 'No, no, of course you are. No woman would *choose* to wear that.' If I stay silent and let it go, then I let them walk away with the idea that I am this weak individual worthy of pity. But if I speak up angrily, I am reinforcing the idea that all Muslims are angry, unpleasant people, undercover extremists hell-bent on causing destruction. And what if I simply tire of trying to defend my side and decide to sit the argument out? I'm accused of shying away from society, not wanting to 'integrate'. With the hijab comes the external burden of wearing it – as well as the uninvited presumptions made on the basis of us covering our hair, as a ubiquitous image of Islam, we carry the unsolicited responsibility of being walking spokespeople for the entire religion. So what options do we have?

I decided the best way to combat it was to be aware of the stereotype people expect me to be and work hard to be the opposite. That might mean that I smile more at strangers, go out of my way to speak to others, and offer you a tissue if you need it. I will work hard to excel in my professional life and put myself out there. You think Muslim women can't *do* things? I'm going to go snorkelling in the ocean. Climb a mountain. Do a postgraduate degree. Get an award. Go abroad to present my research. Get published in magazines and journals. I'll go jogging in the streets. I'll cycle in the park. I will bring you chocolates and gifts when it's Eid. I will send you cards at Christmas. I will be everything you don't expect me to be. I will speak up for myself and not be silenced. My hijab has not led me to shy away; it has forced me to step out. This is my choice, while others equally understandably choose other paths.

I will not let other people put me down and make me feel unworthy. And I will not give them an excuse to hate me purely because of my religion. I am who I am *because* of my religion.

GRENFELL

Shaista Aziz
(in conversation with *Zahra Adams*)

The night our eyes changed
Rooms where love was made and un-made in a flash of
 the night
Rooms where memories drowned in fumes of poison
Rooms where futures were planned and the imagination of
 children built castles in the sky
Rooms where both the extraordinary and the mundane
 were lived
Become forever tortured graves of ash
Oh you political class, so servile to corporate power

— Lowkey, 'Ghosts of Grenfell'

When I was an undergraduate student living in London, I
worked part-time in a children's adventure playground very
close to the Westway, west London, which for the past few
years has been covered in messages of love, solidarity, resistance and calls for justice for Grenfell, in the shadow of the

tower. I used to spend most of my Saturdays in the area, and even though west London has never felt familiar to me in the way east London does, I grew to love this little part of west London for being earthy and real.

I remember very vividly how I first came to hear the news of the fire at Grenfell Tower. It was the early hours of the morning and I was awake, getting ready to fast for Ramadhan. I was preparing suhoor and had the news on in the background. After hearing about the fire I checked Twitter for more details before prayers and returning to sleep. By the time I woke up a few hours later, a partial picture of the extent of the devastating fire was becoming clearer. To this day, the full picture is yet to emerge.

I didn't know anyone who lived in Grenfell, but I understood the magnitude of this catastrophe on the people left behind and the people and communities in the area. And this is what made me feel that I wanted to connect with the women impacted and hear their stories. I first went to Grenfell a month after the fire. I intended to go and pay my respects. I headed to the Westway to do just that. I was very conscious that I was an outsider and many outsiders were in the area and that some of them, at least weren't welcome because of their behaviours – local government representatives, some journalists and members of the media, and those who had come to intrude on the grief and devastation of people and a community. I left a short while after I arrived, after I had read Fatiha and paid my respects.

The more I read about what had happened and was happening to survivors and the community, the more outraged I felt. I wanted in particular to hear the stories of Muslim women in the community, as I wasn't hearing those in the media. So I contacted a friend who was connected with sisters in the area and spoke to her about the possibility of meeting women and finding out if they wanted to speak and tell their stories uninterrupted and in their own words. My friend said she felt this was a possibility and would get back to me. A few weeks later we met at Latimer Road tube station and headed towards Grenfell, with a tin of freshly baked cookies and lots of time to listen actively and respectfully. We created this safe space by explaining that I was there to listen and to capture the stories that women wanted to share. The transcript below is what followed.

Zahra Adams, twenty-eight, lived opposite Grenfell Tower on the twentieth floor of a tower block which overlooked it.

'I've never thought about my identity, I started wearing niqab twelve years ago. When women wear the niqab, we always have to go out of our way to explain that we *chose* to wear it and nobody made us wear it. I honestly have never had anyone bother me about my niqab. It is not an issue for me and I do not believe it is an issue for most Muslims. None of the Muslims I know care about the niqab. I am a white woman, a white woman who chose to become a Muslim, and who chose to wear the niqab. I have lived in west London for twelve years. I loved living here. I'm from east London originally.

I loved the way all of us lived together, all in the same place, sharing the same space. It really is so nice around here, it's so diverse and I love it ... or loved it. You have the Irish and the Moroccans, the Pakistani and Bengali, the Somali and Nigerians and people from the Caribbean, and white people and Europeans.

You hear people from all over the world here, all over.

I took all of this for granted, if I'm honest. It was just part of my life. I thought everywhere was like this. Now I understand. I see more clearly now how special it was to be here in this area – before Grenfell – this place – living here; it was one of the best times of my life, it's the part of my life that I loved the most. It's funny, isn't it? We humans never understand what we have until it's gone.

When you live in a tower block like this one, like Grenfell, people think they know who you are and everything about you without even meeting you. They know nothing. We all loved living around here. We love each other and the community and people – a building is just a building without the bond of love, and that is what we had. I have three children and I live on the twentieth floor of this tower block.

I used to joke around and say to my husband and friends that we have the best view of London from here – who needs the London Eye! On a clear day, I can see across London. I used to love standing at the window and looking at that view. Being up here and seeing all of London below . . .

Now, since it happened, I couldn't look out of the window. I don't even want to pull the curtains back. I can't escape it – it's just there – an empty, burnt-out case. Just there. We will never forget it and we won't ever be able to escape it.

My neighbours are lovely – they have always checked up on me. Always. They asked after my family, after the kids. You know, living here – it made it so easy to be a Muslim! We all looked out for each other – we shared what we had, it didn't matter if you are a Muslim or not – that was not important. It felt safe and you felt like people cared about you and wanted good things for you and your family. It was special.

I had guests over for iftar on that night. A sister came over and we shared food – with our families. It was nice. The kids wanted pizza, that much I remember very clearly. I have chosen to not want to remember a lot, but yeah, I remember everything and there is no way that I will ever forget.

I went to pray Isha in our bedroom. I finished reading and got up, and I remember seeing that smoke was coming out of Grenfell. A small fire – I could see it, and smoke. It was around 1 a.m. I was trying to work out what was going on – I remember thinking to myself, 'What is that? Why is there a fire and smoke?' I went back into the living room and told my husband what I had seen. I asked him to go over to Grenfell to check on our friends. I told him to invite them over for suhoor. It was almost time to start fasting for the day. I stood at the window as he left. I could see more smoke coming out and I was wondering why I could see people in Grenfell. I was asking myself why they were still in there. By now some fire engines had arrived and the fire was spreading. I called my husband. He picked up the phone straight away. I asked him why people were still in Grenfell, why hadn't they left? He told me the fire was bad and that he had told some people to get out and leave, and the fire brigade was here now and everything should be okay. InshaAllah.

I was listening to him as I stood at the window, but my heart didn't agree and I really felt that the fire was getting worse and my heart was beating fast. It was almost suhoor time. I didn't want to wake my eleven-year-old son – I knew if he woke up he would panic at what was happening outside the window. I looked behind me and he was there – my son, he had woken up and walked into the living room. It was so bright, so incredibly bright, because the fire had spread fast, so fast.

The fire was the brightest light I've seen. It was so bright. He was panicking, my son, standing next to me, he was shaking . . . 'Where's Baba? Where's Baba?' he kept asking over and over. I took hold of him and told him it was okay, that his baba had called me and he was okay, he was checking on our friends. After that he was quiet. The colour was draining from his face and he looked like he was frozen still. I took him and held him. My heart was beating so fast. So fast.

The next thing I remember is my neighbours arrived. Everyone was standing looking out of the window – just standing and watching. We were silent and in shock. I spoke to my son and told him to go back to bed. I didn't want him to see what was going on.

I really couldn't do anything other than tell him to go back to his room. I remember saying to him, 'Please do not look out of the window. Do not pull the curtains open.' We were living opposite Grenfell, it's the first thing we see from the window, it's impossible not to see Grenfell. I see Grenfell all the time, I see it on fire, I see it like a bright light, and I see the smoke, the blinding light of the fire.

I called my husband and asked him what was going on. Had he seen our friends? Were they OK? He sounded calm. I didn't sound calm. As I was talking to him I was looking out at Grenfell – I could see people clearly on the top floors – they were running inside their flats. I could see them. So clearly. I still see them. They were running from one end to the other, trying to find a way, trying to find a way to stay alive. Afterwards, this was one of the images I kept replaying in my head, SubhanAllah, it's the image I can't shake.

Next thing, I heard Grenfell mentioned on the news. The news report said there was a fire and the report said that two people had died. I was seeing Grenfell on fire and seeing those people – on the top floors, they were like skittles, moving around, moving, and moving. I thought I was losing my mind. I was hearing the news saying that two people had died, and in front of me, I was seeing Grenfell. I saw ten people overtaken by flames. From my window, in my living room, this is what I was seeing.

I called my husband again. I told him, 'They've been taken, the ten people on the top floors, they've been taken.' He didn't respond. He didn't say anything.

Later, don't ask me what time, because I don't remember the time, my husband told me about a pregnant woman, she was six months pregnant and on the eighteenth floor. She managed to get out, her children passed out on the stairwell, but they managed to get out.

The fire was an inferno, it was so bright, it was so hot, the smoke, and I can't describe it.

Everyone in our tower was out at the stairwells and balcony – looking at what was happening – there was nothing we could do.

People were crying, praying, holding each other. I thought to myself, 'Oh my God, Grenfell is going to fall down'; we thought the tower would collapse, we were terrified. We didn't know what was going to happen.

My husband walked through the door at 6 a.m. He came inside the flat. He didn't speak. He didn't exchange one word with me. He looked pale and like he had seen the indescribable. He went into the bedroom and lay down. I didn't sleep, I felt numb. I felt hollow.

Around 7 a.m. I thought about getting the kids up and ready to go to school but I couldn't. I stayed inside the flat with the kids, but up until 2 p.m. that day I kept on thinking

I should leave the flat and go out – I couldn't muster up the courage to. The curtains were drawn all day. I didn't want to see Grenfell opposite. I couldn't do it. It was embedded in my heart and in my head and it was the only thing I was seeing – but I couldn't physically look at it or see it. But I also felt a strong pull to look at it. I can't explain it. It was the thing I knew I needed to look at, but I couldn't look.

So the curtains remained drawn all day. I also asked myself – what was I going to do outside? Where would I go? Where would I take the kids?

Outside, it was like the carnival, there were so many people everywhere, hundreds and hundreds of people, everywhere.

The people who came to us, who came to Grenfell to help, they were the everyday people, our neighbours, people from the area and people from west London and across London.

It was the people helping the people. We didn't see any officials, we didn't see anyone official – all we saw were the people, more and more of them came, with blankets and food and tears and kindness.

You know, it was when Grenfell was on fire. After that I understood what racism is. It was the first time in my life I understood how racism kills. How racism makes a person vanish and how racism numbs the heart and soul and then the rest of you.

I'm a white woman. I chose to become a Muslim. I married a man of colour and our children are biracial, they are Muslims and have Muslim names, they can't escape this hate. They will never escape it. I was born into my white skin, and into my white privilege. I'm from a working-class family, but we all have the privilege of being white and of never having to justify being who we are. Now, after seeing Grenfell burning and losing my friends in that inferno, I was facing that hate for the first time in my life. It totally threw me. It messed with my head and it hurt. I saw the newspaper headlines about the scroungers in Grenfell. I heard the comments on radio and TV about the illegal immigrants and refugees in Grenfell, the Islamophobia and hate about us Muslims and how we started the fire on purpose to move to a better place. This was so painful for me because, like I said, this was my home. I had lived here for twelve years and my children called this place home, we loved it here and we lived with everyone. The hate and lack of humanity and empathy was destroying my head and heart as much as everything I've seen.

Immediately after Grenfell, workers from the Red Cross came to the door. The white woman took one look at me. I was wearing my niqab when I opened the door, and she called a translator over. The translator asked me what language I spoke. I told her, 'I speak English, I am English – I only speak one language and that's English!'

For the first time in my life I had been reduced to a 'foreigner', an outsider in my own home. And this happened after Grenfell.

When my neighbour heard this – she thought it was hilarious and said as much. After it happened and even now,

GRENFELL

I can't relax . . . it is always there lingering in my mind. I didn't cry for the first three weeks. I couldn't. I was on autopilot. I had three kids to take care of so I had no choice.

The sisters I know were the same. Six months after it happened . . . I started trauma therapy. I found out four of my neighbours had signed me up for it. I told you, I loved living here because this is how my neighbours are – kind and compassionate.

We all looked out for each other, like a family should. I've gone every week and it is helping. I am most worried about my eleven-year-old son. He has been wetting the bed. He is anxious all the time. He is always telling me he feels sick, and he feels scared. He doesn't sleep well. He says he can see the tower in his dreams, it's right outside the window – you can see it from the room he sleeps in. I keep all the curtains closed because of this.

It's the first time in my life that I don't feel safe and I don't feel there is safety for my children, for my family. They will cover up the tower, you won't be able to see it, it will be covered up in white, but nobody can cover up what we have seen, what we have heard and what we feel every day. Our trauma is daily.

A year will pass; more years will pass, we will never forget. It is impossible for us to forget. I just want to sleep. I need safety and security for myself and for my kids and family.

After it happened, our gas was cut off for nine weeks over safety concerns. We were told to shower and wash in the leisure centre under Grenfell.

We are dealing with trauma. I can't face looking out of the window, I can't face leaving my flat, I'm not sleeping, none of us are sleeping, and we were told to walk under the tower and go and get on with life.

These people do not care. They simply have no compassion for us. Every day becomes harder, when you do not see the people you called your friends, the people you used to see, because they've gone. I see the forensic teams dressed in white on the top floors of the flats; I can see them moving around in there working. The traffic whizzes by, the forensic teams are in there, working away, life is going on – except for some of us it's not, is it? For those we lost, for the families and friends and for the rest of us who feel their loss and feel the guilt of their loss all the time.

I lost my friend N. in the fire. When we were looking for a flat – we both looked around Grenfell and the flat we live in now. She got housed in Grenfell and I remember asking her if she wanted to swap flats as a joke. The flats were really nice in Grenfell, they were more spacious, and we all wished we lived there.

So that was my reaction to my friend finding a flat in Grenfell. I feel so guilty now when I think back to this conversation. I lost many people I knew in there. The first named victim, the brother, Mohammed, he was from Syria, a refugee, and he died in Grenfell. His family thought he was safe in London … imagine … SubhanAllah. Sister Rania, she was so brave and beautiful and kind. Nobody will ever forget who they lost – it's just not possible to forget the people who were part of you and where you lived.

When Grenfell happened, along with the racism, indifference and contempt we have been met by, something else also happened.

Grenfell strengthened Muslims, it brought us together, and it brought many people together. But people were also forced to see us. For many, it was the first time they saw us Muslims for who we are and the people around here made a point to talk about us. The young brothers from the masjid, they were the ones who banged on the doors and told people to get out and leave their flats. They were in the masjid reading taraweeh prayers and getting ready for suhoor, they were the ones who acted as the first warning system.

They went up and down the stairs to wake people up. If it weren't for them, more would have been lost. These young men, these are the same men the media and politicians attack, the same men that lies are told about. It is these brothers who saved lives. The media were forced to talk about them because the people around here talked about them, and wouldn't stop talking about them.

It's changed all of us forever. Grenfell has changed our lives, all our lives. It's made me understand more than ever what community is and it's made me want to do more for my community – especially the women here. Most of the sisters I know, they don't even know that they are traumatised. I have white privilege, I grew up in it, and with that privilege, I was taught to seek help, and to know help is there for me, no questions asked. When I seek help, I won't be asked de-humanising questions, I won't be maligned or belittled, what I say will be taken at face value because this is what white privilege is.

Your existence is not questioned. Your humanity is a given. Many of these sisters, they are unable to talk about what they have seen and how they feel. They swallow their words. I see them and hear them. One Somali sister said to me, 'I feel like a zombie.' She isn't sleeping since Grenfell, nobody is, but then to be forced to swallow your words and repress every-thing, to have to let it churn inside and settle inside – to just sit inside you. It's like you have nowhere to go, and no one to release this to, and it hurts and twists away.

The Muslim women I know here – they are zombies. That Somali sister, she described us well.

When I started my trauma therapy it honestly changed everything for me.

I felt like I was breathing properly for short periods of time. I was breathing again. My therapist is incredible; she is a Black woman, who understands and who gets it. She told me she had studied how trauma had impacted Black people and communities post-Hurricane Katrina in New Orleans, and she had looked at how trauma counselling needed to be specified for people of colour to not cause further harm. She is phenomenal. She just gets it. She handed me a leaflet and asked me to read it, it said: 'What is trauma?'

I looked at her and said, 'Oh my God! I'm not crazy!'

That was my first reaction to being asked about trauma.

I told her I have to repress how I feel and how I think, to stay safe and to keep my family safe. No Muslim woman is going to speak to a therapist or a doctor or anyone who is supposed to care about her and show a duty of care to her and tell what is really going on in her head and in her heart. We are policed 24/7 as a community. We can't go to the GP or send our kids to school without everything we are feeling or thinking being put through this filter.

I know Muslim women here who have felt suicidal; they don't use this word, because this is a taboo, but they feel it. At first I felt so guilty for feeling this and for even allowing myself to understand how I was feeling. I felt fear, embarrassment and ashamed that I was feeling this. Also, we don't admit to anyone because we don't want our kids taken off us, we don't want them using excuses to take our kids away.

It was when I confronted myself about how I was feeling that I started to understand how for me it was the racism that created the injustice here, we were less than human, so we were left to die, and then even when some of us died, that racism, it didn't stop, did it?

Post-Grenfell I have experienced levels of Islamophobia I have not experienced before. Grenfell and then the terrorist attacks in London, the pain was deep and indescribable. London is a big city, a big place, but when Grenfell happened and when those attacks happened – London became a very small place. The city shrunk and became claustrophobic. Things changed. The safety and security – it also vanished. I also realised through the trauma counselling that Grenfell, the racism and Islamophobia post-Grenfell, it has given me an identity crisis. For the first time in my life I was left grappling with issues around my identity. I was left to ask myself – can't I be white and be a Muslim? Why can't I be both? Why do people get to tell me what I am? Again, this is my privilege, isn't it? I know this, I'm aware that for my Somali sisters and other sisters, they've never been allowed to belong, neither have their kids. But we belonged here. All of us. I never expected these feelings to emerge because of Grenfell – to be honest I have spent a long time trying not to feel anything. To block feelings out. Most sisters I know are doing the same thing.

There are many things that will stay with me. The light from that inferno, the people on the top floors running, running back and forth in their flats, trapped, but they kept on running, until they were taken.

I will remember feeling nothing for a long time because in order to take care of my kids I had to feel nothing and keep going. I will remember the racism and Islamophobia – how we were just left to pick up the pieces. I will remember the media and how they came and knocked on my door and said, 'You must have a really good view from your flat of Grenfell . . .'

I told one of them, 'Yes, I do, which is why my curtains are permanently closed and why I don't let my kids look out of the window,' and then I closed the door on them.

SMILE

Sabeena Akhtar

> *Smile, though your heart is aching,*
> *Smile even though it's breaking . . .*

I shrink myself as the carriage-full of football fans point and chant the famous Nat King Cole song at me in amusement. Moments earlier they forced me to open my handbag on the packed tube and 'prove' I wasn't carrying a bomb as, grinning, they inspected the contents of my bag (including, to their delight, sanitary towels). They see the fear and humiliation in my teenage face and hold it like triumphant victors, breaking out into chorus, encouraging me to see the bright side of their 'banter'. To just smile.

I hate that song; it's like the soundtrack to the patriarchy. And yet, like most young women who find themselves in a position of fear, I did smile – I still do. I later laughed about the incident, shared it as an anecdote with friends and buried the fear and embarrassment deep behind my laughter.

Pushing the buggy and walking down the street with my three kids one day, I am spat at and greeted with the familiar trifecta of race, religion, woman:

Paki terrorist bitch.

Stunned and scared, my children frantically ask, 'Mummy, what happened, why did he call you that?' I kick into auto-pilot, protective-mummy mode.

'It's nothing.' I smile, allaying their fears, discreetly check-ing my hijab for saliva while we continue skipping along crunching autumn leaves underfoot, grateful that they are young enough to be distracted.

Waiting for a friend en route to the annual Edward Said lecture on Othering, I have to laugh when I am Othered and called a terrorist Paki by a random passer-by who threatens to knock my hijab off my head.

I smile patiently at questions about the hijab, why I wear it, who makes me, and at all the 'kind' curiosities and ignorant nonsense people feel free to ask. I smile reassuringly as my children's school takes measure of my British values and asks me to write an acrostic poem on being British during a 'free' literacy course for children, in which adults were invited to take part. I painfully explain the absurd impracticality of the argument of men who tell me women should not go out alone. I hide my grimace at the elderly neighbours who com-plain about immigrants, and smile compliantly despite being randomly selected at airport security *again*. I switch off the standard TV debates featuring rampant Islamophobes and silently recycle the far-right pamphlets posted through my door. I instinctively stand with my back to the wall on the Underground since a hijab-wearing woman was pushed into an oncoming train on the line I once used daily. I brush off the teenagers repeatedly telling me to 'go home' days after the Brexit vote. I no longer tally the random mutterings of 'terrorist' and patiently listen to the Muslims who tell me it's a cliché to write about 'street-level' Islamophobia – particularly Islamophobia on public transport. These are just things we have become accustomed to as visibly Muslim women, I tell myself. It's often either that or stay indoors, where you invariably end up sifting through Islamophobic bile online anyway. And so, exhausted, I go on absorbing all the encounters with a smile lest my anger, frustration or tears be weaponised against me.

But do not mistake my silences for the easy stereotype of submissiveness. There have been numerous occasions when I have spoken up against prejudice; it is exhausting and not without a personal cost. Most marginalised women, even the most vocal of activists, know the frustration of having to bite your lip and just absorb the violence of hatred. Sometimes we do it because we are tired, sometimes it is in itself a form of self-care and other times it is almost tactical. We save our energy for the institutional and chalk up our own traumas as collateral. All women are used to not being believed, to being told we are too emotional, overreacting or catastrophising, and so you pick your battles. Do I react to this incident, you ask yourself, and risk being branded an angry woman? In a society where the Muslim default is perceived as radical and criminal, can Muslim women, particularly mothers, risk being seen as controversial, as agitators to the status quo?

If, as we have seen in modern discourse, it is worse to call out racism than to be a racist, what does that mean for Muslims who are constantly told that Islamophobia is just a means of shutting down criticism of terrorism? Sometimes our silences are not benign, they are simply the safest option. Incidentally, as I write this, politicians and non-Muslims across the world listen to the adhaan and bow their heads in silence for the victims of the New Zealand terror attacks. I love the adhaan; it is healing and a call to action. But it doesn't matter how beautifully or tunefully it is recited, the solidarity is tone deaf. It is their silence on insidious and pervasive state policy and violence, not ours, that has got us here, to the point where Muslims are executed in our places of worship.

I deliberated over writing this piece. I resisted the urge to just write something funny, trivialising the painful truths. I didn't want to be viewed through the lens of Islamophobia – *I am so much more than that* – but this *is* a cloak that has been thrust upon me and I'm just so tired of it. And if not here, where? Where are the spaces for Muslim women to share openly and heal? To discuss our pain without it inadvertently being minimised by fellow Muslims who tell us that it is a distraction from combating the more serious concern of structural Islamophobia, that we are focusing on the wrong issues. Or without non-Muslims telling us that we bring it upon ourselves. I don't want to exist in the binaries that are expected of me as either funny/rebellious/stereotype-breaker *or* as sad misery-memoir maker. I don't want to write about my experiences of Islamophobia or gendered Islamophobia because, to be honest, there are too many to make it palatable and, let's face it, it's not the 'in' thing to do. We're supposed to be strong and rightfully tell you that Muslim women are not victims, but we can't ignore the fact that Muslim women are increasingly victimised and for some, including myself, the particular brand of Islamophobic hatred that is levelled against Muslim women is beginning to affect our mental health. I can't sugar-coat it or self-censor to make you feel comfortable, I need to share my frustration. Because, try as I might, recently my body will no longer let me just smile.

The first time I have a physical reaction to targeted Islamophobia is at a tube station.

I'm on my way home from a literature festival when, unbeknown to me, supporters of a well-known far-right figure have gathered in Central London. The large group of men spot me on the escalator and deliberately march up behind me and with hot breath, pungent with the smell of alcohol, they scream, 'Free Tommy Robinson', in my ear over and over and over again. The station is packed, I try to move, but they follow. I try to hold back and let them pass, but they wait and continue to tower over me, smirking and shouting for two escalator rides. A man on the opposite escalator observes us quizzically, as if he is witnessing some sort of witty political debate. I wonder if he sees us as equals, both representing opposing ideologies; am I just headgear representing a religion or can he see the fear? Does he see a lone woman being intimidated and loomed over by a group of burly men or is this just Islam versus fascism? Do I represent 1.8 billion or nothing?

I feel my body fold into itself. I want to resist, to stand firm and upright, but the movement is involuntary. Keenly aware that I am hyper-visible to this horde of men screaming in my ear while simultaneously invisible to the hundreds of commuters who pass by without so much as a conciliatory smile, I am caught in flux. The juxtaposition of the joy of the festival and the present fear causes my body to react. I feel faint and shaky and by the time I reach the safety of the platform I am gasping for breath. I feel the swell of tears gather, but I force them back. As commuters obliviously push by I try to compose myself and catch my breath, to shake off the perceptible and involuntary tremor that snakes through my hands. The reaction scares me, but I carry on with my day as if nothing has happened, tucking my quivering hands firmly into my pockets, out of sight.

Weeks later while waiting for a coffee at an Eid celebration at a local centre, I have unprovoked sexualised Islamophobic abuse hurled at me in front of my children. My husband intervenes; he is racially abused and threatened with physical violence by the group as our children look on petrified and crying. My husband defends us and a new fear takes hold. I know the consequences of a bearded Black/brown man squaring up to a group of white people. It rarely ends well for the former, even if in self-defence. On a day when we have brought our children out to have fun and celebrate our faith, they are instead met with an unrelenting tirade of profanity and physical, racial and gendered violence. My eldest daughter stands weeping alone as I try to soothe my younger children and stop them from rushing to their dad. An older Muslim aunty is the only person who consoles her, scooping my daughter up into a bear hug, facing her away. We exchange a fleeting glance, a nod that signifies that she understands, that we both know this situation. The abuse continues and when I tell them that they cannot speak this way, that they cannot just randomly racially and Islamophobically insult people, children, one of them boldly tells us that it's 2019 and they can say what they like now. I am used to facing abuse when out alone, of having to be hyper-vigilant, but this floors me, perhaps because a part of me knows it to be true; after all, we've all read the headlines and felt the growing hostility. We drive home silently, the shadow of Grenfell Tower looming over us. We whisper a dua as we always do, for those known and unknown to us who were left to perish in the fire. Dying as they did in the holy month of Ramadhan, I think of the Eid so many of them never lived to see.

At home, we try to smile and laugh and comfort our children, but when my five-year-old enters my room at 5 a.m. the next day and repeats the words *terrorist, pussy* and *monkey* back to me, asking me if I remember what the man called me and Daddy, apologising for not stopping 'the bad men', I weep after putting him back in his bed. I know that I cannot distract them, that they will likely remember this incident for the rest of their lives. That at their tender ages they have already begun absorbing this violence. My eldest daughter tells me she knows this happened because we are Muslim. She says she never wants to go shopping again. My other daughter withdraws into herself and is uncharacteristically quiet for days. I feel helpless, guilty, unable to protect my children from a pain they should not have to face. In their presence, we talk it through calmly. I smile and offer fun distractions, but I am heartbroken.

I find myself crying when they go to school, and can't face leaving the house for days. I take time off work and for a short time I find fleeting laughter in watching old *Frasier* reruns, until an impromptu Google search throws up the political affiliations of the main actor. Suddenly all the negative encounters and chipping away over the years feel all-encompassing, suffocating, everywhere. Some wider family and friends (both out of a misplaced sense of wanting to shield us and some having never approved of it) ask me if I'd consider removing my hijab. Should I unwillingly change a fundamental part of myself, of a personal undertaking between me and my creator, my most enduring and beloved act of worship, to protect myself, my children? Is this my fault? Should I change the way I dress to avoid being attacked on the street? Are my only options abuse or undress? I am tired and worn down, but know that this can never be the solution we offer women who don't want it, it cannot be the example I offer my children.

Later that week I am due to give a keynote speech on Islamophobia at a conference, but have to cancel. I can't separate myself from the trauma of having suffered Islamophobia, to then talk about it – my emotional labour is spent. I can't compartmentalise and repackage my pain into something to be intellectualised or theorised. To try to convince others that Islamophobia exists and politely listen to conjecture when my kids are too scared to go to the shops. I don't have the energy to opine about how every time there's a terror attack we're a blameworthy monolith of seething brown terror, and yet when we are on the receiving end of hatred, suddenly the diversity of Muslims is recognised as people fall over themselves to proclaim that 'Islam is not a race'. My existence and experience are more than data for research or prescriptive of what constitutes protected characteristics in liberal debate. *My children are scared*.

The invasive pain I feel is hard to admit. It's even harder to explain. How does one give words to a systemic problem the world tells you does not exist? How does one seek help for a problem that 'does not exist', but whose very utterance to health professionals could see you referred to Prevent? Who do Muslim women talk to without fear of reprisal or archaic patriarchal solutions when even elected officials mock and belittle us or, worse still, criminalise us and the articles of our faith? At a time when our prime minister compares Muslim women to letterboxes and bank robbers, leading to a 375% surge in hate crimes against British Muslim women, with whom do we share our grievances without accusation, blame, suspicion or ridicule, when, to paraphrase feminist thinker Sara Ahmed, we become a problem when we describe a problem?

In a bid to get answers, I share the incident online. The responses are as can be expected. There is empathy and kindness from many. Racists, however, tell me I deserved it, akhis tell me I should stay indoors or learn karate, and liberals ask why I didn't call the police™. A relative suggests that I change my body language, saying this happens as I come across as meek. Multiple people ask what I was wearing. *Racism, check. Misogyny, check. Suspicion, check. Internalised Orientalism and victim-blaming, check, check.* Interestingly the experience becomes gendered by Muslims and non-Muslims alike, with the assumption that my dress or behaviour is the sole cause of the incident, that it took place in a vacuum where Muslims at large have not been pathologised. I am tagged in relentless threads of Islamophobic videos and tweets. Before I am even able to process my own pain, it would appear that I am expected to comment and react to every other incident of Islamophobia. The price for naming injustice as a member of a marginalised group seems to be an expectation to comment on every manifestation of it, irrespective of how visceral or painful the hatred is. I receive a deluge of messages from journalists and organisations monitoring Islamophobia, asking me to write articles about my experience. Few enquire about the well-being of myself or my family, of my children. Few treat us with the sensitivity fitting for victims of a crime. It feels as though our trauma is reduced to fodder for headlines or research, the spectacle of Islamophobia to the voyeur more important than Muslim pain.

The responses of women, particularly Muslim women (hijab-wearing or not) and Black women/women of colour are, for the most part, reassuring at least. There is an unspoken understanding, an internal rolling of eyes at the ultra-crepidarian reactions offered by others (particularly men), at the painful specificity of the hatred directed at us that sits at the nexus of misogyny, culturalism, ethnocentrism and racism. We know even when there are no words in our lexicon and no framework in our episteme to comprehensively describe the hatred and racialised misogyny levelled against Muslim (and perceived Muslim) women from all aspects of society.

The expectation for women to just cope or put up with certain behaviours is not a new one. We are of course *taught* to plaster that smile over things. Muslim women, and indeed many of our non-Muslim counterparts, are expected to just cope. Coping in the face of strange men attacking you, coping to keep your children safe, coping to keep conversations at conferences civil, coping online at the deluge of requests for you to talk about your experience or shut up about it. Coping at being confronted with the violence of gendered or racial hatred, or both, has become part of the quotidian. It seems we must steel and anchor ourselves against the waves of hatred, or risk being set adrift.

For almost every Muslim woman, irrespective of hijab, every aspect of our lives is monitored – by the state, by upholders of the patriarchy, by feminists, by men. We are policed from within our communities and outside them. We are supported when we speak of Islamophobic attacks from outside of the community, but less so when we address internal issues (even though there are elements of the far right and the Muslim community whose interests align solely in the harassment of Muslim women). Similarly, wider society is generally only interested in our concerns when they can be manipulated into demonising Muslim men. The media will greedily consume abhorrent tales of forced 'veiling' in far-flung countries such as Iran, while wilfully ignoring how they perpetuate a climate so hostile that increasing numbers of British Muslim women feel pressurised into removing the hijab, simply to avoid harassment or gain employment. There is, of course, the term 'gendered Islamophobia', which goes some way towards addressing the issues faced by Muslim women, but it too can be limiting. Just as the term 'anti-Muslim hatred' is limited in its usefulness in describing the systemic and structural barriers of Islamophobia, perhaps 'gendered Islamophobia' doesn't quite cover the full breadth of our lived experiences either. In reality, the particular blend of hatred directed towards Muslim women does not just come from non-Muslims, or men, it comes from Muslims and other women and marginalised groups also, often from those who share aspects of our racial and religious identities. The harassment of Muslim women is, after all, the confluence of otherwise opposing ideologies. It is the meeting point where feminist and incel align, where the deeply racist Hindutva and white nationalist movements greet 'lefty do-gooder' liberals and toxic elements of the Muslim community, however they wrap it up. Muslim women see it, feel it and encounter it on an almost daily basis; the internet alone is rife with it. And still there is no readily available term in our corpus to accurately describe it. While there are no Muslim-specific terms, the closest academic framework that could be applied to examine the levels and nuance of discrimination encountered by Muslim women can be found in the pioneering work of Moya Bailey, whose term 'misogynoir' encompasses the very specific prejudice directed at Black women from differing facets of society. Bailey's definition of misogynoir expands upon misogyny and cuts across race and gender to highlight the particular discrimination Black women face from within and outside the Black community for their position as both Black and woman. I am not an academic and have no wish to detract from or appropriate the scholarship of Black women, but I cannot help but wonder if Bailey's framework could be utilised to help understand and interrogate the complex nature of gendered Islamophobia too, particularly considering the overlap of discrimination that disproportionately affects Black Muslim women. Perhaps the racialised misogyny levelled against Muslim women would probably be more accurately described as a type of MUSogyny? I cannot pretend to have the answers, but as Bailey mentioned in a recent interview with *MIC* magazine, 'I think we have to refine language in a lot of different ways so we can actually come up with solutions that help the communities we want to address.'

I wonder if there are no terms because our positionality is politically expedient; Muslim women have been reduced to defenders or accusers of Muslim men, we are either weak and submissive victims or harbourers of their radical terrorist tendencies. The inherently dangerous carriers of culture and violent heritable pathologies. We're infantilised and patronised, spoken over or in constant need of someone's rescue (usually white men, brown men or white feminists), when the reality is that these parties who position themselves as liberators often work in tandem, mutually reinforcing animus towards Muslim women; sometimes it comes from women of Muslim backgrounds themselves. Perhaps there are no terms because we have learned to self-censor our experiences as a means of protecting our communities from further harm, but what is the mental toll of our political silencing? Who is caring about or collating the effect? Where are the spaces to heal? Perhaps there are no terms because some women are disposable. *Perhaps there is no perhaps about this cognitive dissonance at all.*

In the weeks that follow, I am repeatedly told to just remove my hijab, to 'integrate'. Well-meaning liberals offer apologies on behalf of British people. Both are Othering and assume Britishness as an identity of which Muslim women are on the peripheries.

I realise that I have become so preoccupied and exhausted by conversations around my cultural identity and defending my right to practise my religion that my actual practice is impacted. In the quest to defend perceived Muslimness, one's Islam can begin to suffer. In my moments of reflection, I turn to the Qur'an for comfort. While our identities as Muslims may be attacked, for me the most soothing of balms, and the most logical solution to Islamophobia, is to turn closer to Deen, rather than away. Despite the distractions and inevitable dips in imaan. I know that my liberation and healing will always be with my Lord.

And to everyone who is conscious of Allah, He grants a way out

– Surah At-Talaq, 65:2

I can't help but feel that the systemic silence on the positionalities that Muslim women are forced into in the mainstream functions as a very deliberate type of structural gaslighting. If we can't name a problem, how can we begin to tackle it, and if we are consumed with defending our identity, positions and faith, when do we find the time to practise that faith? If our existence as women is perceived solely to act as conduits of faith and culture, then there is no distinction between the personal and the political. Do we then actively destabilise one, to impact the other? Does the targeting of Muslim women serve a deliberate and useful social function for the state? When Islamophobic hate crimes against Muslim women are steadily on the rise, yet we are simultaneously bombarded with headlines like 'We need more Islamophobia', at what point do we accept that this indifference to our physical and mental well-being is in fact a carefully constructed, state-sanctioned gaslighting of Muslim women? A deliberate trickle-down trauma and arm of endemic racist policy that seeks to target Muslims in their places of worship and work, hospitals and homes, bodies and mind? When do we name it?

Exhausted, angered and upset, I make the decision to actively resist this feeling of listlessness; of being seen to exist in the liminal spaces of hyper-visibility and invisibility, of too Muslim or not Muslim enough, too covered or not covered enough, of being denied agency and having trauma weapon-ised, of being caught between racialised and politicised toxic masculinities, of being attacked for being Muslim, woman and Other, of being expected to smile. I refuse to be gaslighted, to be expected to put up with violence by state or stranger, to debate or second-guess my reality to appease the epistemological myopia, to abandon or become distracted from my religion. I refuse to just smile.

O you who believe! Stand out firmly for justice, as witnesses to Allah, even as against yourselves, or your parents, or your kin.

– Surah An-Nisa (The Women), Qur'an, 4:135

THE GLOBAL REVOLUTION OF HIJAB

Yvonne Ridley

It was a look of pure, unadulterated hatred that caught my attention initially. There was so much venom in that one stare that it took my breath away and sent a chill down my spine.

I couldn't for the life of me account for it and, without staring back, I tried to go back through my memory files. Did I know this woman? Had we been on opposite sides of a demonstration? Just what was her problem with me, for her angry eyes were definitely focused on no one else?

It was an encounter several years ago on the Docklands Light Railway. The train was heading towards Canary Wharf, a journey I'd made many times before but this one will remain with me forever.

As I hid behind my free copy of the *Evening Standard* I looked up again and this time noticed two men sitting opposite on the right giving me what *Little Britain* character Vicky Pollard would call 'the evils'.

I looked around, just in case I was inadvertently sitting in a seat reserved for the elderly or disabled. The whole journey was uncomfortable, and I was relieved when I reached my destination and was able to escape the looks from these unknowns on the DLR.

Later that day I met a friend of mine for lunch. I mentioned this awkward encounter, and asked her if I looked fine or if there was a blemish on my make-up, maybe a piece of toast wedged in my front teeth; something, anything which would earn such disapproving looks from three total strangers.

Like a true friend, she was frank. 'Surely you've noticed this before? I certainly have! It's your hijab. People don't like it, especially on someone with white skin. Every time we go out, I see people gazing over in a disapproving fashion. I can't believe you've never noticed this; you're supposed to be a trained observer!'

Up until 2011 I'd spent the last two decades living in London, probably the world's most diverse, multicultural capital – somewhere where you could move around freely without being judged, or so I thought.

From that day on I did become more aware of what was happening in my immediate surroundings, and I began to notice the looks, the stares and the feeling of discomfort. I found it difficult to believe that I hadn't recognised this hostility before, but once I'd been made aware of it the hatred was very perceptible.

I was blessed to live in Soho at the time, and so when I converted and 'came out' as a hijab-wearing Muslim not an eyelid was batted – most of the residents living there are among the least judgemental villagers in the world. Nestling in the heart of the English capital, Soho is the capital of LGBTQ+ nightlife and home to London's gay community; it's also most tourists' first port of call for those wanting to embrace the culture, go to drag nights or enjoy some of the trendiest bars and restaurants in the City of Westminster.

Yet there are those – predominantly men – who will still try to make us women feel guilty about how we dress and how we cover ourselves; about what we wear on our head and how we wear it. I would explain to these controlling men that Islam is such an easy religion to follow, and has more to do with what we can do than what we can't. Yet some seem determined to be forever listing rules and regulations, many of which have no bearing in Islam.

The truth is, I used to look at veiled women as quiet, oppressed creatures until I was captured by the Taliban just fifteen days after the horrific events of 9/11. I had sneaked into Afghanistan under the cover of the all-enveloping blue burqa, intending to write a newspaper account of life under the repressive regime.

As an investigative journalist, I must admit the burqa was extremely liberating in as much as I had become invisible. No one looked at me, judged me, gave me a first – never mind second – glance. I was only arrested after falling off a donkey!

After being rumbled, I spent ten nights and eleven terrifying days in the hands of the Taliban. Believing they would kill me and therefore realising I'd nothing to lose other than my life, I spat and swore at my captors; they called me a 'bad' woman but let me go after I promised to read the Holy Qur'an and study Islam.

That triggered my spiritual journey to Islam. I have to laugh at critics, bigots and Islamophobes who call me a victim of Stockholm Syndrome. Trust me, there was no bonding with my captors, and I'm not sure who was happier when I was released . . . them or me! They were glad to see the back of me and I them, although I did keep my promise.

Two years later I embraced the Faith, provoking a mixture of astonishment, disappointment and encouragement among friends and relatives. However, it wasn't until I began wearing the hijab that the real anger was unleashed.

Even to this day, my eyes fill as I remember the cruel taunts and sneers from one of my ex-Fleet Street colleagues, a very well-known columnist for a national newspaper, over my hijab. I've named him previously, but I won't here as I'm told he's suitably embarrassed by his vile behaviour, although I'm still waiting for an apology.

Why he bellowed out such a vile diatribe I will never know. I do know that as Western converts we are open to a deluge of hate and criticism from all sides. We are viewed as traitors by those from our original community while being treated with suspicion from within the Muslim community.

Moving from Soho to the Scottish Borders I soon realised the hijab would prove to be more of a negative distraction than a symbol of faith, especially after learning one local resident had already referred to me as 'Mrs Al-Qaeda' within a week. My hijab was soon replaced by a tweed cap and later a bandana, enabling me to go about my business unhindered.

The hijab, you see, propels women onto the frontline the moment they step outside their front door. It has proven to be a powerful, almost iconic garment that evokes all manner of reactions.

Muslim women who wear the hijab are largely demonised or romanticised, mainly by men who cannot see the person beyond it other than in fantasies of their own making. It does provoke strong reactions – both positive and negative – and is, in many ways, a form of self-expression and a reflection of the political landscape. It is a strong symbol in the politics of identity not only for the wearer but for those on the outside looking in.

For many years I have investigated the bizarre case of the Pakistani-born Dr Aafia Siddiqui who, in my opinion, is a victim of a grave miscarriage of justice, serving an eighty-six-year sentence in a US prison following the alleged shooting of US soldiers in which no one was injured other than Dr Siddiqui herself, in 2008.

She has now become a poster girl for just about every jihadi group in the world today, who use her hijab-wearing image to rally people to their cause. What they never show is the Westernised academic who graduated from MIT in Boston and happily posed for photographs without her hijab. Aafia is used and abused by all manner of people who have their own agenda.

As I portray her as a victim of injustice and the most wronged woman on the planet, someone else will change the narrative and present an image of a violent, convicted Muslim extremist. There are a variety of photographs to promote both images, with and without the hijab.

Depending on people's own politics and understanding, a woman going about her business in a hijab can be viewed as helpless, vulnerable and oppressed, someone who needs to be rescued. Paradoxically the sight of a veiled woman can also evoke all sorts of romanticised fantasies about the wearer and what exotic secrets she is hiding beneath her scarf or niqab. Others simply see a religious fanatic and extremist.

Images of hijab- and niqab-covered women in bombed-out cities across Syria have emerged during the civil war and these have been used by Western observers and supporters of the secular regime as evidence of radicalisation and Islamist control. The reason for the recent proliferation of the wearing of the hijab in war zones, I believe, is because it offers some form of protection and security, real or imagined.

During a visit to Idlib, the last rebel stronghold in Syria in 2019, I was advised to put on a niqab and abaya. Not a garment I would normally wear, I felt it gave me a protection, limiting the danger of moving around in a war zone undetected for ten days. As I engaged with other Syrian women, it became clear that it wasn't a garment of choice for everyone, but most women chose to wear it out of necessity because they felt it enabled them to move around anonymously and with a minimum of hindrance.

Some of those women told me they had never worn a scarf in peacetime, and while a veil would give no protection from a sniper's bullet, Syrian-regime barrel-bombs or Russian chemical weapons, they said they felt safer covered. I certainly did.

From a practical point of view, when living in a rubble-strewn war zone, an all-enveloping abaya also provides protection to clothes underneath. Sadly the largely culturally bereft mainstream media has already laid the groundwork for an oversimplified narrative about what clothes say about a Muslim woman.

During the brutal siege of Aleppo, for instance, Syrian women were barely seen or heard and so the images sent to the rest of the world were those of rebel fighters, including the Syrian Free Army, clashing with their male counterparts in President Bashar al-Assad's regime. Veiled women weren't interviewed; they had no voice.

Not only were they invisible in their own country, they appeared to be absent from the United Nations' brokered peace talks as well. Women represent half the population of this planet and should not be airbrushed from the landscape, but men, from the East and West, often overlook our presence with or without the hijab.

The story was slightly different in eastern Ghouta, where by early 2018 women were playing a dominant role in getting the news out to the English-speaking world, detailing the vicious bombing campaign by the regime. Many women, using social networks, became the first point of reference for journalists who wanted accurate details of war crimes and massacres.

Sometimes anonymously and sometimes not, hijab-clad Syrian women became the face of eastern Ghouta with their powerful and heroic use of Twitter and Facebook to keep us all informed. In their case, the identity of politics was not important. They had a story to tell and were determined, come what may, that the outside world should know about the atrocities they were enduring.

Even the less well-informed, who saw the hijab as a symbol of oppression, hardship, extremism and even terrorism, put aside identity politics as they listened to these women and their compelling stories in the besieged area.

While I don't wish to fuel negative stereotypes, the hijab is open to all manner of different expressions from both within and outside of the Muslim community.

For instance, in Palestine two female icons have emerged in recent years. One is Rouzan Ashraf Abdul Qadir al-Najjar, the volunteer paramedic killed by the Israel Defense Forces in 2018 during the Right to Return marches at the Gaza border.

The other is blonde-haired Ahed Tamimi who, at the age of sixteen, became the international face of resistance in the occupied West Bank after a video of her slapping and kicking an Israeli soldier stationed outside her home in Nabi Saleh went viral in December 2017.

While the media obsessed over Rouzan's colourful hijabs and turned her into an icon (long before she was slain by Israeli snipers), rather than focus on why her life-saving services were needed during peaceful protests, other Western journalists preoccupied themselves with Ahed's luxurious, wild mane of curly hair, calling her 'Shirley Temper' and using playful headlines like 'Illegally Blonde'.

Author and journalist Ben Ehrenreich, who in 2012 profiled the Tamimi family for the *New York Times Magazine*, observed of Ahed that she is blonde, with light eyes and skin, which does not fit the Othering media view of Palestinians. But 'when suddenly the kid doesn't fit into those stereotypes – when she actually looks like a European kid or an American kid – then suddenly all that work of dehumanization can't function . . . And then people freak out.'

Less nuanced were the words of Danish journalist Søren Willemoes, who wrote in a Facebook post that she was a 'Lolita on the barricades', adding, rather creepily in my view, that photographs of her wearing a tight T-shirt enabled him to just about see her nipples.

Such focus must be greeted with dismay and disdain by all Palestinians, not least the women who want an end to the eight-decade struggle to get back their stolen lands; sadly, some journalists are easily distracted into fixating on external appearances and not the real issues of the Palestine–Israel conflict, the brutal occupation, the siege of Gaza and the continued building of illegal settlements across the occupied West Bank making the prospect of a two-state solution ever less likely.

Palestinian women, whether they cover or not, are united in their just cause for Palestine and appear not to care who wears a hijab and who doesn't. To them it has no bearing on their heroic struggle.

And from my own experiences in the Middle East, especially during the Arab Uprisings, the decision to wear the hijab or not was irrelevant. Standing in Tahrir Square in Cairo during the height of the Egyptian revolution, I saw women of all faiths and none come together as one. What they wore, how they wore it, mattered not, as their sole focus was ousting a ruthless dictator.

Talking to some Egyptian women at the time, I was told the issue of hijab had quietly undergone its own revolution and evolution starting in the late-nineteenth century when Muslim women from across the country, spreading through to others in Turkey, Lebanon and Pakistan, ditched their hijabs.

It was neither a political nor religious statement and no scholars were predicting its return any time soon. During the huge political shifts in the Middle East and Asia it had virtually disappeared as more women embraced Western fashions. Ditching the hijab wasn't a sign of losing faith, it was merely a sign of keeping up with fashionable trends.

There was some resistance to this abandonment of the hijab from the Muslim Brotherhood, which was founded in 1928, but it was largely taken up by their own female members, who very much regarded the retention of the veil as a symbol of resistance and identity.

By the 1970s, as the Muslim Brotherhood increased its influence, the hijab began to return on Middle East university campuses, which were once hotbeds of influence from the Communist-driven Soviet Union. While there may have been an antagonism between sisters in Islam, by the time of the Arab uprisings the differences had gone and activists, veiled and otherwise, worked together.

I personally saw this in Tunisia, Libya and Egypt, where the hijab was nothing more than a religious symbol; it certainly wasn't a fashion accessory nor a sign of patriarchy or politics. Women activists were on the same page, united in a common cause.

Visiting Baghdad under the merciless Saddam Hussein regime back in 2002, there was little evidence of the hijab unless you ventured into the poorer, working-class areas. However, in the war-torn destabilised country today, which falls heavily under Iranian influence, the all-enveloping black abaya has a huge presence, especially among the Shia community.

It is becoming increasingly obvious that in times of crisis, war and disaster, women become sidelined, and when the patriarchy kicks in very often the women retreat and instinctively cover themselves (although as was evidenced in Raqqa when Daesh emerged on the scene, a strict regime in which all women adopted the niqab was enforced).

The actions of the so-called Islamic State really fuelled Islamophobic bigots everywhere to draw comparisons with the hijab, niqab and veil as clear signs of religious extremism and the oppression of women. The vile actions of Daesh/ISIS produced endless debates and discussions about Muslim women and their hijabs, which in reality had nothing to do with women wearing hijabs, but ironically provided an opportunity for those with an Islamophobic agenda to exclude Islam and further silence Muslim women.

While Western countries seem to be preoccupied with meaningless culture wars around the wearing of the headscarf, what really has concerned me is the deafening silence from the international community and, in particular, Muslim countries with regards to the plight of up to three million Muslim Uighurs in the Xinjiang region of China, who have been interned in what the Chinese government euphemistically refers to as 're-education camps'.

Female Kazakhs, Kyrgyz, Uzbeks and other Muslim minorities as well as the Uighurs have had their hijabs ripped off, now live in constant fear of arbitrary detention and can expect swift retribution for any expression of Turkic or Muslim identity. Wearing a hijab in 2020 can make you a target for an intolerant Beijing regime.

At the time of writing this, US President Donald Trump appeared to be resisting calls for sanctions against Beijing over its attempt to wipe out the Uighurs' separate identity, language, culture and history. In September 2019 both Trump and

British Prime Minister Boris Johnson did, however, embrace humanitarian issues during the United Nations General Assembly by presiding over a forum addressing China's treatment of Uighur Muslims. However, the cynic in me tends to think that since both leaders were burdened on the domestic front with growing calls for their resignation and impeachment, they probably saw the plight of the Uighurs as a welcome relief and useful distraction. Suffice to say nothing productive has so far emerged from the UN with regards to China's treatment of the Uighurs.

Both leaders have a history of making Islamophobic remarks and treating the Muslim community with contempt. When then Foreign Secretary Boris Johnson wrote a column in 2018 referring to veiled Muslim women as 'letter boxes' and 'bank robbers,' it led to a dramatic increase in anti-Muslim attacks and incidents of abuse.

Far from promoting gender equality, the fact is, Muslim women have to bear the brunt of the politics of exclusion, because when politicians like Johnson demean the hijab they are effectively belittling and excluding the wearer.

France banned Islamic veils and hijabs in schools in 2004, while the issue is still being actively pursued by right-wing elements elsewhere in Europe today. Heated debates about Muslim women wearing headscarves rarely involves direct input from the women themselves about the role of Islam or gender equality.

When the German Chancellor Angela Merkel suggested

banning the burqa and niqab in December 2016, she was reacting, I fear, to criticisms over her refugee policy which had led to her country providing a safe haven for around one million refugees. Following the lead of a number of other European countries – in France niqabis can face fines, and in Belgium up to seven days in prison if they step out publicly wearing a full-face veil – she was obviously trying to give proof of taking a hard line. The politicisation of the veil has a long history in European politics and often becomes a sideshow for politicians who want to take cheap shots.

Meanwhile, in Iran the hijab is compulsory. I've visited the country many times and, depending on the mood of the religious police, I've seen Iranian women wear their hijabs in various styles and still show off masses of hair. It appears that the dress of Muslim women (whether to add or remove more) is policed in most countries.

Former world number-one air-pistol shooter Heena Sidhu dramatically pulled out of the 2016 Asian Airgun Shooting Championship being held in Iran's capital, Tehran. In a series of tweets, the two-time Olympian shared that she had withdrawn from the competition because of the compulsory hijab rule for all women athletes, which she said went against the spirit of sport.

Since the head-covering rule is strictly enforced in Iran, regardless of someone's faith, it naturally provokes a certain amount of resistance, which has led to the unjust jailing of a number of Iranian women.

So what does a Muslim look like? We come in all shapes, sizes and shades these days. Some of us think it is a religious obligation, while others prefer not to be identified by faith. Throw in the hipster phenomenon of massive, bushy beards and the picture becomes even more confused.

When I first embraced Islam I didn't wear the hijab. I was told it was an obligation to cover, but so many sisters asked me not to wear it, while just as many begged me to put it on. The truth is, there are a great number of on-off hijabis out there today.

I've watched fathers and mothers from religious homes lose their daughters because of insistence they wear the hijab. I've seen brothers, wearing tight jeans and clinging T-shirts, berate their sisters for not wearing the hijab, without realising how inappropriate their own dress is in terms of modesty. There are just as many male bum cracks on show in east London during Friday prayers and yet many of these men, wearing the latest tight jeans and slavishly following fashion trends, fail to see the irony.

We are living in an unprecedented era in which it is becoming increasingly difficult to tell the heroes from the villains, the heroines from the harridans, and the hijab is no indicator of whether you live in a Western society or one of those Muslim countries where covering is encompassed within the law.

I now live in the Scottish Borders, where Muslims are about as rare as hens' teeth. If I wear a scarf I will attract the attention of everyone I encounter. It's a point recognised by my husband, who is probably more conflicted over the issue of hijab than I am, although I think this has much to do with fearing judgement from some of his male friends who reside in an Islamic bubble of their own making!

Just for the record, I absolutely love and adore my husband, who is from Algeria where, in the 1950s, the hijab played an important role during the Algerian War of Independence against French colonial rule. The brutal colonialists decided that if they were to succeed in destroying the fabric of Algerian culture, they needed to indoctrinate the women with European values, trends and fashion. The French held 'unveiling' ceremonies involving the wives of French military officers, and some compliant journalists portrayed these as acts of spontaneity.

Living in the Scottish Borders, you're more likely to see me in a hoodie, flat cap or Celtic FC green beanie – the latter of which I would never wear near the Rangers football ground otherwise I'd get my head kicked in (some headwear will inflame others even though it has nothing to do with Islam!).

I love the story of the girl who was challenged as she walked through Glasgow wearing a hijab: 'Are you Rangers or Celtic?'

'I'm a Muslim.'

'Is that a Rangers Muslim or a Celtic Muslim?'

There's no getting away from the fact that the hijab is a religious symbol, but there's also nothing wrong with wearing a flat cap, hoodie, beanie, or any style of titfer – or not.

One of the greatest Islamic scholars, Taqī ad-Dīn Ahmad ibn Taymiyyah, who was born in 1263 in Turkey, wrote:

'If the Muslim lives in a non-Muslim country, regardless of whether or not that country is hostile with the Muslim countries, he is not obligated to make himself appear different than them. This is on account of the difficulties that doing so can pose. Indeed, it might become preferable or even obligatory for him to conform to their outward standards of appearance if there is a benefit for the faith in doing so like inviting them to Islam, or preventing hardship for the Muslims, or for realising any other wholesome intention.'

RACIAL PERCEPTIONS

Khadijah Rotimi

As a biracial Muslim woman whose faith is automatically recognised by my choice to cover and wear the hijab, I often feel
like a site of different identities, cultures and customs. Islam is
my faith, my nationality is British and I am ethnically half
Nigerian, half Pakistani. It can sometimes feel like I am not
able to express my appreciation of all aspects of my identity at
once without certain aspects clashing. I think that people in
general feel a need to box other people into a category that
makes sense to them, and I have never felt like I fit completely
into any category, despite being a whole Muslim! At times it
feels like other people try to dictate my identity to me based
on their own ignorant perception of what I am, rather than
accepting my own perception of my identity.

My faith has always been very personal and intrinsic to my
identity; the concept of hijab is something that I view more in
terms of the way that one conducts oneself in a modest

manner and wearing clothing that isn't revealing or tight-fitting, rather than the physical act of covering one's hair. However, despite my faith being the strongest aspect of my identity, I have often felt alienated from the Muslim community due to my ethnic background; it is clear to me that colourism and anti-Blackness are still rife.

My father moved from Nigeria to Britain when he was ten, and my mother was born in London but her ethnic background is Pakistani. I decided to start wearing the hijab when I was fifteen and have worn it consistently since then. My father's family are mainly Christian, as he is a revert, and my mother's family never put a heavy emphasis on hijab. However, my mother wore the hijab throughout my childhood, so I did grow up accustomed to the concept of it in Islam. Although my mother decided to stop wearing the hijab when I was fifteen, this was at a time when I had already come to the decision that I wanted to wear it, so her decision didn't have an effect on my choice. It was something I felt strongly about; I had always told myself I would wear the hijab once I came of age. Every Saturday and sometimes after school throughout my childhood I went to various Islamic schools and mosques to learn Islamic studies and how to read the Qur'an. I would always wear modest clothing and the hijab when I went and I felt proud doing so. This limited experience of wearing a headscarf is perhaps responsible for my naive outlook about the real struggles I would face by choosing to wear the hijab every day. As a fifteen-year-old in Year Ten I suddenly felt less attractive and more invisible – some of my so-called friends who were mainly non-Muslim and Black stopped saying hi to me in the corridors. I didn't realise what a big part of my identity my hair was – my tight bouncy curls had always been my main identifier and the first thing everyone noticed about me. Now I was just 'Khadijah', not 'Khadijah with the curly hair'. In truth, I felt less pretty, as my hair was my only feature that I felt proud of and consistently looked after. However, at the same time I was happy that it had weeded out those around me who were shallow and didn't have my best interests at heart.

When people hear the words 'mixed race' they automatically think of 'Black and white'; growing up, I became accustomed to most people assuming I fell into this category since my hair colour, skin colour and features all fitted the stereotype. In my primary school, which was predominantly white and Indian, I did sometimes feel alien because of how I looked. For the first time in my life, as a five-year-old I suddenly became very aware of my physical appearance, something that I had never given much thought to until kids decided to belligerently point things out to me. I remember being called 'poo skin' and 'noodle head' by some of the ignorant bullies who were no doubt echoing the bigoted ideologies of their parents. Or people asking questions like 'Why is the end of your nose so flat?', 'Why is your hair like that?' Once my peers found out that my mother is Pakistani and not white, that's when one relentless white boy started calling me a 'Paki' (much to the amusement of some of the Indian kids). After the London bombings the same kid who had been made to write me a letter of apology for calling me 'poo skin' the year before decided she now hated me because I was a 'dirty Muslim'.

Despite the taunts, even as a young child I was always confident in my identity and equally proud of both of my ethnicities. I think this is partly because I was brought up in a family that taught me not to value a hierarchy based on race or skin colour. My Nigerian side are proudly Nigerian and my Pakistani side are proudly Pakistani, but crucially reject the anti-Black views held by a large number of Asian communities; perhaps the most cultural thing about my Pakistani family is the food! People are often shocked when I tell them my mix and ask, 'How was your mum allowed to marry your dad?' as if to imply that World War Three must have started over the marriage. I always find this question by Asians an interesting tell on the scale of anti-Blackness within the community. For a people who often claim that anti-Blackness is not a pervasive problem among Asians, why is the instinctive question always 'How was this allowed?' As it happens, I don't have a single first cousin on my mum's side who isn't mixed with something else other than South Asian. Islam teaches that no skin colour or race is superior to another, and it's sad that culture, and indeed cultural Muslims, still get in the way sometimes and ruin things.

I remember towards the end of primary school I had just begun to feel like I had found my place and I was comfortable in my own skin, as now it was cool to have curly hair and be mixed race. Isn't it funny how something you were once ridiculed for can suddenly become sought after, then eventually appropriated (#KylieJenner)? However, I remember one day walking into our class during break, and the same boy who I had got into countless fights with over the years looked me up and down and said, 'You know you're half Pakistani, half Black, right? That basically means you're a Pakistani monkey.' I was so shocked and lost for words – I didn't know what to say. I decided to tell my teacher after school, but, much to my dismay, all he said was, 'Well, you can write a letter of complaint that I can pass on to the headmistress if you really want to, but X is going through a hard time at home at the moment, what with his parents being on holiday without him, so it's up to you really.'

My eleven-year-old self wrote that letter of complaint vehemently, but X didn't even get so much as a detention, so I'm pretty sure the teacher never sent the letter to the headmistress. His reaction alone showed his lack of concern.

One thing that bothered me growing up was constantly feeling Othered and the lack of representation in the media. I remember wondering why Barbie always had to be blonde or why there wasn't a brown Baby Annabelle doll with curly hair available on UK shelves. It's a misconception that children don't notice these micro-aggressions of feeling Othered on a daily basis. I've had to tick 'mixed other' on every form that has ever asked for my ethnic background. However, I do recognise the fact that although there wasn't (and still isn't) nearly enough positive representation of a wider scope of ethnicities in the media, light-skinned women are always the go-to when it comes to showing your 'token Black girl', whether it be on a TV show or magazine cover. I mean, let's face it, the original Aunt Viv from *The Fresh Prince of Bel-Air* (who was indisputably the best) was replaced by a lighter-skinned actress. Claire from *My Wife and Kids* was replaced by a lighter-skinned girl. As a young 'light-skinned' girl with curly hair I had *Sister, Sister* and Beyoncé to identify with and look up to; I can't think of any mainstream TV shows that cast dark-skinned girls as being intelligent and beautiful, even the so-called Black shows like the ones I have mentioned.

When I started high school, the bullying stopped, as I went to an all-girls' school which was very ethnically diverse and had a lot of Muslim girls; in fact, there was only a handful of white girls in my year group. For the first two years of high school, I didn't wear the hijab, and as usual everyone assumed I was either Black (usually Jamaican) and white, or mixed Indian and Black Caribbean. No one had any idea that I had any Pakistani in me until they asked me where I was from. However, since wearing the hijab, the way that people racially perceive me has changed drastically, and this has given way to a different set of identity issues. It's almost as if people can't see past a headscarf, and a piece of cloth has now become my main identifier. The assumption is that being Black and Muslim cannot be synonymous (even though Nigeria is 50 per cent Muslim, and Islam came to Africa before the Indian subcontinent!). People usually assume that I am either fully Asian (Pakistani or Bengali), or Sudanese, Bravanese, Egyptian or Yemeni. It's always a shock when I tell them I am half Nigerian. I've been told many times that I don't look 'Black', which I always find quite odd because I have African features, such as my lips and nose. But wearing the hijab has hidden my curly hair, my most obvious indicator of being Black. I often struggle with my relationship with my hair, which is an important part of my identity. Sadly, I sometimes miss showing my hair because I feel that my Black side wouldn't be questioned as much if my hair was uncovered.

One of the main challenges for me has been the fact that, since wearing the hijab, my Nigerian side is often overlooked and/or insulted by certain Muslim communities who have a very ignorant perception of beauty. I've developed a very thick skin towards racism and backhanded compliments, particularly from the South Asian, Arab and East African communities. I'm often told that I'm 'too pretty to be Nigerian'. I think my least favourite is 'Wow, you look completely Pakistani, mashaAllah', as if to congratulate me for my apparent 'lack of Blackness'. My eyes automatically rolled even having to write that stupidity. It's as if because I am half Asian, the Asian community has a sense of familiarity towards me which makes them feel it's perfectly acceptable to 'compliment' me in this way, as they assume I share their racist beauty standards, which stem from a history of colonialism (and two-faced aunties who want their grandkids to look as gora – white – as possible!).

A lot of the time I am guilty of ignoring these awkward encounters with new people as I know I am not likely to see them again and I can't be bothered to educate them. However, in situations where I have called someone out for their ignorance I usually see a variation of the same response: immediate shock and embarrassment that I took their so-called compliment as an insult; then the incessant pleas that they're not racist because their 'friend is Jamaican' or one of their relatives married a Ugandan; last but not least I get bombarded with more lovely compliments, as if to shut me up – 'Aww, you really are so lucky, you're so unique, mashaAllah'. This false sense of familiarity which gives them the confidence to be so outright means that, in a way, I probably experience more explicit, in-your-face day-to-day racism from the Asian community than a fully Black person would. Out loud anyway.

I remember the first time I went to Pakistan, when I was fifteen. I had mentally prepared myself for the sly digs and stares. I was convinced that I would be the black sheep, and everyone would be able to tell from my deeper skin tone and features that I was different. Much to my surprise no one even batted an eyelid; everyone tried to speak to me in Urdu. I think my younger cousins didn't even realise that I wasn't fully Pakistani until I took my hijab off and they stared in amazement at my hair and asked if it was real then started playing with it. Everyone thought I had had some type of treatment to make it so curly, assuming that must be the fashion in London. I do, however, remember one aunty saying my skin colour was nice and I was 'very fair'. I'm definitely not 'fair' by Pakistani standards, so I presume she was insinuating that I'm dark but not 'too dark', considering my dad is a dark-skinned Nigerian man. In other words, it could be worse. I can't help but wonder if my younger sister, who tans more easily because she doesn't wear hijab and has very Afro-textured hair, went to Pakistan, would she have the same warm reception? Would her hair be perceived as cute and bouncy or too coarse and not beautiful by their standards? With her hair on display, would people in the street treat her like a local or rudely stare and touch? When we went as a family to Nigeria I was fourteen and hadn't started wearing the hijab yet. Nigerians are generally very welcoming, and they would treat you as their own and try to claim you even if you were only a quarter Nigerian. If I went back now as a hijabi I doubt I would be treated differently to when I last went as a non-hijabi, although with my hair covered it might be harder for people to tell that I am mixed-race. There are a lot of mixed-race people in Nigeria, and hijab is nothing unusual there.

That being said, in my experience wearing the hijab has alienated me somewhat from the Black British community. When I first started wearing the hijab in high school, most of the non-Muslim Black girls who I thought were my friends suddenly walked past me like I had become irrelevant. Some of them said things like, 'Oh, I didn't know you were Muslim', as if being Black and Muslim are two separate things that cannot mix. When I started college my Nigerian classmates would be shocked when they found out my mix, and while most of them had a positive reaction, some wouldn't believe me until they had quizzed me enough to be satisfied that I wasn't making it up. I was asked questions such as 'Name a Nigerian dish other than jollof rice if you're really Nigerian', or 'Where is your dad originally from in Nigeria? You can't say Lagos.' It sounds silly but it felt like they were forcing me to 'prove my Blackness' by answering these questions until they were sure I wasn't an imposter trying to seem 'cooler' by pretending to be half Black.

One of my best friends is Somali and recently we decided to make a YouTube channel where we mainly vlog about halal food places in London. We were getting a lot of questions about our ethnicities, so we decided to film an ethnicity tag. While the majority of the responses to this video were positive, there were a lot of comments from trolls accusing me of 'trying to jump on the Black bandwagon' (whatever that means) and saying that 'It's pretty clear you're not Nigerian', etc. I also received more of the usual non-compliments such as, 'You're very light skinned for a Nigerian <3' and the truly awful, 'Nigerians are ugly monkeys, she's only pretty because she is mixed.' The sad thing is that these comments mainly came from Nigerians who were accusing me of lying, or from East Africans with a superiority complex. My friend also got comments from Somali people saying that she's not Black because 'Somalis aren't black, they're Arab', while a Nigerian man told her that 'Somalis aren't Black and have never been considered as Black by real Black people'.

One of the things that struck me out of all of this is the disunity among the African diaspora in Britain. Some East Africans do not consider themselves to be Black; they look down on other Black people as if they regard themselves as higher up in some racial hierarchy. Similarly, some West Africans do not regard East Africans as being racially Black. As well as experiencing racial prejudice from the wider Muslim South Asian community, I have also had similar encounters with the Somali community. I have many Somali college friends and have been introduced to some of their acquaintances who hold racist views about my West African heritage. Just a few weeks ago I met a friend of a friend who, upon learning that I was half Nigerian, exclaimed, 'Wow, you're lucky God really saved you, mashAllah.' Before befriending Somali girls in college, I always assumed that I would be able to relate to the Somali community, given that they are probably the largest Black British Muslim community in north-west London. I was blissfully unaware of how they – like the South Asian community – have such deep-rooted issues around colourism and anti-Blackness.

Last year I was sitting at the bus stop next to a middle-aged Somali woman who complimented me and asked me where I was from. I said, 'I'm half Pakistani,' and she smiled sweetly and nodded in approval, then I continued, 'and half Nigerian.' Her face dropped and her mood changed. She stared at me in disbelief and exclaimed, 'No, no, no! Nigerians are very ugly, you are not ugly, Pakistanis are beautiful, you are not Nigerian.' When I told her that the Nigerian side of my family are also beautiful she shook her head and laughed. She then said, 'You know Somalis are not like other African people? We are beautiful because we are mixed blood with Arab, that is why we are not ugly like Nigerians.' This woman was obviously set in her views (and the effect of years of internalised hatred) and a lot older than me, so I didn't bother putting her in her place; I couldn't find the words to protect myself from the violence of anti-Blackness, from a fellow Black woman. I just quickly ended the conversation and sat far away from her when the bus came soon after, much to my relief.

While these racist encounters upset me, I am aware that as a lighter-skinned woman I do have privilege. Some people do treat me better than they would if I were a darker-skinned Black woman because I am closer to their ideal of what is beautiful. If I wanted to marry someone whose family held these same backward views, they would be more likely to accept me and sweep my Nigerian heritage under the carpet than they would a fully Black and darker-skinned Muslim woman. I have come across half Black mixed-race girls who do not acknowledge their light-skinned privilege and add fuel to the fire by putting down women of a darker shade; they act like they are on a pedestal and expect men to find them more attractive than their darker-skinned peers. It is as if, in order to continue feeling like they are on top, they perpetuate these harmful notions of colourism. Especially considering the fact that many lighter-skinned women often end up in relationships with dark-skinned Black men (a whole separate essay topic of its own), so their children are likely to inherit a much deeper skin tone. These same men also sometimes ridicule dark-skinned Black women and call them unattractive; it's a vicious cycle of colourism and misogynoir which exists in many communities, including Muslim and non-Muslim communities, in Britain and globally.

From the age of seventeen I have encountered men who only try to talk to me because they want a Muslim woman with desirable Black features but lighter skin. Yet these same men ridicule dark-skinned Black women who have these same features and say they don't find dark skin attractive. I have had Asian men DMing me making rude remarks saying words to the effect of: 'I wanna marry you but I'm not gonna tell my mum you're half Nigerian.' It amazes me that these idiots think that's some form of flattery and expect a response other than 'fuck off!' I have also experienced similar encounters with Arab and Somali men. It is disgusting how these men seek out and fetishise women who have certain African features, such as curvaceous backsides and fuller lips, while systematically degrading Black women.

Multi-racial Muslim women like myself often feel alienated from all factions of society unless they give into their 'light-skinned privilege' and in effect become the bully by perpetuating colourism and proximity to whiteness. However, it is important to emphasise that while issues of colourism sadly exist in all Muslim communities, from African to South Asian, Islam does not teach that any race or skin colour is superior to another. These ideas arise from the mentality and internalised hatred that colonisation gave birth to. I think that Muslim biracial women need a space to explore our experiences within the Muslim community at large. We as a community must create a space in which all Muslims feel safe and able to live and celebrate our identities.

TICKING THE 'INTELLIGENCE' BOX

Raisa Hassan

'So let me get this right: You're a British, female, Asian, hijabi, disabled graduate – with a degree in creative and professional writing . . . ? Wow! You tick a lot of boxes!'

I know: it's a mouthful. But – have you got your head around it yet?

I'll wait.

Where do I begin?

Here's something I want you to remember and understand: disability can happen to anyone, and strike at any time. If it does happen, as ridiculous as it sounds, try your best not to dwell on it. The truth is that of course your disability will define you, but is not all that you are. This is how I felt as I wrote the opening of my dissertation, 'My Humanity: Life with a Disability – A Poetry Collection', in 2017:

THE CRACKED SKULL

The Doctors Fucked Up in the Delivery Room –
And said that I'd Have the Brain of a Vegetable.

Yet,
I Sit Here,
Fully Aware –

Proof –

That They Were Wrong.

I Am the Doctor of Words and Emotion.

These Poems are My Testimony.

I was born with cerebral palsy, which affects all of my limbs. Because it's a brain injury, it basically prevents your brain and body from collaborating. To call it frustrating is an understatement. I was one of the lucky handful that had the privilege to go to a special-needs school up until the age of seven. Technically, it wasn't just going to school. It meant constant physiotherapy – day in, day out.

You learn everything there, aside from the standard school stuff. From holding cutlery so you can eat, holding a pen so you can write, doing buttons for your shirt, laces for your shoes –

fine motor skills. And then there's the whole physical strength side of things. Sitting up straight, getting up from a chair, going to the bathroom by yourself, and of course walking without falling over. Classes were small; you got the help you needed. To my knowledge, there was no gender or racial bias.

I haven't always been sure whether being in a special-needs school was a definite good or bad thing. I mean, I have always understood the concept of a disability and I felt a sense of solidarity with my fellow students, but part of me knew that wider society wasn't just about disabled people. None of the staff had disabilities, and I could spot the difference between the disabled and non-disabled community. And I was one to always talk about it, more than anyone.

I've always wanted to be able to do things for myself, you know, be independent and all that kind of thing without asking for help. I've always been under the impression that being dependent on a wheelchair was a 'bad' thing – because you are perceived to be 'stuck in it'. I was wrong. It's actually liberating. I just didn't, and still don't, want to be labelled 'stupid 'or 'incompetent'. I've always had the 'I'll show you what I can do' attitude – not that I was bullied there or anything, I was just frustrated with myself. I suppose it wasn't easy when you constantly compared yourself to your twin sister who had no disability at the time. I just wanted to do what she did so effortlessly.

I was lucky though – my disability and culture never clashed. My family wouldn't allow it. I was treated as an intelligent individual. What I had to say mattered. I didn't have to worry about breaking social barriers, because I had backing. There was never any pity, or the feeling that I was 'a burden to society'. I was never hidden away or silenced. That has given me courage.

I suppose one thing that *didn't* really help was the fact that my bus driver, Dave, who must've been in his late forties at least and took me to school for four years from the ages of three to seven, was a bully. I was the only one he teased out of seven passengers – purely because he knew I would retaliate and call out his stupidity. He would constantly threaten to 'chuck me off the bus' – and then he would laugh, wholeheartedly. I can still hear his voice in my head. He really enjoyed it. Too much. To this day, I really fucking hate him. No apology will ever be enough. It has shaped who I have become. For all I know, he's dead. I think this is how I developed my defensive side. People still find it funny when I'm angry – which makes me angrier. I really don't understand it. More often than not it was for two reasons – either to insult my intelligence, or they believed I was too nice to object, and treated me like a doormat.

Sounds fun, doesn't it?

Can you tell that I'm angry?

Excuse me while I go and break something.

I dislocated my left hip at the age of eight and a half. That's when my disability actually became real to me. Surgery and rehabilitation pushed me to my limit – and nearly cost me my sanity. As if one surgery wasn't enough, I had to 'start from zero' three more times by the age of sixteen. They said that I wouldn't need another one for at least another decade. That's basically now. Fantastic.

I was twelve (and in Year Eight) when I started to think about wearing the hijab seriously. I used to go to the mosque wearing the type you could pull over your head instead of using a headband, pins and safety pins. (My mum or my sister still do it for me whenever I want to go out.) My sister started to wear a hijab first – in August that year. Then my mum followed two months later in October. I found myself putting it off, even though I promised myself that I would do it. Of course, then I realised that I was playing with fire – I'm not the sort of person that makes a promise I can't or won't keep. I also decided that if I was going to wear it, it would be out of sincerity. I knew that even if I decided to take it off, I could still say that I had the experience – but the bigger part of me knew I wasn't going to backtrack. So on 30 December 2007 I made the choice to wear the hijab in public, and I haven't taken it off since (aside from my Year Eleven prom, but that's a different story) – and here we are thirteen years later.

High school wasn't great; being an outspoken disabled person who didn't fit in anywhere wasn't going to end well (I was picked on the second I got there – 6 September 2006), and to then suddenly wear a hijab after a whole term of not wearing one only meant to be interrogated even more than usual. Clearly didn't think that one through, did I? Long brown hair in a ponytail before Christmas, and a hijab after New Year. In Year Eight I got three death threats in the space of six months. It wasn't the first time in my life that I wanted to kill myself. It took a lot of strength to pretend that I was OK. When asked by people who didn't like me why I decided to wear the hijab, all my responses were along the lines of 'Because I want to, and it's none of your business' – which was sufficient. I wasn't going to waste my energy on them.

My form tutor for Years Seven and Eight was also a Muslim woman. Miss Zaidi. She had to be in her late twenties at the time. She was a science teacher, her room was number 50 in the science block, and you could always tell it was her from behind because of her long, flowing brown hair. We didn't talk much, but I liked, trusted and respected her. After the hype had died down, she asked me why I had decided to wear the hijab. Her tone I remember being polite and curious, unlike the others. I told her that it was what I wanted, and it was the right thing to do. She said nothing, but smiled. She interacted with me more after that discussion.

A few weeks went by, and then I got the biggest shock of my life. I walked with my walking frame into room 25 – my form room. And there she was. Her signature long brown hair was gone, and in its place, a hijab. I said nothing. I nodded and smiled at her. In reality I was having heart attacks on the inside, and jumping for joy. I remember one day afterwards when she assisted me to walk to the bathroom after I had waited for my henna to dry at lunch on a fundraising day. She made the effort to ensure that I had nothing to worry about.

By Year Nine, she was no longer my form tutor – and I barely saw her. I did see her once though, that is for certain. I was late for my science class because I had come from a hospital appointment in the morning. I remember running into the building, but I had to stop because I was exhausted. In the hallway, I had stopped outside a classroom, and as I peered through the glass, I discovered that it was Miss Zaidi who was teaching. She spotted my exhaustion, stopped her class and stepped outside for a minute to talk to me. She asked me if I was OK and I said I was tired from running and we both laughed. I said that I had to dash off and, frankly, I didn't want to hold up her lesson, that it was good to see her, and that I would see her later.

For once, our eyes locked. She smiled with a light in her eyes – a light I cannot explain. I will never forget that look in her eyes. Or her face. Never. Little did I know that that would be the last time I ever saw her. That year, in the summer of 2009, Miss Zaidi died in an accident on holiday. It was hard to go past room 50 for the remaining four years, let alone walking through or being taught in there. Every time I think about that last encounter, I cry. I still miss her. This is one story that will always be connected to my hijab, with pride – for as long as I live. She respected me for who I was. A disabled Muslim hijabi. People now say that I had influenced her to wear the hijab. If I did, what an honour. We will never know for sure.

MISS ZAIDI'S GOODBYE

For every time I wear a headscarf, my thoughts turn to
    you.
How I wish I could thank you –
For always treating me with respect, unlike anyone else.
I took you for granted. Because I never did.
You left us too soon, and I, for one, will make sure that
    you will never be forgotten, and forever will be missed.
Eye contact spoke louder than words between us,
For I will never forget that sparkle in your eyes from our
    last conversation –
Were you trying to say goodbye?
I'm sorry that I left it too late.
Forgive me.

It was not until recently that I realised that my hijab was
respected by other members of staff. I can recall going on a
sports trip for disabled students in Year Nine. When on a break,
I went to the bathroom. My hijab was a mess; you could see my
hair peeking out from everywhere. A learning support assistant
(who was Eastern European) instinctively began tucking in my
hair, saying that I looked like a princess. I couldn't stop smiling.
I laughed and said that my name meant queen – to which she
replied, 'You'll be a queen when you're married, you can be a
princess for now.' It was immensely sweet of her. She evidently
knew what my hijab meant to me.

I started wearing a wraparound headscarf when I started sixth form. The first few months it kept on falling apart – both irritating and embarrassing. So much so that one day I actually asked a learning support assistant who also wore the hijab to redo mine at lunchtime. I thought she would say no in all honesty, but she said yes. She even asked me how exactly I liked my scarf done – where to put the pins and safety pins and how low my scarf should go (down to my neck or my chest). I gave her my specification, and she did it perfectly. I don't know if she broke any rules, but I really did appreciate it.

My life changed drastically when I was fourteen. That's when my opinions really began to take shape. I have always said that I started to feel 'physically old' from this age. And that's when I discovered the importance of emotional intelligence and 'looking at the bigger picture'. Me voicing my opinion was still an issue among those I knew. For example, we were in a citizenship class in Year Nine. The government had amended the law in relation to what the homeowner could do to a burglar and still claim self-defence. The majority of my class said that if it was self-defence it was OK to kill them, even if they didn't attack you. I was alarmed at this, and I said, 'Unless you genuinely feel like you are going to die, by all means, beat the shit out of them, send them to the hospital – but don't kill them, they're human too!' And that was it. All hell broke loose – everyone talking over each other, looks of disapproval towards me, and no one in that class spoke to me for weeks after that altercation. Even my teacher raised an eyebrow.

What do you want me to do? Sit there and pretend it didn't happen? The things that stick in my head become borderline photographic memories – and it bothers me until I actually do something about it. The strangest part is that, most of the time, I'm not even trying to be rude or start a fight – I just want people to see an alternative perspective. Obviously if you're going to blatantly insult my disability, core beliefs or family then (like anybody else) of course I'm likely to flip out. I'm also always trying to be polite and to sugar-coat things so I don't hurt people's feelings, but still all I get in my ear (particularly in high school) is, 'You're a nutcase, and wrong, and what do you know? You're a spaz.' Why can't we respect difference? And I hate to break it to you, I am one of the lucky ones.

Maybe that's what people find threatening – that it isn't the norm, coming from a British disabled hijabi. Being so aware and connected to what is going on around me and not keeping my mouth shut.

Of course, it's a dangerous game. You can clearly see that I am Muslim, female, a hijabi, Asian, and disabled, if I am in one of my walking aids. But because I am in pain every second I am awake, in recent years, particularly after my last surgery aged sixteen, I have decided to put my sanity first. Most of the time that involves saying something controversial. I don't need the added psychological strain of regret that I hadn't said anything when a person's comments were particularly unjust.

When I went to university, everyone knew me as a hijabi from the start. As the only Muslim hijabi disabled person, they somehow assumed that I was really religious and wouldn't want to joke around. I referred to myself as the 'silent ninja', as I developed a great skill in the form of going up to somebody in my electric wheelchair without them realising and scaring them, just by saying, 'Hey, what's up man!' It was absolutely priceless every single time. That's when they discovered my light-hearted nature, and that they really needed to chill the fuck out! One of my classmates asked me how my Christmas was one year and then she said, 'Oh my God, I just realised that you don't celebrate Christmas, are you offended?' It was absolutely hysterical! Bless her!

I have one single Muslim friend now – and I'm perfectly fine with that. One is enough. All my closest friends have now fully accepted my disability, soul and religion – what more could you possibly want?

Going to university for four years straight was both fun and exhausting for me as a disabled person. As much as I appreci-ated the human interaction with my classmates, I sometimes wished my classes were available online with the other resources in order to catch up properly – it would make a disabled stu-dent's life easier. Before coronavirus, we were told this was 'impossible'. And now, in 2020, I'm thinking: 'Hypocritical, much?!' I'm so mad at this fact.

Stereotypes are disgusting. In any capacity, and for any reason. Especially about what a person is capable of. The worst thing you can do for anyone is just sympathise. This means your intentions are clouded by passivity, pity and are possibly patronising. I don't want that. I don't need that.

Because of all I represent, I understand what it's like to be misjudged and disrespected. At university I always felt the need to connect with everyone in some shape or form, no matter what the person's background was. I became friends with everybody. From the teachers, academic advisers, residential team, to the cleaners. From the disability team, shop staff, to security. Everyone knew who I was – and I didn't care. I respected them, and I expected the same in return. It worked out most of the time, I just wanted to fix problems that were heading my way in the long run. Can you blame me?

Of course, there was going to be at least one memorable fuckup. A male Muslim security guard not much older than me was testing my patience by asking me stupid questions and being generally immature. He was with his colleague, Shirley. I said to her, 'Can you believe this guy?! Wow. Just. WOW.' She smiled weakly. And that's when he said, 'Can you spell that?' I was furious. I wanted to hit him and was on the brink of tears. And I said, 'Mate, for the record, I am about to finish my creative and professional-writing degree, can you spell that out?

HOW DARE YOU! You know what? Screw this!' And I walked out on him at the library security desk. It felt like being with Dave again. He came after me to apologise; it wasn't out of sincerity, it was to save his job – I could tell. I yelled at him to 'never come near me again'. People were staring at us, and it probably humiliated him. I don't regret it though. After all, his job was to make others feel safe. He took the joke too far. I should've got him sacked. Bastard.

This is another thing that I want to emphasise. Sympathy and empathy are two completely different things. Empathy is active, inclusive and respectful. It creates change. While this world is focused on the masses, the marginalised trail behind. To put it simply, from my 2017 dissertation:

INCLUSION

Inclusion Seems to Be a
Perplexing Concept.

Exclusion and Segregation are
Easy Enough to Understand –

Exclusion is Like Watching Events
In the Liminal State at the Door –
Seen and Not Heard,

And Brushed Off –
Much like Social Groupings.

In High School – No-one Wanted
A Disabled Student on their Team!

Segregation was much like Lunchtime –
The Logical Thing to do was to have
A 'Disabled Students' Table, Always
Crammed –

To Oppose it was Unspoken Of –

It Just Happened.

This is Where Things Get Slippery:

Integration and Inclusion <u>ARE NOT</u>
The Same Thing!

Integration Leads to Saying:
All Disabled Students are in the Same Group –
With 6 Other Potential Groups to Disperse them into:

Passive,
Tolerant.
Separate Standards to Everyone Else.

It Screams – 'We haven't Left Out the Disabled Students,
They're Just
Over There in the Corner!'

NOT GOOD ENOUGH!
There's no Interaction with Anyone Else!

I Hang my Head in Shame and
Contain my Rage.

Inclusion is an Experience and
Exposure of the Disabled Community.

Active to Help,
Active to Listen,
Active to Enforcing Change!

A Disabled Person per Group.

A Group Where:

My Thoughts are Just as Valid and
Important as Yours.

The Only Way you'll be
Able to Understand
The World of Disability –

Is If You Allow Yourself –
Physically, Psychologically and Emotionally –
To be Immersed in It –

With Pride.

From the second I left high school, I felt free. I had no more duties towards a place I never loved, or trusted for that matter. But it was my degree which really highlighted the significance of what I represent. In order to complete my degree, I had to go out there and attend events which interested me as a writer, public speaker and poet. I couldn't turn down being on the first UEL Uni Slam team, could I? Or performing at open mic nights. Or continuing to give speeches on disability discrimination. I have something to say. And yes, some (if not all) of my work is immensely personal – to the point that it has caused me to have severe mental breakdowns. I don't regret it one bit. It was my dissertation supervisor and personal tutor, Dr Tim Atkins, who kept me and my spirit alive. I could probably write another 10,000-word essay about the statement above and still go over the word limit, but obviously I won't! In a nutshell, hand on heart, there's no way I could have got through my work in one piece without him.

My life is so different now. I'm actually happy. While 2017 was the year from hell (regardless of the fact that I achieved my 2:1 in creative and professional-writing from the University of

East London, which was bloody hard work), the future is already looking brighter. I can finally say that I have been horse riding, swimming, performing, writing, tutoring English to disadvantaged high-school students, and have completed basic training to become a mentor. I'm now an advocate for disabled people with Scope for Change, and a Trustee of disability charity CPotential. I want to run creative-writing workshops and disability-awareness workshops in the future – a goal which finally seems within reach. I can't wait to see what the next few years hold for me!

It has been nothing less than a privilege to have been able to write this essay for the world to see.

Alhamdulillah.

Yes, I do tick a lot of boxes. Boxes that matter. We need to make sure that we celebrate that.

Don't let society dictate what you can and can't do. It's your life.

TICKING THE INTELLIGENCE BOX

With the weight of expectation
On your shoulders,
Both society's
And your own –
It can become

A deadly combination.
But
Your words
Your history
Presence
And your world –
Will matter.
Without you
It will never be
The same again.
Remember,
You are here to leave
Your mark.
So there is no need,
No matter how much
It hurts,
To crack under the pressure.
There will always be
Only one of you.
And you WILL be
Good enough.
So please,

Breathe.

SO I CAN TALK TO GUYS NOW?

Fatha Hassan

All of my life I was told to stay away from the opposite sex while my age-mates were linking high school mates, college mates and even their university peers. Even if I'd wanted to, I wasn't very lucky – my university did badly in the diversity department. And let's not even talk about high school, as I took on the role of the fat Black comedian. There was no chance of anything happening there anyway.

Growing up, I was given the same speech that I'm sure every Muslim Somali girl has received: 'It's haram to date', 'You can't talk to men', 'Once you are married', etc. Suddenly though, after university, aunties have flipped and come flying from all corners of London asking if I am talking to a man or when am I bringing a man as they can't wait to see me married. Well, bitch! Where was this same attitude when you used to tell my mum that I was outside of the school gates with a boy?

This wasn't in the Muslim-girl handbook on 'how to sud-denly find a husband'; no one prepared us. They say practice makes perfect, but I'm now entering a swimming pool with a full belly of Nando's and I don't know how to swim. I was constantly told not to do this and that, but now I have completed jumping through hoops – education, career – I am magically expected to produce a family out of thin air. This is exactly what happens when parents avoid giving the talk on sex – we're just left stumbling around in the dark. The thought of bringing in the opposite sex as 'marriage material' after being told to stay away for so long is crazy! Suddenly the fictitious man you've never spoken to materialises in their mind: 'Is he Somali?', 'Does he work?', 'Is he Muslim?' (I don't know what's been going on for this question to suddenly arise) and 'What's his tribe?'

As a Somali girl, tribal ties are important, so not only do I have to complete my own checklist that everyone in the Somali community has, but now the person I'm supposed to be bringing in has his own set of rules. I understand that this is the case for everyone and there must be certain precautions to take when talking to individuals, but how am I supposed to do this when I haven't even figured myself out yet? It's hypocritical that I'm expected to know how to talk to men and on top of that bring in someone I'm supposed to marry and lie in the same bed with, when I've been told never to speak to men. I mean, he could wear socks in bed – how would I know?!

I've binge-watched TV shows where parents prep their children for the big world. They were able to discuss topics such as dealing with the opposite sex and how to avoid unwanted advances, as well as how to prepare to get serious with someone. I would have loved to have had the same talk but just slightly tweaked to make it more muslamic. But I didn't.

I've lived quite a sheltered life and never had the chance to become myself. I've lived vicariously and it was only at university that I was able to live the real Hannah Montana life. 'I'm at the library' became my favourite line, as I was out exploring Oxford Circus and finally being the Londoner I had been prevented from being. Once that was done and I was searching for a job, questions of marriage started to come up. I'm not going to deny that I have always had crushes and liked boys, but it was never reciprocated and I'm fine with that. However, it's having my phone blow up and constantly being told by family that male attention is suddenly meant to give me a sort of validation of my womanhood that annoys me. Five minutes ago I wasn't allowed to speak to them!

The fact that I am still learning about myself and not mixing with male counterparts would, you think, somehow simplify this equation, whereas in reality, I still can't find X in this sum. It's the thought of pleasing everyone and having nothing for yourself that grates. I want to find myself first.

Let's just say I do get a husband (insert shuddering) and it's time for the wedding – have you even been to a Somali wedding? They're absolutely amazing – I'm not going to deny it, Somali weddings will always be top-tier for me – but it's the aftermath that I'm discussing right now. It's when every-one goes home and – let's digress from the newly married Somali couple; that discussion will come later. Let's talk about Somali aunties.

On one occasion my mother and her friends went to a wedding. When they returned, I stupidly asked how the wedding was, but I somehow forgot this was old Somali women I was talking to.

'The bride is fat.'

'You could see her arms from the dress.'

'I think her make-up made her look older than her hus-band. They are the same age but she looks older.'

'She has big breasts.'

That was the point at which I decided I will probably never have a wedding, and will announce my marriage through a group WhatsApp message instead. I have never been so shocked in my life, hearing the post-wedding discussions. I just sat there listening to a detailed deconstruction of this woman's wedding with a long running commentary from a bunch of women who could have birthed her. I'm glad Hooyo (mum) wasn't part of this gossip because I would have probably marched her back home. However, I still couldn't help but say, 'You guys just came from a young person's wedding; what would you say about mine?' The room went quiet and they started backtracking as they began to say the standard 'no we would never say that' and 'we would be overjoyed if you got married'.

These discussions that take place after weddings really make you think twice as a woman who would love a wedding but not the comments. The fact that there are beauty standards, gossip and intense criticism at a time you should be at your happiest makes you wonder if a woman is ever allowed to be truly happy. Not if bitter aunties can help it, anyway.

I shall now bring forth the word that we are all dreading talking about . . . sex. I said it – sex, sex, sex, sex, sex, sex, sex. I want to say this as much as possible because when will I ever have a chance to say *sex* in writing again? I never had the sex talk. I was the one who brought up the conversation with Hooyo – I probably fell on my head a lot as a child. I was especially brave, as I asked how we are to produce children if not by sex, but obviously the conversation was brought to a complete standstill by Mum because I was promptly told that it was God who gave us children. I completely agree that it's the will of God to grant us a child, but that does not help when trying to understand how we get from A to B. But what could I say? You can't question things when God is brought into the equation.

I learned for myself and had come to understand during my twenties through porn – book porn. Don't judge; I'm being honest and I was curious. Also I have already admitted this to Hooyo, so nothing can shock her.

I had to find out about all this myself, and if it wasn't through those weird *Cosmopolitan* magazines, it was through

Fifty Shades of Grey. That's right, I was a huge fan of the book until I really went down to the nitty-gritty and figured out there were a lot of sections that had escaped my notice. Ropes and chains?!

But that and other erotic novels really made me look into sex without having to look into sex, if you know what I mean. I became a reader of erotic novels and they taught me a lot. The fact that this whole genre exists and I can read it with no one knowing (make sure it's on Kindle) and discover how different people meet each other and view sex is mindblowing. I do understand that erotic novels have their own problematic takes, but it was a real eye-opener nevertheless. My own Muslim girl cheat-sheet. If I am expected to bring a husband home now, I need to know this stuff, right?

No one discusses sex in the Somali community; that and mental health have been such taboos that I've always wondered who taught my parents about sex, because if they weren't taught, there are a lot of questions to be answered. I remember thinking when I was younger that when the time for sex came on my wedding night it would be something that would come naturally to me and my husband. That innate instinct will take over and we'll just do it, like some animal documentary or something.

I would hazard a guess that all these bitter aunties who always have negative things to say about women have never experienced an orgasm. The fact that we are prevented from discussing such things and are constantly told to button it makes me wonder if they even know what one is. For their generation, when it comes to having a husband, it's all about *his* pleasure and making sure *he's* happy, and this refers to outside the bedroom too.

But that's enough of the older generation; let's bring it forward to millennials. How do you even meet or talk to the opposite gender? This has been the basis of this whole discussion but I've been getting ahead of myself, already jumping into the bedroom when nothing has even been discussed, and no man has made an appearance.

The dating game has changed people (or so I've heard!). There were the good old times of shooting your shot through social media, but now we swipe right or left. Sounds familiar, right? My experience with online dating started during my final year of university. I was sitting making observations with my supervisor for my dissertation. I had decided to write chapters of a novel for my final project and so we started talking about plot points and one of them was a romantic encounter. Because I'm enthusiastic about social media it was suggested my characters meet through a dating app that starts with an 'M' instead of a 'T'. I laughed it off, saying I might give this a go instead as a social experiment. But who knew I would actually sign up to all this and discover a whole new world of online dating post-graduation?

I've never tried online dating. I believed that there was some sort of secret society through which people met and found their dates. I felt left out, until I realised that social media was the new way to date and interact with men.

I talked to a lot of interesting characters along my journey. The first man who messaged me wanted to see a picture of my feet – and that right there is when I knew there are a lot of weird individuals on the internet. I was in class when I showed a friend and we giggled like schoolgirls over the trivial messages that I received – it was a great source of entertainment. There was definitely no marriage material there!

There was one interesting conversation with an individual who came from a mixed-race background; the conversation about my skin colour came up as I had a profile picture. He said that he had always loved Black girls, to which he then added 'the darker the berry the sweeter the juice'. I immediately felt nauseous. I didn't feel the conversation was genuine but I felt vulnerable to his unwavering desire to put me on some sort of pedestal. I could deal with flattery, but I was unable to deal with the constant barrage of 'I like Black women', 'you're beautiful', and 'I only want to talk to Black women because you are so sexy'. I was constantly being fed one-liners about his fantasies and how he only deals with Black women until it started to feel creepy and obsessive. I felt like a special doll being stroked by a hot and heavy hand. Ugh.

I thought to shift the conversation and thankfully he followed, and then he decided to inquire about my ideology and asked, 'Are you a feminist?' I replied, 'Yes I am.' He added emoticons as though to say, *So this is why you speak your mind.*

Every question he asked received a quick answer, sometimes a challenge back, but for him the easiest catch-all response was that I was a feminist. I began to challenge him more aggressively, and had the advantage because I was unwilling to back down. This was my internet space, my free space, and I didn't have to hide and just say, *let's agree to disagree*, and then move on. I defended, argued and made sure my points were clear. I was a visible Black Muslim woman on this social app and I was determined not to let myself be pushed and trapped into a nonsensical question-and-answer session. I felt empowered enough to navigate and shut down the conversation. If this had been a face-to-face date I would not have been able to continue with the conversation but would have been more inclined to sit there awkwardly.

Starting off by using the internet to talk to men prepared me to be able to test myself with how I deal with questions that at first would have thrown me off. But now I can handle them with ease (even if I can't use the angry emoji in real life).

I've come to the conclusion that dating as a millennial is tough, but starting off online taught me at times to walk away from conversations that I don't enjoy or feel comfortable with. I now know that I can safely manoeuvre myself through online conversations. So if someone does slide into my DMs I'm much better prepared and can handle myself much more confidently.

The whole thought of trying to date and find a soulmate in the age of social media leaves me cynical though. There is hope, but nothing is looking up at the moment. I ask my friends and they seem to have their own misgivings about what to do to get a man's attention and I wonder if there is even any point in trying.

There are so many expectations, advice and self-help options that it has come to the point where I don't know what to do any more. Everyone has something to say. Don't talk to strangers, but somehow attract and marry strangers. It's all so confusing.

There isn't the 'milk the cow before buying it' clause. We don't test-drive anything; we just hand over the payment plan and take the car out of the dealership without even knowing if we have a licence to drive. We can't live together (which has its pros and cons), we don't know anything about the other person, but the woman is meant to show good faith and believe that it'll all work out and this man isn't going to be a weirdo like the men in her DMs.

There is no manual, and there is no one to tell you what you should know, because they don't know. The fact that I'm in my twenties and I have no clue is the result of this conundrum. I was supposed to write a fancy conclusion once I got to the end, but, dear reader, Fatha hasn't figured anything out. There is no man.

RIOT, WRITE, REST: ON WRITING AS A MUSLIMAH

Sumaya Kassim

There is an essay I did not write.

This is not the essay I planned for this collection. I have another essay that I might finish someday; it's sitting on my hard drive in a sea of other unfinished essays (on topics such as video games, serial killers, the figure of the orphan in Islam, heritage, whiteness, modernity). I get waylaid a lot. I'm interested in a variety of subjects, and my projects grow in multiple notebooks and lists and diagrams – and there is nothing as exciting as the start of a new writing project.

I originally pitched an essay about cities. Cities are multiple, heterogeneous, exciting; when I think 'Muslim', I think of London and Manchester and Birmingham. England is not a home to migrants: the cities of England are. And I've lived in two of the largest cities; the intricate and intimate ways we dwell together in urban spaces have always fascinated me.

And yet something felt fundamentally wrong. Each time I started writing, I second-guessed myself. I made an inventory of all the racialised encounters I'd experienced in both cities. Everything felt weirdly performative. Who would be interested in this?

I am so much more than these encounters. I put the inventory away. I think about how boring racism is, how it evinces a lack of imagination, and how sad it was that this boring quality had leached into me, so now all I could produce is bad writing about sad people who can't face themselves and so would rather attack people based upon their forebears' bizarre insistence that their culture and phenomes cohere into static brilliance that exerts itself in a supremacy, an ahistoricity, an atemporality, that edges towards the divine. In a word, whiteness.

We are more than just anthropologists of whiteness; we have lives outside other people's fantasies of us.

I put the essay away, and continue with a piece of fiction. I take the essay out again, write words like 'cosmopolitanism' and 'multiculturalism' and 'gentrification'. I research the Trojan Horse case. *You're trying too hard not to be 'that Muslim'*, a wry voice sounded in my mind. Savvy, cosmopolitan, in control – an exceptionalist Muslimah, who is always on the right side of the political game. A woman on the defensive, scared of her own story, scared of what it might do, who it might hurt.

But a good reader always knows when you're holding back.

When attempting to write an essay for this collection, my mind was so filled with argument and counter-argument, with the white noise of white anxiety – preternaturally concerned with women's clothing, with my (a)sexuality, curiously incapable of comprehending my complexity – that I struggled. What had the current Islamophobic culture done to my creativity as a writer? What had all the op-eds on the burqa, debates over my humanity, my interior life, done to me, personally, imaginatively and professionally? How can I write about the Muslim subject when the voices that hate her are so loud? If my audience are people who suspect, in their heart of hearts, that they are modern and I am an anachronistic relic or an aberration, how can my work be heard?

As a Muslimah who writes, I am keenly aware of the ways society has been purposefully designed around my erasure and how this has impacted both my imagination and also the pathways to disseminate my work. Muslim women are searching for forms to articulate our experiences in ways that do not fall prey to the binary narrative trajectory, from patriarchal Islam to the liberal, secular subject. What happens when we direct our work to Allah, without a particular audience in mind? What happens when we view writing and creative practice as a site of radical transformation for the writer? How have I been made to collude in my own silence?

One of the archetypes of Muslim women is that we are forever in a double bind, stuck between a racist society and a disapproving community. It is not for me to say if this is true or not; when I reflect upon my own experience it is archetypal, in the way all families are archetypal, Muslim or not. Writing through archetype is exhausting. As a writer, my medium is what has not been determined; the realm of chance and change. In an environment which considers me as a foreclosed conclusion, irresolvable, my work suffers. Repetition is a sign of trauma, but it is also a tool used to traumatise others. The interminable 'debates' on what Muslim women wear and on terrorism serve to traumatise Muslims into believing we should feel ashamed, that we are inherently disloyal, that we are uncivilised, beyond redemption. Some have used repetition to their advantage, writing about women, veils and silence. And yet here we are, partaking in conversations that are designed to humiliate us, that hinge upon our being irredeemable subjects because we refuse to relinquish our belief, because we are useful as irredeemable subjects. Only art and writing which relies upon binaries, the simplicity of free/ unfree, secular/religious, barbaric/civilised, are deemed worthy, a sign that we are educated barbarians, if nothing else.

Whatever you fight, you strengthen. Whatever you resist, persists. When we work hard to humanise ourselves, the battle is already lost.

These repetitious 'debates' serve to diminish our imaginations. We are forever oriented towards the questioner, the colonial centre, the white subject/audience, the one who has trained us to consider Islam from a place of fear. We are programmed to write only about certain subjects of interest to white people. As the bombs rain down on Black and brown bodies overseas, we who live here are forced to contend with the fragilities and psychosis brought on by the cognitive dissonance white supremacy relies upon. A culture that seems adamant to drive Muslim women crazy, and then to make them feel that our madness is entirely our own responsibility. Apparently, we are not even entitled to own our pain; we are discouraged from looking at the sources of our oppression. We are purposefully kept from our own histories, from how Britain's history shaped the present world, how its current political machinations rely upon racism, on fear, on dividing people based upon hierarchies of race, class and gender. We are asked illogical questions again and again (notably, 'Why do you not apologise for the actions of others?' and, beneath it all, the spectre of 'Why remain Muslim at all?').

Even my constraints, my personal tragedies, are viewed as exotic. Thus our stories are imminently commercial, more easily packaged. Trauma is a currency. Anger is a product courted by the mainstream; the personal story is powerful. Editors are infamously disinterested in how reiterating trauma is, in turn, traumatising. On the one hand, there is the pressure to perform one's trauma. On the other, the pressure of being a spokesperson. And then comes the fact that creating, writing, is a challenging process that requires immense psychological strength, discipline, a strong support network and, of course, money and time.

Yet whenever we put pen to paper and answer deceptively simple questions with simple answers, we are diminishing ourselves, we are relinquishing something that is worth fighting for: it keeps us reactive, not creative. If we continue to respond to bigotry, everything becomes an account of things that were meant to be, but did not happen – a symptom of how our future is overdetermined, that each move feels mapped, each creative act pinned down by those who have convinced you they are powerful. When we write, we are grasping in the dark. If you have already made your conclusions, are you doing your job properly? Or do you view your job as an informant?

I am not interested in disrupting stereotypes, or readers' expectations. Rather, I am invested in dissolving the internal barriers, the internalised misogyny, homophobia and racism, the shame, the silences, and in unpacking our implicit beliefs. Those definitions and the rhetoric we inherited from hardened men drawing boundaries and borders on their imaginations and on lands they pretended had no one living there already.

A change in process, a change in how we conceive of writing, could be one of the ways we do this work. Writing is spiritual practice; a searing honesty, a commitment to the discipline, a refining of what some call 'craft'. It also entails giving yourself the permission to create imperfectly in a culture that expects perfection from us, giving yourself the permission to fail, to recognise whatever you make is imperfect, to love your mistakes, to embrace your vulnerability.

This may very well confound readerly expectations. But that is not my intention.

It is important to note that this is not prescriptive: I'm not advocating for a particular style, aesthetic or medium. Instead I am drawing attention to the ways creative industries train creatives – through their funding applications, their diversity drives, in meetings held in pubs, etc. – to perform a palatable Muslim identity, demanding that we mute our spirituality, for instance. I am drawing attention to the power of refusing to back down, of refusing to indulge racist sensibilities, orientalist assumptions. Saying no, when your conscience tells you to, no matter what treasures are dangled under your nose, is an incredibly powerful thing to do. I am advocating that we look inside ourselves when creating, checking in, ensuring what we're doing is coming from a place of love rather than fear. I am stating that instead of confessing to our audience, we should see our practice as writers as a spiritual practice, one where khushooa'a (closeness to Allah), ikhlaas (sincerity) and humility are goals within the writing process.

To get away from these expectations, we must refuse. This refusal does not have to look like a particular kind of resistance. However, there is a big difference between performing your pain from a place of fear, from a desire for recognition from people who are culturally bound to be blind to your pain and your humanity, and writing from a place of love. I look at work from writers who identify as Muslim and often I am deeply aggrieved; so much is being written from a place of self-interest, self-aggrandisement, mercantile careerism. This is an environment which encourages surface engagement with deep subject matter, disconnection from the body, disconnection from the social body.

This is what I am running from.

We rarely consider the writer as a person with a body, with needs, with pressures, desires outside our own – especially women writers, especially Muslim women writers.

Growing up, I didn't believe that writing was an option for me. This is despite the fact I wrote constantly and read voraciously. My family despaired of my reading, my father in particular. I lived in one of those contradictory households that was full of books (full of other worlds and possibilities), but that demanded its inhabitants – its women especially – live narrow, sequestered lives. My father is what one might call a zealot. I do not attribute Islam as the defining factor of my father's views: men controlling women is hardly unique to Islam. My mother writes too. She burns everything she writes in the sink each night.

After I went to university (without my father's knowledge), I became acquainted with a different kind of tyranny: that of the Individual Genius Author who creates in a vacuum and also a conceited secularism. Anne Carson can speak of 'leaving room for God' in her poetry, but I felt no such freedom. In this sense, there is a double standard for non-Muslim, particularly white, writers, who can write about their beliefs, but also maintain an ironic distance from it. Like their coloniser ancestors they can explore, discover and steal for their ostensibly universal art. White people get to move in and out of spirituality, the occult, their struggles with faith without much pushback. But Islam is fixed in people's minds as inherently anti-literature. When I was a student, I attended a literary event at SOAS. During the Q&A, an author misunderstood my question ('Will the Qur'an be treated in English literature in the same way as the Bible, as a source of literary inspiration?') and became visibly enraged. Muslims, he said, do not read fiction. The only book they read is the Qur'an. And it was for this reason that they are held back politically. For me to mention my reliance on God within this creative context, and not on my own singular genius, is somewhat paradoxically blasphemous. So much of what we think of as good practice and good writing is founded on the ideal of the singular genius of the author (usually a white man).

Another factor is that it simply isn't respectable for a woman to write. Creative work is so often seen as frivolous by caring (and not so caring) migrant parents and families. I don't consider writing a choice because it is something I must do and I'm lucky enough to be passionate about it. But I fought valiantly against the urge for years: I wrote in secret, I published nothing. It wasn't legitimate work, it wasn't productive. And if you 'don't work' (i.e. if you do not follow the incredibly narrow definition of work developed by able-bodied men over the centuries), you're lazy. So many outsider figures – the migrant, the homeless, the sick, the old, the very young – are seen as politically unimportant because they are not part of the workforce. Even the most radical people are often deeply attached to notions of productivity and labour that lack spiritual and bodily dimensions.

But then I became ill. Developing a chronic condition forced me to confront many of my deeply held assumptions, particularly about use and usefulness. Suddenly, I recognised how my obsession with achievement was tied to how unworthy I felt – and that this was a widespread generational malaise. It was also un-Islamic. Allah has asked us to worship Them, not to be useful to other people just for the sake of it. I am not the only woman writer who found writing, or came to new phases in the work, through physical and mental illness: Ali Smith, Flannery O'Connor, Audre Lorde, Susan Sontag, Han Kang, Johanna Hedva, all women (though Hedva identifies as queer) whose conditions bred their writing, a contagion of understanding that came from having to evaluate themselves not through the mind – rational, objective, independent – but through bodies that are sacred in their limitedness.

Before this, I was still under my father's wing. I had been disowned by this point, but I was still guilt-ridden, still convinced of my own guilt, that the only way to God was through being a dutiful daughter. But my body forced me to make a choice, to choose myself, and to choose my tribe: those who are silenced.

How radical, then, to write.

And how difficult. It requires resilience, discipline and upholding strong boundaries. It takes time to write. As I carved out time for myself, for my craft, I found that people melted away. I've lost friends for asserting boundaries over my apparently 'free' time. Some cannot understand the necessity to be protective, even to the point of obsession, about one's time at work. A woman writing or reading is a woman asking to be interrupted, to be disturbed. It is an affront to people's deeply held beliefs about what a woman should be: women should be available, kempt, smiling, accommodating and, above all, practical. It is eccentric, even today, for a woman to claim autonomy over time, over her creativity, above her 'duties' as a friend, a daughter, a wife.

I have grown to be grateful for being disowned by my family, painful as it was (and still is). It taught me something about relationships, their inherently transient nature, about the necessity to listen to that small voice inside yourself insisting on your purpose, insisting that it is loving to be at your desk and it is loving to write from the deep communal wells of the collective unconscious for yourself, and for your communities, even as they reject you. It is courageous, and it is radical, and it is kind. My heart knows that if I am tethered to the formlessness through my pen – tied to this desk, and to the discipline – I am tapping into reserves of power that most ignore.

It is because words are so powerful that many consider writing a form of betrayal. My mother doesn't know what I do. It is one of the paradoxes of patriarchy that a woman who writes, who speaks out, is treated with suspicion, while the crimes she may speak of are minimised and justified. Our societies betray us, our families; that is ordinary. And so generation after generation, we lay out the workings of injustice, questioning values, making unduty an artform . . .

But it is not a betrayal; sharing our stories with radical vulnerability can be a sacred act, a duty. Words are powerful, words are transformative. Sitting across from her, my mirror, my double, my sister, I have seen how meditating upon words with precision has uncovered decades-old wounds, conditions shrouded in shame and betrayal. I've sat opposite women and we've grieved the time lost to families and institutions and states who colluded to entrap us, to ruin us with subtle tools, to make emotion itself an enemy. As Audre Lorde shows us, the rage we feel is what will save us. I've seen revolutions ignite behind women's eyes every time we share our stories and get angry for ourselves and for each other.

It doesn't feel like resistance: it feels restful, tender and healing.

When I write, I want that energy to come from a place of peace and love: love for anyone who has felt as I have – and still do, at times – that all the doors have closed, that no one will listen even if I share my truth. Love for every person who grew up as I did, for every person who has ever felt dehumanised or unloved, and love for Allah, without whom my practice is meaningless. As a Muslim, writing and making art isn't separate to the act of living, and living cannot be separated from the act of worship; the intention is the same. We can choose to tell stories about one another that serve our growth as a community, or that deplete us. That is the real choice. To love enough that we embrace our traditions, to love enough to critique and better our work and our lives.

When we write, it needs to be a kind of falling, a kind of dislocating, something akin to the fear when falling in love, rather than the fear of an abuser's displeasure. Creating from a space of fear will only further traumatise us – what kind of art will emerge from that place?

All of the noise: we lack intimacy with ourselves. A part of us that is ancient knows that all of the noise is just noise, and yet that part of us is buried deeper every hour we are subjected to trauma without self-awareness. In this environment, we do not have intimacy with our beliefs, with ourselves, with each other, with that ancient part of ourselves.

We who live in majority non-Muslim countries are testament to the coming together of different origins and sources (ta'leef). We must beware to take on the mantle of those who reject the edges that cannot fit into the narrow strictures of secular, humanist interpretation. What if my body is not resistant to their interpretation? What if my body is in repose, even as I write?

I cannot be read in parts. I will be read in my totality.

Writing is an act which mediates the private and the public, drawing together a breadth of experiences and voices, and inspiration that is collaborative not didactic; to work is to re-mediate and re-formulate how we conceive of the personal when writing and when reading Muslim women's writing. You are not receiving the unmediated, raw thoughts of a woman writer. Writers play with received forms, with genre, with language, with the ebb and flow of culture, with the conversations we are surrounded by. Our work is edited, crafted, moulded – it is rigorous. It bears the mark of many hands. Writers mould the forms and make the words that set the terms of the debate. In this version of reality, where you write without fear, writing is testament to *possibility*. It creates conceptual space, where we breathe different air.

Because, as much as some would like us all to believe that the future is already determined, it is not. Many assume that being Muslim entails a deterministic view of life and for human creation, but that is not the case. The beginning of the Qur'an invokes the ghayb, the unseen, the unknown – the unknown of the future, and the unknown of other people's intentions, their interiorities – it is not for anyone to assume an individual's or a people's trajectory. One of the cruellest after-effects of colonisation is the insistence that the future is set. To create is a vulnerable position to be in; it indicates a willingness and courage to imagine a different ending. When we listen closely, we find voices that say – we survive through you, and the future is in Allah's Hands. The unknown is a central principle in Islam – it can mean the divine's nature, it can mean the future, which is only known by the divine. If our medium is the unknown, the future and the past, then it is only through relying on Allah that the writing struggle – and the struggle of life – is meaningful at all.

There is a story that must be told, but there is also a life that must be lived. Living within the perception of others, to be held captive by your audience, is no way to live. Our role is to refuse, and reconvene on some other ground, and for it to be elsewhere, outside of the city, but also somehow within it. There are interior architectures that deserve our time, our love, our attention. Enough wasting time writing for others. Our role is to make space for ourselves, and to write, just write, and read each other's work with generosity and patience – allowing for possibility and future to emerge for us, a selfhood that we share.

NOTES

From 'I am Not an Answer, I Am the Question' by Suhaiymah Manzoor-Khan

'Living as we did – on the edge – we developed a particular way of seeing reality . . . a mode of seeing unknown to most of our oppressors, that sustained us, aided us in our struggle.' bell hooks, *Feminist Theory: From Margin to Center*, 3rd Edition (Routledge, 2015) © Gloria Watkins, 2015. Reproduced by arrangement with Taylor & Francis Books UK.

'a special vantage point . . . to criticize the dominant racist, classist, sexist hegemony as well as to envision and create a counter-hegemony . . . the margin is more than a site of depravation . . . It offers to one the possibility of a radical perspective from which to see and create, to imagine alternatives, new worlds.' bell hooks, *Feminist Theory: From Margin to Center*, 3rd Edition (Routledge, 2015) © Gloria Watkins, 2015. Reproduced by arrangement with Taylor & Francis Books UK.

From 'The Gift of Second-Sight' by Sofia Rehman

'If you are never to see yourself depicted . . . Not in story, nor song, nor poem, nor painting, nor prose . . . No shred of a tale by some distant kindred soul who saw and knew and felt then as you do now, and else another who loved and bore witness . . . Never see yourself

except as crude caricature, mythical beast, or Magdalene penitent ...
You believe no other like you ever existed. Unquiet women, defiant
women – we live invisible lives, and if we are seen and seen by strangers, we are reduced to monsters. Vampires, who have no reflection in a
looking glass. Mermaids, who die and become seafood, blown away by
the wind. We will take up and take back the tools to tell our stories as
our own. Civilisations may rise and fall and rewrite the history of the
dead, as is often they do. But we are here ... and we lived, and loved,
and mattered.' Marguerite Bennett, *InSEXts Vol 2*

From 'Hidden' by Asha Mohamed
'capitalism requires inequality and racism enshrines it.' *Geographies of
Racial Capitalism* with Ruth Wilson Gilmore (Antipode Foundation) <https://www.youtube.com/watch?v=2CS627aKrJI>

'affirmed by the yearning of the oppressed for freedom and justice, and by their struggle to recover their lost humanity', Paulo
Freire, *Pedagogy of the Oppressed*

From 'Grenfell' by Shaista Aziz with Zahra Adams
'*The night our eyes changed
Rooms where love was made and un-made in a flash of the night
Rooms where memories drowned in fumes of poison
Rooms where futures were planned and the imagination of children built
     castles in the sky
Rooms where both the extraordinary and the mundane were lived
Become forever tortured graves of ash
Oh you political class, so servile to corporate power'*
  from 'Ghosts of Grenfell' by Lowkey, with permission of the artist

GLOSSARY

abaya long dress garment worn by some Muslim women, particularly in the Middle East

adhaab manners

adhaan Muslim call to prayer

affu forgiveness

akhi Muslim brother (colloquial)

Aalhamdulillah Praise be to God

alif, baa, taa beginning of Arabic alphabet (equivalent of the ABC)

Allahu Akbar God is great

Apa big sister (Urdu)

Aqeeqah Islamic celebration at the birth of a child

Ayatul Kursi a verse in the Qur'an

Baytullah house of God (ie. place of worship)

Daesh pejorative term for ISIS

deen religion (i.e. Islam)

dhihaar a form of divorce among pagan Arabs

dua private or group invocation (prayer) asking God for something

Eid Islamic festival

Fatihah opening chapter of the Qur'an

fitrah state of purity all humans are born in

ghayb the unseen

gora Urdu word meaning white

hajj Muslim pilgrimage

hijabi person who wears hijab (colloquial)

hooyo Somali word for mum

'ibadah worship

iftar meal at the breaking of the fast

ihram a state of consecration assumed by Muslims on pilgrimage

ikhlaas sincerity during worship

imaan simply defined as faith

InshaAllah God willing

iqra read

Isha evening prayer

jama'ah congregation/community

Janazah funeral prayer

Jumuah Friday prayer

kalimah Urdu/Arabic word for the Muslim declaration of faith

Kali Urdu word meaning black, often used as a perjorative

khushoo' calmness during prayer/closeness to God

madrassah Islamic school

masjid (pl. masajid) mosque

mashaAllah God has willed it

minbar pulpit in a mosque

mithai sweets (Urdu)

Muslimah feminine of Muslim (i.e. a Muslim woman)

naseehah sincere advice

nasheed Islamic song

Nikkah wedding contract/ceremony in Islam

niqab face veil

Qaa'idah (or qaida) a book used for beginners to learn Arabic

Ramadhan holy month of fasting

sabr patience

Sahabah companions of the Prophet Muhammad (SAW)

salah prayer

salafi a member of a strict Sunni Muslim group who seek to follow the methodology of 'The Pious Predecessors (Salaf)', often viewed as dogmatic

salwar kameez Pakistani dress (Urdu)

sharia Islamic law

Shia second-largest sect in Islam

SubhanAllah Glory to God

suhoor pre-dawn meal before fasting

Sunni majority sect in Islam

taraweeh night prayer during Ramadhan

ta'leef the coming together of different origins and sources (to reconcile)

Ummah nation/community (i.e. the global Muslim community)

ummi mother

ustaadji teacher (Urdu)

Wahhabis pejorative word for a member of a strict Sunni Muslim group that originate in Saudi Arabia (subset of 'Salafi')

wudhu the ritual washing performed by Muslims before prayer

CONTRIBUTORS AND
ACKNOWLEDGEMENTS

Negla Abdalla is a freelance journalist, digital marketer and founder of Creative Faces who seeks to help empower the BAME community to believe, progress and achieve in the creative field. She is published in *gal-dem* magazine and the Middle East Monitor, and is currently the only person in the UK to have graduated with a degree in Journalism with Contemporary Arabic studies. She has appeared on TRT and Al Jazeera and on the BBC's *Beyond Today* podcast. Negla created a range of workshops in collaboration with the City of Westminster Council that were introduced in schools and colleges across London. These workshops aimed to tackle the gaps she believed were missing from standard education, such as money management, importance of networking, crime and self-confidence, as well as creative workshops that covered the arts, music, graphic design, photography and much more.

Zahra Adams is a pseudonym.

Fatima Ahdash is a British–Libyan Lecturer in Law. Her research examines the interaction between counterterrorism and family law in the UK. She has an LLB and an LLM in Human Rights Law and has worked for a number of international and domestic human-rights organisations. She lives in London.

My sincerest thanks to my sisters, Zainab, Nusieba and Hajer, for reading and commenting on earlier drafts of the essay. I also thank my friend Tasnim Qutait for her kind encouragement and insightful feedback. My gratitude also goes to my friends Zainab Asunramu and Yousef Al-Shammari for the conversations that inspired a lot of what was written here. This essay is dedicated to my wonderful friend and colleague Samah Al-Mashadani; without you it would have been unbearable, impossible.

Sabeena Akhtar is a writer, editor and an arts and culture programmer working across a variety of literary festivals. She is the Festival Coordinator of Bare Lit, the UK's principal festival celebrating remarkable writers in the diaspora; a co-founder of the Primadonna Festival, which spotlights the work of women writers; the Primadonna Prize for Writing; and Bare Lit Kids, the UK's first children's festival showcasing the work of writers of colour. She is also Senior Programmer at the WOW Foundation. A keen advocate for Partition commemoration, in 2017 she partook in the BBC's coverage of the seventieth anniversary of Indian independence and, alongside her daughter, filmed a programme for children on the Partition of India. She has since been invited to discuss the subject on various media outlets. She has published a wide variety of work and is currently working on her debut novel. She is a mother of four. You can find Sabeena tweeting at @pocobookreader

Thanks to everyone who supported this project and helped make it a reality. To Unbound, for taking us on, to Tilted Axis Press for their support and to Jannatul Shammi, whose generosity is not forgotten. To my co-authors, who truly are the most remarkable and talented group of women. To Joelle, for all the calls and emails – we got there! To Martha for the final hurdle. And to my best friend, Sof, for her unwavering love and support. A special thanks to my family, especially my parents for all their help and to Ismail, Sumayyah, Ruqayyah, Yusuf and Zayd for their love, support and laughter.

Mariam Ansar is a writer, teacher and graduate of the University of Cambridge. Her freelance work – which ranges from feature writing to politics to film studies and music – has been featured in *NME*, *gal-dem*, *VICE*, *Dazed*, *Catapult Story*, *Buzz-Feed*, *Rookie Magazine*, *Teen Vogue*, *Elite Daily*, and many others.

My endless thanks to my family, who encourage me beyond limits, who love me whether the writing for the day is good or not. And to my friends, who have become part of my family, too. Praise always to the Almighty alhamdulillah. Any good seen in me comes from Him.

Shaista Aziz is a freelance journalist and writer specialising in identity, race, gender and Muslim women. Her work has appeared in the *Guardian*, *Globe* and *Mail*, *New York Times*, *Huffington Post* and on the BBC. She's a broadcaster and political commentator and the founder of the Everyday Bigotry Project, seeking to disrupt narratives around race, Islamophobia and bigotry. She's a former Oxfam and MSF aid worker and has spent more than fifteen years working across the Middle East, East and West Africa and in Pakistan with marginalised women impacted by conflict and emergencies. Most recently she was working in Borno state, north-east Nigeria. She is also a member of the Fabian Women's Network Executive Committee. Shaista is the co-founder of Intersectional Feminist Foreign Policy, seeking to influence the creation of an ethical feminist foreign policy that does no further harm to women and girls and that brings the voices, lived experiences and expertise of women excluded from policy discussions based on their intersectional identities.

Suma Din is an author and freelance researcher based in Buckinghamshire. Her titles focus on social justice, education, faith and women. She taught in the supplementary and adult-education sector for many years and has written non-fiction resources for children. One of her writing passions is to bring marginalised voices to the fore, as she did through her book on Muslim mothers and their children's schooling. Suma is married with three children and lives with her pet fascination for bodies of water and recreational painting. Further details of her publications are at therootedwriter.co.uk. *Thank you to Sabeena for your dedication in creating this space for women's writing and for the team at Unbound for facilitating the* *way. I'm also grateful to my family for their reflections on earlier drafts of this chapter.*

Dr Khadijah Elshayyal is a specialist in British Muslim history based at the University of Edinburgh. Her research looks at activism, advocacy and political engagement among British Muslims. She is the author of *Muslim Identity Politics: Islam, activism and equality in Britain* (IB Tauris, 2020) and *Scottish Muslims in Numbers: Understanding Scotland's Muslims through the 2011 Census* (University of Edinburgh, 2016). She tweets at @drkelshayyal.

Thank you to Yusuf, my number one reader.

Ruqaiya Haris is a freelance writer who graduated in Islamic Studies from SOAS and is currently studying an MSc in Islam & Christian-Muslim relations at Edinburgh University, in 2017, and has written on niche aspects of Muslim identity for *Dazed*, the *Guardian*, the *Independent* and the *New Arab*. She has presented short videos for media platforms such as i-D and the BBC, and led panel discussions on Islamophobia, racism and mental health. She enjoys following digital trends and particularly how religious communities carve out spaces for themselves online, and may be found getting into Twitter arguments with misogynists (@Ruqaiya_H) or obsessing over her cat.

Fatha Hassan is a writer who aspires to publish a novel. She is regularly on Twitter @FathaaaOnline posting memes as well as discussing her love for reading. As an avid reader Fatha maintains ties with the publishing industry by reviewing books and talking about her journey towards her first novel. She writes stories on FGM and poetry that dives into the sexuality, religion, cultural values and impulses of women, taking inspiration from her Somali culture and religious background as a Muslim. You can find the majority of her book posts on Instagram @Fathaaaa_online. A supporter of #ownvoices and feminism, she enjoys fighting with others on the internet and getting in on the diaspora wars. A graduate in Creative Writing and English Literature, she is also studying for an MA in Digital, Professional and Creative Writing.

Raisa Hassan is a graduate in Creative and Professional Writing from UEL. She is also a disabled-rights activist – as the founder of the campaign 'Right Words. Right Mind.' in collaboration with Scope, a trustee of a disability charity, and a performance poet. She works with Action Tutoring as a volunteer English tutor in east London.

Sumaya Kassim is a writer, cultural critic and independent researcher. She has published short stories and essays and has given talks across Europe on museums, decoloniality and writing. She was one of the co-curators of the exhibition 'The Past is Now: Birmingham and Empire' at Birmingham Museum and Art Gallery (2017–2018). She chronicled this experience in her essay 'The Museum Will Not Be Decolonised' (Media Diversified, 2017). Her article 'The Museum Is the Master's House: an Open Letter to Tristram Hunt' (Medium, 2019) challenged the director of the V&A to question his assumptions about what it means to live in colonial aftermaths. Her understanding of museums and institutions is informed by her writing practice, particularly the role of memory and futurity in making ourselves and our communities. She is writing her first novel and a set of essays. @SFKassim.

Rumana Lasker Dawood is a junior doctor training to be a general practitioner, with a special interest in Medical Education. Alongside her day job she juggles motherhood and a passion for crafts which she documents on her blog, The Little Pomegranate. In 2016 she was a quarter-finalist on *The Great British Sewing Bee* on BBC2. Since then she has continued to share her sewing and the benefits of crafts for mental well-being. She is a vocal advocate for increased inclusivity within the sewing and crafts communities and works to raise awareness of these matters.

To my daughter, who inspires me to be the best I can be. I hope this book reminds you that only you define who you are and that your potential is limitless.

Suhaiymah Manzoor-Khan is an educator, writer and poet from West Yorkshire. Her work seeks to disrupt narratives of history, race, knowledge and power – interrogating the political purpose of conversations about Muslims, migrants, gender and violence in particular. She was runner-up in the Roundhouse National Poetry Slam 2017 and shortlisted for the Outspoken Prize for Poetry in 2018. Suhaiymah is the author of poetry collection *Postcolonial Banter* (Verve Poetry Press, 2019), co-author of the anthology *A Fly Girl's Guide to University: Being a woman of colour at Cambridge and other institutions of power and elitism* (Verve Poetry Press, 2019) and hosts the *Breaking Binaries* podcast. She is a contributor to the *Guardian, Independent,* Al Jazeera, *gal-dem* and more and her work has been featured across radio and TV stations, magazines and digital media. Her poetry, articles and books can be found on university and school syllabuses.

Thanks to Sabeena for the vision, determination and execution – putting this all together and her resilience in seeing this through.

Asha Mohamed is an illustrator, photographer and short-story writer whose work can be found on AFREADA, *Unbreakable Bonds Anthology* as well as in literary magazines such as *TOKEN Magazine, Claim* and Hargeisa Literary Magazine. Her art and writing centre on self-reflection and knowledge -seeking with a focus on how these processes are affected by the external world. Her work also explores brevity and capturing what exists within the snapshot. Twitter: @iftiinwadaag Instagram: @iftiinwadaag.art

I would first and foremost like to thank Allah without whom I wouldn't be where I am today, protected, guided and surrounded by so many opportunities and so many genuinely kind and wonderful people. Thank you, Hooyo, for not only your never-ending advice and duas but also for introducing me to the concept of the hidden curriculum! Thank you, Layla, for patiently reading and rereading my work. Ladan, Bas, Jamal, Anisa and Anab, just because, and of course Bolu for being the first to read anything I've ever written, thank you for not cringing at the cringeworthy and for choosing to encourage and push me instead! Endless thanks to everyone I love, too many to name in such a short space but you know who you are.

Dr Sofia Rehman completed her PhD from the University of Leeds. Her research excavates a feminist hermeneutical approach to reading the hadith, with a special focus on the statements of Aisha bint Abu Bakr. She has worked with the Muslim Women's Council as an Impact fellow for her department, has featured as a scholar activist for the Shiloh Project, and is currently involved in a project to explore and challenge everyday sexism, sexual harassment and abuse, together with secondary-school students. She is a mother to four spirited little individuals who keep her feet firmly on the ground and her heart soaring high. She also runs the baddest book club in town. You can find Sofia on Instagram @sofia_reading

I would like to thank Sabeena for not only having the confidence in me to allow me to contribute to this collection, but for all her tireless work behind the scenes to bring the project to fruition despite all obstacles that came her way. Sabeena, you are a force for so much good, you have so much more to give yet and I can't wait to witness it all. I'd also like to thank the other Sabina in my life (Sabina Qadri) who read over my piece and gave me so much moral support and encouragement as always.

Yvonne Ridley is a British journalist, committed trade unionist and feminist. After becoming the first female editor of *Wales on Sunday*, she entered Fleet Street working for several titles including the *Sunday Times*, the *Observer* and *Daily Mirror* before joining the *Sunday Express*. In 2001 she became headline news when she was captured by the ruling Taliban after sneaking into Afghanistan days before the US-led war. Few expected her to survive but she emerged unscathed eleven days later, released on humanitarian grounds. The Taliban described her as 'A very bad woman with a very bad mouth!' Two years later she confounded critics by embracing Islam. In 2019 she wrote a book called *The Rise of the Prophet Muhammad: Don't Shoot the Messenger* and in 2020 *The Caledonians* marked her foray into historical fiction. Yvonne helped launch the English Language division of Al Jazeera in Qatar before returning to the UK for broadcasting start-up ventures Islam Channel and Press TV. She has also contributed to BBC TV and radio, CNN and numerous Middle Eastern broadcasters. In 2019 she was nominated for the Nobel Peace Prize for work with Rohingya refugees and Syrian women prisoners and in 2020 she was awarded an honorary doctorate in journalism by the International Academy of Diplomatic Action in Bern, Switzerland.

For the unstinting support of my husband Samir Asli, who takes a lot of stick for my outspoken views but gets little credit for being my anchor in life.

Aisha Rimi is a British–Nigerian Postgraduate Journalism student and writer. Raised in a small village in Cambridgeshire, she has been writing from a young age. Looking for a place with a little more excitement (and diversity), Aisha was drawn to the bright lights of London, where she obtained her degree in French and German at Queen Mary, University of London. Over the years, she has used her voice as a tool to express her views on identity, particularly living in Britain as a young, Black, Muslim woman. Aisha's writing has covered a broad range of topics, including race, gender, disability, pop culture and faith. You can find her work featured on online platforms LAPP the Brand and Amaliah. She is also currently one of the co-hosts of *The Black Muslim Girl Podcast* and is the founder of a platform for Black Women writers called Black Girls Write Too. Apart from her obvious love of writing, Aisha's favourite things include travelling, finding new series to binge-watch on Netflix, and eating out a lot more often than she should. You can find Aisha on Twitter and Instagram @theaisharimi

I'd like to say a huge thank you to my sister Maryam, my honorary editor who I've made read every single piece before I've clicked send. Thank you to my parents for their continuous support and for always encouraging my love of writing. To my youngest sister, Zara, thank you for always telling me how it is. Thank you to my friends who've been a part of this journey from beginning to end. And a big thank you to Leomie Anderson and LAPP the Brand, without whom this opportunity never would have arisen.

Khadijah Rotimi is a twenty-four-year-old mixed-race Nigerian–Pakistani creative from north west-London. In her day-to-day life she works as a child contact supervisor and mentor for children who require supervised contact sessions with their parents. She is also a creative who enjoys writing, sketching, painting, food blogging and creating YouTube content. You can find Khadijah on Instagram @khads._

I would like to thank all the supporters who made this book happen and Sabeena for believing in me.

Sophie Williams spent her early- to mid-twenties trying to Find Herself. She ended up finding Islam instead. After the usual series of new revert mishaps (accidentally joining a cult, marrying a sociopath and wearing slip-on hijab), she ended up on Twitter and married her Twitter crush. Sophie now lives in London with her husband and three children, editing other people's books because it's more fun than writing her own.

Hodan Yusuf wears many hats (or should that say hijabs!). Among other things she is an essayist, poet, mediator, multi-media freelance journalist, actress and playwright. She has delivered workshops, spoken at and read her poetry at many events, universities and festivals. Her on-screen debut role saw her land a part in a J.J. Abrams & Warner Bros series. Her first play, *Refuge[tree]*, which she wrote, directed and per-formed, was selected for an international festival. A graduate in Human Geography and Environmental Policy, she also has a Diploma in Journalism and an MSc in Conflict Resolution and Mediation Studies. Hodan continues to develop her crafts while working on her debut poetry collection.

Twitter: @hyfreelance

Thank you Aabo (may Allah have mercy on your beautiful soul, Ameen), Hooyo, Walaalahay, Caruurtayda and all who have supported me. I appreciate everyone who pledged their support for this anthology on the level that included my poetry.

THANKS

To Joelle Owusu-Sekyere, for commissioning this anthology, and to Imogen Denny and Martha Sprackland, and all at Unbound, for seeing it through the editorial and publication process.

Unbound is the world's first crowdfunding publisher, established in 2011.

We believe that wonderful things can happen when you clear a path for people who share a passion. That's why we've built a platform that brings together readers and authors to crowdfund books they believe in – and give fresh ideas that don't fit the traditional mould the chance they deserve.

This book is in your hands because readers made it possible. Everyone who pledged their support is listed below. Join them by visiting unbound.com and supporting a book today.

Patrons

Jannatul Shammi

Tilted Axis Press

Supporters

Nabila Abbas

Ayesha Abdul Hai

Kia Abdullah

Zainab Jumoke Abdullahi

Aysha Abdulrazak

Muhammad Abdurrahim

Leila Aboulela

Sana Abubaker

Jacqueline Achermann

Martha Adam-Bushell

Mary Adeson

Maria Afsar

Samayya Afzal

Mohammed Ahad

Wajiha Ahad

Faaria Ahmad

Zahra Ahmad

Akeela Ahmed

Khwaja Ahmed

Mediah Ahmed

Muna Ahmed

Nasima Ahmed

Ruqiya Ahmed

Saba Ahmed

Sarah Ahmed

Hanna Akalu

Habeeb Akande

Latifa Akay

Afsa Akbar

Aaisha Akhtar

Ahmad Saleem Akhtar

Saleem Akhtar

Shazia M. Akhtar

Zainab Akhtar

Zuhura Akhtar

Paula Akpan

Tasnim Alahdal

Hafiz Alako

Umber Alam

Zakirah Alam

Lara Alamad

Reem Alfahad

Shuruq Alfawair

Ahlyah Ali

Sana Ali

Zarrin Ali

Verity Allan

Katie Allinson

Sarah Almahmoud

Zahed Amanullah

Audrey Ampofo

Nida El Amraoui

andykisaragi

Saima Ansari

Tahera Ansari

Sandra Armor

Alba Arnau Prado

Richard Ash

Juwairiyya Asmal-Lee

Amy Atkinson

Dean Atta

Magali Aurand

Samantha Austin

Djibril al-Ayad

Bushra Azim

Eva Bahnsen

Nafisa Bakkar

Selina Bakkar

Emily Bamford

Aziza Bangue

Siana Bangura

Catherine Banner

Adrian Banting

Martin Banting

Yuliya Barannik

M. Barkley

Ondine Barrow

Sarah Anne Barrow

Stuart Bartholomew

Andrew Barton

Hafsah Aneela Bashir

Subat Bashir

Wanda Batman

Andy Bean

Suzanna Beaupré

Loz Bee

Dulon Begum

Kazi R. Begum

Mamataj Begum

Rehana Begum

Peter Adrian Behravesh

Rachel Belward

Sarah Benafif

Jendella Benson

Amanda Berriman

Sarah Berry

Sasha Bhat

Nikki Bi

Asma Bilal

Elizabeth Billinger

Anne-Marie Blackburn

Cara Blaisdell

Chris Blewitt

Margaret Bluman

Clare Bonetree

Gracie Bradley

Monica Brady

Hanain Brohi

Christine Bronstein

Luis Bruno

Victoria Adukwei Bulley

Ed Burness

Clare Burroughs

Laila Butt

Samina Butt

Sam Byers

Naomi Byrne

Sara C.

Rosie Calthrop

Sophie Cameron

Finlay Campbell

Lucy Campbell

Deborah Cannarella

Susan Carey

Poppy Carpenter

Anna Carruthers

Celine Castelino

Nathaniel Catchpole

Shannon Chakraborty

Ollie Chamberlain

Megan Chandler

K. J. Charles

Catherine Charrett

Pascal Chatterjee

Afia Chaudhry

Kristen Cherry

Anish Chhibber

Jo Childs

Alex Chisholm

Shaista Chishty

Vera Chok

Iqra Choudhry

Kantha Choudhury

Shahima Chowdhury

Julie Cipolla

L. C. Clarke

Anna Coatman

Kathryn Coll

Simon Collinson

Anastasia Colman

Jane Commane

Brittany Constable

Joanne Conway

Georgie Cosh

Madeline Cowen

Arthur Cradock-Medcalf

Alison Craggs

Jessica Craig

Tinuke Craig

Tomas Cronholm

Annabel Dian Tara Fatima Crowley

Elizabeth Curwen

Richard D'Souza

Meera Damji

Darkowaa of African Book Addict!

Thalaya Darr

Sian Dart

A. M. Dassu

Rishi Dastidar

Masarat Daud

Maryline David

Patricia Davis

Adam Dawkins

Taufiq Dawood

Margaret Decker

Simon Demissie

Jenny Denton

Liz Dexter

U. Bava Dharani

Sandy Dillon

Sam Dixon

Ciar Donnelly

Kirsty Doole

Tiernan Douieb

Fiona Dove

Alice Duddy

Anais Duong-Pedica

Natasha Dyer

Saimma Dyer

Katrina Eastgate

Shelley Edwards

Farhia Elmi

Khadijah Elshayyal

Imogen Ely

Ilana Estreich

Fergus Evans

Anna Fargher

Nizrana Farook

Abdul Hamid Faruki

Lucy Fawcett

Fazia Fazal

Rahnuma Feist-Hassan

Abi Fellows

Saima Ferdows

Charles Fernyhough

Claudine Field

Will Fihn Ramsay

Sally Fincher

Miriam Fine

Spicy Fishcake

Jean Flack

Charles Forsdick

Hannah Fort Teller

Jackie Fox

Katherine Foxhall

Naomi Foyle

Magdalena Frankiewicz

Rosa Freedman

Naomi Frisby

Maxwell Frost

Laura Fry

Julie Furlong

Laura Gallagher

Miss Gamaz

Valerie Gauld

Claire Genevieve

Miranda George

Friederike Gerken

Aisha Ghani

Divya Ghelani

Daniele Gibney

Abi Gilbert

Eliza Gina

Jodie Ginsberg

Bruno Girin

Salena Godden

Mary Goodhart

Pippa Goodhart

Sakura Gooneratne

Jane Gould

Bhavini Goyate

Roshni Goyate

Edward Grande

Philip Green

Rose Green

Lewis Greener

Aoife Greenham

James Gregory-Monk

Danny Griffiths

Hannah Griffiths

Alexandra Gruian

Bryony Gundy

Murshad Habib

Bina Haider

Sarah Hale

Ben Hall

Bridger Hamilton

Donna Hardcastle

Eleanor Harding

James Harding

Clare Hardy

Beverley Harper

Becca Harper-Day

Lorna Harrington

Emily Harris

Abby Harrison

Kate Harrison

Lauren Harrison

Christopher Harrisson

Raisa Hassan

Shaira Hassan

Francesca Haswell-Walls

Sarah Hatch

Amina Hatia

Zainab Hayder

Anwen Hayward

David Hebblethwaite

Sareh Heidari

Grace Helmer

Lori Helmstetter

Claire Heuchan

Anna Marie Hill

Rachel Himbury

Em Hodder

Antonia Honeywell

Helen Hood

Katharine Howell

Shane Huddleston

Bekah Hughes

Heather Hugs

Heather Hunt

Jacinta Hunter

Khalida Huq

Laura Hurley

Hamzah Mohammed Hussain

Lynsey Hussain

Noreen Hussain

Nuzaifa Hussain

Rabiah Hussain

Rozia Hussain

Saania Hussain

Zahra Hussain

Leisha Hussien

Lizzie Huxley-Jones

Mahin Ibrahim

Natalie Ibu

Nadia Inha

Afshan Iqbal

Hafsah Ismail

Ittai

C. Jacob

Muhammad Jaffer

Zehra Jaffer

Adiba Jaigirdar

Charley James

Fyeza Janjua Sharif

Isra Jawad

Michal Jaworski

Eva Jeffreys

Natalie Jester

Theodore Johnston

Anna Morris

Rebecca Morris Knight

Abebech Moussouamy

Ms Jill Petty

Sara Muhr

Nicky Muir

Caroline Mukisa

Aayesha Mulla

Clare Mulley

Carolle Murray

Jawwad Mustafa

Katie N.

Carolyn Nakamura

Claire Napier

Kasia Narkowicz

Carlo Navato

Tamie Needler

Sasha Nemeckova

Chris Newsom and Jasmine Milton

Ben Nichols

Lena Nisula

Julian Norman

Lena Nuechter

Rachel Nye

Jamie O'Brien

Jenny O'Gorman

Shona O'Keeffe

Erika O'Reilly

Ros O'Sullivan

Elie Ochôa

Constance OConor

Office for Contemporary Art
    Norway

Mairi Christine Oliver

Mohamed Omar

Karen Onojaife

G. Oommen

Fiz Osborne

Malika Oubella

Joelle Owusu-Sekyere

Sarah P.

Camilla Pallesen

Jun Pang

Saskia Papadakis

Steph Parker

Kayleigh L. A. Parle

Michelle Payne

Rosie Pearson

Hugo Perks

Daisy Perry

Sabbiyah Pervez

Grace Eliza Phillip

Hafsah Pirzada

Sahar Pirzada

Katherine Pole

Justin Pollard

Laura Pollard

Patricia Pollock

Annelie Powell

Satish Prabhakar

Tara Pritchard

Emma Pusill (Plum Duff)

Dr Q

Sabina Akhtar Qadri

Abdulla Qmsz

Phillippa Quinn

Asim Qureshi

Sadiah Qureshi

Sarrah Qureshi

Emily Rader-Neely

Leah Raftis

Imdadur Rahman

Zara Rahman

Zareen Rahman

Fatima Rajina

Julia Rampen

Jenny Ramsden

Madiyah Rana

BibaMaya Randle-Caprez

Holly Ranger

Naaz Rashid

Jinny Rawlings

Simon Raybould

Sabila Raza

Daria Reaven

Naida Redgrave

Andy Reeve

Asia Rehman

Sajida Rehman

Trish Reilly

Madeehah Reza

Lowri Rhys

Marguerite Richards

Jane Richardson

Hafsa Al Rifai

Emma Ritch

River Spirit Films

Miriam Roberts

Anna Robinson

India Rome

Saeida Rouass

Catherine Rowley

Beck Roy

Lisa Rull

Jonathan Ruppin

Umm Ruqayyah

Caitlin Russell

Efea Rutlin

Bethany Rutter

Alysha S.

Niroshini S.

Tamim Sadikali

Tania Saeed

Safina-Ship-Amy

Tayyaba Sajid

Samaira Saleem

Saba Salman

C. M. Samala

Cathy Sangsue

Parveen Sarwar

Hina Sarwar-King

Nada Savitch

Bareerah Sayed

Suanne Schafer

Ruth Scheidegger

Carina Schneider

Kira Schumacher

Nadia El-Sebai

Natalie Sedacca

Helen Sedgwick

Najma Shaheen

Barry Shapiro

Aoife Sheehy

Mustapha Sheikh

Caroline Sherwood

Miriam Sherwood

Theresa Shingler

Daniel Shodipo

Nikesh Shukla

Nicky Siddall-Collier

Julie Siddiqi

Sabah Sikander

Emma Simovic

Amandeep Singh

Sid Singh

Sunny Singh

Usha Singh

Ala Sirriyeh

Beverley Rosemarie Smith

Deborah Smith

Immy Smith

James Smith

Ken Smith

Maddy Smith

Matthew Smith

Emma Southon

Wendy Staden

Henriette B. Stavis

Katarzyna Stawarz

Gabriela Steinke

Ashley Stephen

Adam Stoneman

Louie Stowell

Iga Strapko

Aleksander Sumowski

Rosmita Syarief

Susie Symes

Vicky Syred

Anita Szatmary

Hashashin Tag

Zeba Talkhani

Preti Taneja

Nicolas Tantot

Emilie Tapping

Claire Taylor

Dorothy Taylor

Rachel Taylor

Phil Teer

Sümaya Teli

Ruth Temple

Emily Thew

Adam Thomas

Siân Thomas

Clara Thompson

Lucy Thompson

Hannah Thomson

Hannah Tometzki

Anthony Trevelyan

Wendy Tuxworth

Rebecca Tye

Jack Underwood

Anna Vall

Roderic Vassie

Kanessa Visuule

Valerie Vitzthum

Jo W.

Amina Wadud

Daniel Walsh

Rory Weal

Siyang Wei

Kate Whitley

Claire Whitmore

Trudi Wilkes

Helen Williams

Kathryn Williams

Katie Williams

Catherine Williamson

Mark Williamson

Grace Willow

Naomi Woddis

Coin and Rachel Wright

Salma Yaqoob

Naomi Young-Rodas

Shahed Yousaf

Zahbia Yousuf

Imran Yusuf

Mohamed Yusuf

Soraya Zahid

Rafidah Al-zeer

Sabeena Zeghum Ahmed